Last Resort

Last Resort

THE FINANCIAL CRISIS AND THE FUTURE OF BAILOUTS

Eric A. Posner

The University of Chicago Press • CHICAGO AND LONDON

The University of Chicago Press, Chicago 60637
The University of Chicago Press, Ltd., London
© 2018 by The University of Chicago
All rights reserved. No part of this book may be used or reproduced in any manner
whatsoever without written permission, except in the case of brief quotations in critical
articles and reviews. For more information, contact the University of Chicago Press,
1427 East 60th Street, Chicago, IL 60637.
Published 2018
Printed in the United States of America

27 26 25 24 23 22 21 20 19 18   1 2 3 4 5

ISBN-13: 978-0-226-42006-6 (cloth)
ISBN-13: 978-0-226-42023-3 (e-book)
DOI: 10.7208/chicago/9780226420233.001.0001

LIBRARY OF CONGRESS CATALOGING-IN-PUBLICATION DATA

Names: Posner, Eric A., 1965– author.
Title: Last resort : the financial crisis and the future of bailouts / Eric A. Posner.
Description: Chicago ; London : The University of Chicago Press, 2018. | Includes
bibliographical references and index.
Identifiers: LCCN 2017017174 | ISBN 9780226420066 (cloth : alk. paper) |
ISBN 9780226420233 (e-book)
Subjects: LCSH: Financial crises—United States. | Bailouts (Government policy)—
United States. | Intervention (Federal government)—United States. | Global Financial
Crisis, 2008–2009.
Classification: LCC HB3722 .P666 3028 | DDC 338.5/430973—dc23
LC record available at https://lccn.loc.gov/2017017174

♾ This paper meets the requirements of ANSI/NISO Z39.48-1992 (Permanence of Paper).

Contents

Introduction

[The] Federal Reserve was the only fire station in town.

HENRY PAULSON[1]

IF ONE THING WAS CLEAR AFTER THE FINANCIAL CRISIS OF 2007–8, it was that the government would no longer bail out helpless financial institutions. President Obama said so. Congress wrote this principle into the preamble of the Dodd-Frank Act,[2] the major post-bailout statute. All high-level government officials confirmed this policy.

There was good reason to. The bailouts enraged the public. They spawned the Tea Party and Occupy Wall Street. Public officials agreed that bailouts were anomalous in a market economy, where people who take risks must be allowed to lose their money. Bailouts reward irresponsible rich people for foolish investments that harm ordinary people who do nothing wrong. They were needed in the financial crisis only because a global economic meltdown would have harmed people even more. Or maybe they were not needed at all. Financial institutions should have been allowed to immolate in a purifying *Götterdämmerung*, or perhaps bailouts would not have been needed if people had acted sensibly in the first place.

Bailing out firms is wrong, or so it seems. But the word "bailout" is used by people in different ways, and here is where the trouble starts. The Federal Reserve Board—like central banks around the world—possesses a function known as the Lender of Last Resort (LLR). The Fed has had this function since its establishment in 1913. The purpose of the LLR is to lend money to financial institutions that are unable to borrow money during a financial crisis, a systemic withdrawal of credit and hoarding of cash across the economy. The LLR makes loans to banks and other financial institutions until confidence is restored. Then it is paid back, with interest.

In the financial crisis that began in 2007, the Fed exercised its LLR function just as it was supposed to. While the crisis did not take the form of a traditional run on ordinary commercial banks, it did conform to the classic definition of a financial crisis. People withdrew their funds first from certain financial entities operated by banks and investment banks, and then from investment banks, money market mutual funds, and other financial institutions, but these "shadow banks" had become so important to the economy that their failure would have caused economic collapse (and taken the regular banking system with them). Because of the unusual nature of the financial crisis, the Fed responded by making credit available to nonbanks as well as banks; later Congress appropriated funds for the US Treasury to boost the financial system.

Did the Fed "bail out" the financial system? It depends on how one defines a "bailout." The dictionary says that a bailout occurs when someone provides financial assistance to a person or business that cannot pay its debts. But that definition is pretty broad. Suppose I don't have enough money to pay my $1,000 credit card bill, so I go to my local bank and take out a home equity loan, which I use to pay off the credit card bill. Then I pay off the home equity loan over the next several years. The bank loan qualifies as a "bailout" under the dictionary definition because it saves me from defaulting on my credit card debt. But there is nothing wrong with such a loan. The bank isn't doing me a favor; it's charging me interest and making a profit.

Suppose instead I go to my rich uncle and explain that I can't pay my debts. My uncle hands me $1,000 in cash and tells me to give it to the credit card company. Or he gives me an interest-free loan, knowing that I'm a deadbeat and unlikely to repay him. The uncle not only bails me out according to the dictionary definition. He bails me out, some might say, in a morally questionably way. He relieves me of responsibility for my debts, perhaps teaching me that there are no consequences to my actions. He incurs a loss and does not expect to be paid back. Knowing that my uncle will rescue me, I may continue to act in a financially irresponsible manner.

Now consider a classic LLR loan during a financial crisis. A bank or other financial institution cannot borrow money because no one is willing to lend. As its bills come due, it faces bankruptcy. The bank possesses numerous assets that it could sell off to raise cash to pay its bills. But no one wants to buy those assets because everyone is hoarding cash. If the bank nonetheless sells them at fire-sale prices to the handful of hardy souls who have cash and believe that the financial crisis has peaked, it will be driven into insolvency because the fire sales do not raise enough cash to pay its debts. Instead, the bank applies for a loan from the LLR, using its assets as collateral. The LLR can lend because it has an infinite time horizon. It doesn't matter how long it takes for the bank to pay it back because the LLR can keep itself in business by printing money—subject to some vague macroeconomic and political limitations.

If all goes well, the bank will either pay back the LLR with interest or lose its collateral to the LLR, which the LLR can resell to the market once the crisis ends. The scenario is much closer to my first example than to my rich-uncle case. The only difference is that in the first example, I go to a private bank, while in the financial crisis, the financial institutions sought loans from the government. But they did so only in the sense that if someone's house is on fire, that person calls the fire department rather than looks for a private company to douse the fire. No such private company exists. The government is a kind of credit monopolist during a financial crisis; if the LLR is operated correctly, the government should make rather than lose money—as, in fact, it did during the crisis of 2007–8.

Of course, it need not work out this way. If the LLR makes loans to insolvent institutions and against inadequate collateral, it will lose money, possibly a great deal of money. Economists distinguish between the pure type of liquidity support of solvent banks, which I have just described, and the rescue of banks that have been badly managed and driven into insolvency. Such banks make bad loans that are not repaid. During the S&L crisis of the 1980s, many savings and loans made bad commercial loans and were shut down. The government paid their depositors. Because the liability to depositors greatly exceeded the value of the banks' loans, the government lost billions of dollars.

The S&Ls were not bailed out and the government lost billions of dollars; the banks in distress in 2007–8 were bailed out and the government made billions of dollars.[3] And while people were angry about the S&L crisis, the anger was not remotely as sharp and politically damaging as their anger after the 2007–8 bailouts. What accounts for the rage?

At least among the public, hardly anyone knows that the government made rather than lost money. This misunderstanding probably stands in for a more realistic assessment: that in some way the government was responsible for the financial crisis and the economic pain that resulted from it. One idea is that the government established a financial system that rewarded bankers in good times and protected them from losses in bad times at the expense of taxpayers. As we will see, while this idea contains a kernel of truth, it is not a good assessment of the problems that gave rise to the crisis.

Among experts who criticize the government rescue, the view that the Fed went too far, or acted questionably, during the financial crisis can be attributed to several features of the crisis response. First, conventional wisdom about the LLR is that it should lend to banks and not to other financial institutions. In contrast, the Fed gave huge loans to nonbank institutions. Second, many people think that the Fed should support the financial system as a whole rather than specific firms — and the Fed violated this rule as well. It made numerous customized loans, including to the investment bank Bear Stearns and to AIG, an insurance company. Third, during the crisis many commentators claimed that the Fed was lending to insolvent firms rather than to illiquid but solvent firms — in effect, this was the S&L crisis all over again, except in the S&L crisis the Fed properly withheld liquidity support. This criticism was mostly wrong — though it is likely true that some of the borrowers were insolvent as well as illiquid. Fourth, the sheer scale of the Fed's activities — along with those of the Federal Deposit Insurance Corporation (FDIC) and Treasury once Congress authorized rescue money — placed the government response outside the range of precedent.

Finally, many commentators claimed that the government saved firms that acted recklessly. This was unfair; it also set the stage for future crises by informing markets that investors will not bear the consequence of bad decisions. Knowing that they will — or might — be bailed out in the future, investors today have every incentive to gamble, expecting to reap profits if markets rise and avoid losses if they collapse. This bad incentive is known as moral hazard.

The moral hazard charge is more complex than it first appears. A firm can act recklessly in different ways. One way is to make investments with negative net present value (NPV). A firm will do this if it is careless or believes that the government might rescue it. Another way is to make positive-NPV investments with only a remote probability of success. Unless the firm carefully hedges its bets, it may find itself in a liquidity crisis—unable to borrow enough money to keep itself going until the investments pay off.

While many firms acted recklessly in the first sense (and indeed some firms acted illegally), it is unlikely that their reckless (or illegal) behavior caused the financial crisis. Reckless behavior might have caused some, or even many firms, to fail; but there was never any reason for anyone to believe that it would cause a crisis. For that reason, it is unlikely that the bailouts of 2008–9 will encourage anyone to act recklessly in the future. A firm that today loads up on risky derivatives that sour will very likely go bankrupt—unless it is a too-big-to-fail firm—a special case that I will return to later—and even then its shareholders will be wiped out.[4] And it is impossible for financial institutions—except in unusual circumstances—to guard against a liquidity crisis. For protection, they depend on the government, as the law provides.

However, the focus of this book is not the policy debate. It is another topic, largely neglected but equally important: whether the government acted lawfully.

During and after the financial crisis, Congress grilled the top officials who managed the crisis response. These officials included Ben Bernanke, the Fed chief; Timothy Geithner, the president of the New York Federal Reserve Bank and then secretary of the Treasury under President Obama; Hank Paulson, the secretary of the Treasury under President Bush; and Sheila Bair, the head of the FDIC. Congress created commissions to evaluate their behavior, and other government watchdogs joined in. A recurrent question in these inquiries was whether the crisis-response officials violated the law. Did they act beyond the authority that Congress had given them?

The answer is—yes. The government frequently violated the law. In some cases, the law violation was clear; in many more cases, the government advanced a questionable interpretation of the law. The Fed acted unlawfully by seizing nearly 80 percent of the equity of AIG, while Treasury broke the law by seizing nearly all the equity of Fannie Mae and Freddie Mac. The US government violated the spirit, and probably the letter, of bankruptcy law when it rescued many of the creditors of GM and Chrysler. The Fed may well have broken the law by purchasing rather than lending against various toxic assets, and Treasury by using congressionally appropriated funds to help homeowners. The FDIC broke the law in major instances as well.

In some of these cases, affected parties—shareholders and contract partners—have brought suit to vindicate their claims. In other cases, no one has sued because no one has standing to challenge the conduct. From the standpoint of commentators who complain about the bailout, the ironies are salient. The critics believe that the victims of the bailouts were taxpayers, not shareholders. If anyone should sue, taxpayers should. But taxpayers are not allowed to bring lawsuits against the government to stop regulatory actions—except in limited cases not relevant here—or to obtain damages as a result of illegal regulatory actions. Instead, the shareholders (and other stakeholders)—thought to be unfairly helped—get to bring the lawsuits.

Lack of sympathy toward Wall Street, understandable as it may be, has obscured some important questions about how the government behaved during the bailout. The illegality of the government's conduct is tied to the underlying question of what bailout policy should have been, and what it should be in future crises. If we think the government's illegal actions advanced the public interest, then we'll need to change the law so that next time around regulators will know what is expected of them. It turns out that the lawsuits—whether the plaintiffs win or lose—reveal a great deal about the problem of bailouts and how bailout policy should be formulated.

The lawsuits all center around two closely related claims. The first is that the government exploited emergency conditions to expropriate the property of the plaintiffs. The second is that the government treated the plaintiffs unfairly—worse than shareholders (or other stakeholders) in similarly situated firms that received bailouts on favorable terms. The claims are closely related because fair terms are just those that do not expropriate. During the financial crisis, countless financial institutions found themselves unable to borrow funds. Many plunged into bankruptcy, but many others borrowed money from the government without being required to give it equity or even pay substantial interest rates.

A number of complications need to be understood. First, many firms benefited from government emergency lending even when they did not borrow from the government. When the government "bails out" firm X, it typically bails out its *creditors*, which X is able to repay, thanks to the government loan. Indeed, X's shareholders might be wiped out, as occurred with Fannie and Freddie. Many other firms benefited directly from government loans; these firms did not sacrifice equity and paid very low interest rates. In both cases, shareholders retained their equity stake because the government either enabled their firm to pay its debts or enabled other firms to repay debts to their firm. The plaintiffs claim that the government treated them shabbily relative to this baseline.

Second, a question arises why the government treated certain firms worse than others. Theories abound. One theory is that certain firms exercised outsized political power because of the shrewdness of their executives or the connections between those executives and government officials. A related idea is that "Wall Street" obtained favorable treatment compared to firms in other locations and other industries. AIG's shareholders argue that the government seized AIG's equity to make a scapegoat of it at a time when the public and Congress sought scapegoats. Others argue that too-big-to-fail firms benefited from government largess while too-small-to-save firms did not.

While these explanations reflect elements of the truth, another explanation has escaped attention. A significant but often overlooked problem with bailouts is that firms do not want to accept emergency loans; and even when they do accept emergency loans, they hoard cash rather than lend it out. Firms do not want to accept emergency loans if they can avoid it because they fear that the market will single them out as the weak member of the herd and stop lending to them, hastening their demise. The emergency loan turns out to be a death warrant rather than a reprieve. And firms do not want to lend out money they receive because they want to have enough cash in case creditors stop lending to them. This is the "pushing the string" problem: the government cannot force borrowers to relend funds they receive from the government. These are both significant problems for the government because it cannot restore confidence to the credit markets until traditional lenders like banks begin lending again.

I will argue that the government was, for largely adventitious reasons, able to gain control over AIG, Fannie, and Freddie early in the critical stage of the crisis, which began with the bankruptcy of Lehman on September 15, 2008. It was able to gain control over Fannie and Freddie because of those firms' peculiar status as hybrid public-private entities. It was able to gain control over AIG because, in the wake of the government's failure to rescue Lehman, the government could credibly threaten to let AIG fail unless AIG's board turned over control to it. Once it controlled these firms, it could direct or at least influence their activities. Pushing a string was no longer necessary. The government encouraged Fannie and Freddie to rescue the mortgage market[5] and forced AIG to help remove toxic assets from the balance sheets of other firms.

These examples illustrate some of the themes of the book, but many more examples will be discussed. My basic claims are as follows. *First*, at the start of the crisis, the law did not give the LLR—the Fed, the FDIC—sufficient power to rescue the financial system. Even after Congress appropriated funds for the rescue and placed them at Treasury's disposal, the authority of the LLR—which now included Treasury—was not adequate for addressing the crisis. *Second*, the agencies were not fully constrained by the law, but they were partly constrained by the law in important ways. In some cases, they disregarded the law. In others, they improvised elaborate evasions of the law. In the end, a combination of legal and political constraints forced them to go to Congress for additional authority, which was still not sufficient. *Third*, the legal constraints were damaging. During the crisis itself, the harm was limited because the agencies—with a few significant exceptions—violated or circumvented the law. But after the crisis, the legal violations led to political damage, which may well hamper the response to the next financial crisis. Moreover, the legal violations may make the government liable for damages in lawsuits. *Fourth*, even so, the LLR agencies used their power to play favorites to manage public perceptions and limit political opposition to their rescues. *Fifth*, while the current mood, reflected in the Dodd-Frank Act, is to limit the LLR's powers, the right response is to increase them while subjecting the LLR to equal-treatment principles that restrict favoritism.

Economists and lawyers, even those of a free-market bent, have always believed in a strong state, even while they sometimes deny that they do. Only a strong state can enforce property rights and contracts. Without reliable, routine enforcement of property rights and contracts, businesses and consumers cannot engage in sophisticated market transactions. These commentators do criticize other aspects of the strong state—subsidies for favored industries, heavy-handed regulation of market transactions, and the like. They tend to lump in bailouts with these wrong-headed interventions. But this view is mistaken. Once it is recognized that the role of the state in a market economy is not only to enforce property and contract rights, but to ensure liquidity, then the bailout, properly understood, is no different from the enforcement of property rights. A host of legal consequences follow from this observation. This book gives an accounting of them.

1   The Transformation of the Financial System

At this juncture, however, the impact on the broader economy
and financial markets of the problems in the subprime market
seems likely to be contained.

BEN BERNANKE (2007), MARCH 28, 2007

IN HIS SHORT STORY, "THE LIBRARY OF BABEL," JORGE LUIS BORGES
describes a library with more books than there are atoms in the universe.
Books about the financial crisis are not numerous enough to fill Borges's
library, but one should be forgiven for thinking that they might be. While
we don't need another description of the financial crisis, I provide a brief
version in this chapter and the next, emphasizing those points that are
relevant to my arguments about law and policy.

The Transformation of the Financial System

Many things caused the financial crisis, but the major cause turns out to be
simple and, with the benefit of hindsight, even obvious. The financial crisis
took place because the financial system had undergone a transformation
that left behind the legal structure that was designed to prevent financial
crises from occurring.[1] The transformation took place in part because that
legal structure created costs for financial institutions and their customers,
and, as in the natural order of things, these institutions developed meth-
ods for evading the law without breaking it—"regulatory arbitrage," in the
lingo of economists. The transformation also took place because the world
changed: the needs of borrowers and savers changed, and the financial system changed so as to serve them; and technology changed, allowing for
financial innovations that created new types of transactions and institutions. While many experts—including financial economists, industry prac-

titioners, and regulatory officials—recognized the transformation as it was occurring, they did not realize that the transformation outstripped the law and created new risks of a financial crisis.[2] In fact, they believed the opposite: that the transformation created a safer financial system rather than a riskier one. This is why the legal developments leading up to the financial crisis were, in the main, deregulatory, which (unknown to nearly everyone) enhanced the risk of a crisis rather than (as nearly everyone believed) reduced financial instability; why the crisis was a surprise; and why the Fed was forced to innovate, in some cases breaking the law, to respond to it.

THE (NOT SO) GOOD OLD DAYS

The backbone of the financial system was banking. A bank took deposits from ordinary people and businesses and lent them out long term to people so that they could buy homes and cars, and businesses so that they could buy equipment and pay their employees in advance of revenues. In this way the bank acted as an intermediary between short-term savers—people who needed access to their funds on demand—and long-term borrowers, who needed assurance that they would not be required to repay loans in full until they had lived in their houses for 30 years, driven their car for 5 years, or (if they were businesses) obtained revenues from the project that the loan financed. This process is called maturity transformation—the short-term maturity of the savers' loans to the banks is transformed into the long-term maturity of the loans that the banks make to their borrowers.

The key to maturity transformation is a statistical law—the law of large numbers. A bank takes money from thousands of customers, who are constantly depositing and withdrawing money from their checking accounts. Often, when a customer withdraws money from her checking account she is merely writing a check to another bank customer—so the bank does not actually pay out cash but instead notes that it now owes less to the first customer and more to the second. While different customers are withdrawing and depositing, closing out old accounts and starting new ones, the bank can assume that on average a balance of incoming funds will be maintained, and it is this balance that the bank, in effect, lends out to borrowers for the long term. No one will finance a home purchase by taking short-term loans; the bank does that for the home buyer, and this is how the bank generates economic value, creating a valuable long-term loan for the home buyer while compensating savers by giving them interest and payment services like checking.

Unfortunately, this system is also fragile. It assumes that the probability that the decision by one depositor to withdraw money from the bank is uncorrelated (or sufficiently uncorrelated) with withdrawals by other depositors. The assumption holds in normal times, but it can be violated. If the only big employer in a small town shuts down, nearly all depositors may withdraw money to carry them through hard times. Or if a rumor starts that the bank is being mismanaged, depositors may withdraw their money because they fear the bank will not have funds to repay them. In both cases, a run can start. A run occurs when people withdraw money from a healthy bank because they lose confidence that it will be able to repay them—even if the bank actually can repay them. A run can quickly empty the vaults of a bank—banks do not keep much cash on hand because they can earn more money by lending it out. Banks may be able to borrow from other banks to stem a run, but in the worst case, they must sell off their assets (mostly long-term loans like mortgages) at fire-sale prices to raise cash to pay the withdrawing depositors. When assets are sold at fire-sale prices, they rarely generate much cash. The healthy bank becomes illiquid (it lacks cash), and then in selling assets at low prices to raise cash, it becomes insolvent and shuts down. The bank fires its employees, who lose their relationship-specific knowledge about borrowers, and calls in loans where it can—and all of this causes economic damage unless other banks can quickly take up the slack.

Banks do not stand alone; they operate through networks consisting of numerous banks. There are two reasons for this. First, banks offer payment services, and these take place through bank-to-bank interactions. If a customer of bank A writes a check to a customer of bank B, banks A and B manage this transaction by adjusting the balances of their customers and adjusting the balance in the account that one of the banks keeps with the other. Second, banks lend money to each other short-term because at any given time one bank will have money it doesn't need and another bank will need additional money. The network system helps banks in one way but makes them vulnerable in another way. If a single bank is subject to a run, it can quickly borrow money from other banks and use it to pay off customers until they come to their senses. Those banks will lend to the first bank against the valuable home mortgages it owns and other assets. If the bank is located in a town suffering from factory closures and long-term decline, the bank can borrow enough from other banks to sell off its loans in an orderly fashion over a long period of time, in this way avoiding the destructive fire-sale consequences of a run.

However, the network also creates a kind of fragility because a run on one bank can be transmitted through the network to other banks. If a run starts on bank A, and bank A raises cash by withdrawing its deposits with banks B and C, then customers of bank B and C might worry that those banks will not be able to honor their debts as well. If the customers of B and C start running on those banks as well, then the entire system might collapse, converting a local crisis into a regional or national crisis in which money is sucked out of the economy and commerce grinds to a halt.

In the old days, banks guarded themselves against runs by maintaining cash on hand and capital cushions, but their incentives to do so fell below the social optimum because the costs of a crisis extend across the economy and are not fully internalized by banks themselves. In response, governments created a regulatory regime with two major elements. First, governments imposed a rigorous, extensive system of regulation on banks, whose goal was to ensure that banks engaged in safe practices—made low-risk rather than high-risk loans, maintained diversified portfolios, stayed out of risky lines of business, kept sufficient cash on hand, and maintained large capital cushions. Second, governments guaranteed deposits—through explicit insurance like the FDIC system, and a vaguer promise to make emergency loans to banks that are in trouble, the Lender of Last Resort (LLR) function. The two elements were closely tied. The insurance system reduced the incentive of depositors to choose safe banks over risky banks and monitor the behavior of banks. This created moral hazard, which the ex ante system of regulation tried to counter.

THE TRANSFORMATION

This system of financial regulation came to maturity in the United States during the Great Depression, and it seemed to work well enough over the next several decades. But by the 1970s, it was in disarray. One of the problems with the regulatory system was that it went too far. In the interest of safety and soundness, banks were kept out of lines of business—insurance, securities underwriting—that might have allowed them to reduce risk (through diversification) and provide financial services more efficiently to their customers. They were also—for the most part—not allowed to branch across state lines or even within states. This kept the banks small and fragmented, insufficiently diversified across geographic space. The banking system was also artificially divided into savings and loans or thrifts, which were oriented toward consumer depositors and home buyers, and "commercial banks," which were oriented toward business. Regulators and, eventually, Congress dismantled many of these barriers. The inflation shock of the 1970s caught the S&Ls in a squeeze between their legacy 30-year mortgages, which they had issued at low interest rates, and their financing needs, which required payment of high interest rates. Much of the now-maligned movement of financial deregulation, which began in the 1970s and accelerated in the 1980s and 1990s, was a sensible response to these problems.

Deregulation was not the only response to the perceived excesses of the regulation; transformation within the industry was another. The transformation reflected two sources of demand. First, because regulation imposes costs on financial intermediaries and their customers, customers sought ways to avoid the most heavily regulated portion of the industry—banking. This was a form of regulatory arbitrage—although it is not clear whether it should have been condemned for evading safety-promoting regulations needed to prevent a crisis or praised for evading excessive regulations that created costs. Probably a bit of both.

Second, the transformation responded to growing demand across the world for highly liquid and safe assets. Under the old system, pension funds, insurance companies, sovereign wealth funds, and other huge institutions that sought liquid and safe assets were limited to insured bank deposits. These were zero risk (at least in the United States) and more liquid than the only other zero-risk asset, US debt. But as Pozsar (2011) notes, there was an upper limit on the supply of insured deposits. Under US law at the time, a deposit account was insured up to $100,000, and while investors could spread their wealth across banks, they could choose among only so many banks—and mergers were rapidly shrinking the number of banks. The increasing demand for safe, liquid investments—Pozsar (2011, 5) estimates that the holdings of "institutional cash pools" increased from $100 billion in 1990 to $2.2 trillion in 2007, or possibly as much as $3.8 trillion— spurred the financial system to construct new securities thought to be as safe and liquid as insured deposits. Pozsar's analysis turns the traditional, moralistic account of the financial crisis on its head: its cause was not the drive for risk—for gambles based on the promise of socialized losses—but the drive for safety.

The new system, which would come to be called shadow banking, provided an answer. That sinister name was bestowed on the system by a financial executive—in 2007!—decades after it had come into effect.[3] It was not entirely new and drew on many established financial practices, which may be why no one fully understood the nature of the transformation.

Consider a bank that issues a mortgage to a home buyer. Under the traditional system, the bank kept the mortgage on its books and the homeowner made payments to it every month for the next 30 years. The bank had a strong incentive to screen mortgage applicants for credit risk because if the borrower defaulted, the bank would be forced to go through the expensive process of foreclosure and may not be fully paid back from the proceeds of the sale. For this reason, the bank also had a strong incentive to keep tabs on the homeowner and renegotiate the loan if he had trouble making payments. But while the bank had very good incentives, the necessity of keeping this asset on its books exposed it to considerable risk. If interest rates rose or housing prices fell, the risk of default increased, and there was little the bank could do about it. Moreover, if depositors needed their cash back, the bank would have trouble selling off the mortgage in short order and would take a loss. In the traditional model, banks were vulnerable to runs; FDIC insurance along with government regulation ensured financial stability. But government regulation imposed costs on banks, costs that the banks sought to minimize or avoid.

Under the modern system, the bank or other financial entity, generically called a mortgage originator, initiates the mortgage to the home buyer and may temporarily hold it on its books, but sells it off as quickly as possible. The buyer of the mortgage is Fannie Mae or Freddie Mac, two quasi-private entities that I will discuss later; or an investment bank; or a trust operated by a commercial bank or its holding company; or another similar private financial institution. The buyer collects a large portfolio of loans, diversified across various dimensions (for example, region), and converts them into securities. These securities are sold to investors. The securities give investors a right to a stream of payments, just like any bond, with the payments coming out of the principal and interest payments made by the homeowners to the intermediary. The payments are structured so that some securities are super-safe, while others are highly risky. The super-safe securities are super-safe because their owners have the right to be paid from the entire pool of cash generated from the homeowners' payments before the owners of the less safe securities are paid. If a few homeowners default, the safe tranches are unaffected, while the lower tranches take the hit. That is why the super-safe tranches came to be regarded as good as bank deposits, effectively money—liquid and safe, and hence ideal for pensions, insurance companies, banks, and other investors who needed to be certain that a portion of their holdings could be converted into cash and paid to customers, depositors, or short-term lenders on a moment's notice. Credit-rating agencies formalize this arrangement by stamping AAA on the safe bonds.[4]

These securities are called mortgage-backed securities (MBSs), and they have existed since the Great Depression, thanks to the involvement of Fannie and other government entities. But their volume, and significance for the financial system, grew exponentially in the 1990s and 2000s when private financial institutions also got into the act. These institutions created a range of related securities, including asset-backed securities (ABSs), which used other assets, like car and credit card loans as well as mortgages, and collateralized debt obligations (CDOs). These asset classes had many differences, but they all followed the logic of the MBS.

Another innovation was the credit default swap (CDS). A CDS is just an insurance policy, typically on a bond or another financial instrument. Imagine that an investor owns a bond issued by IBM. She worries that IBM will default on the bond. She could unload this default risk by selling the bond, but she could also protect herself from default by buying a CDS from an investment bank or other financial institution. Under the terms of the CDS, the insurer pays the investor the par value of the IBM bond if IBM defaults on the bond. In return, the investor pays the insurer a small amount of money, akin to an insurance premium. If IBM defaults, the investor hands over the bond to the insurer and receives the payout. Note, however, that the investor takes on the "counterparty risk" that the insurer will be insolvent when payment is due.

Firms sell CDSs on all kinds of bonds—including sovereign bonds, for example—but they played a specific role in the financial crisis of 2007–8. When investment banks constructed CDOs, they needed to meet the demand for super-safe, AAA-rated tranches. In many cases, a guarantee from a top-rated firm—like AIG—did the trick. Monoline insurance companies—companies that, because of regulations, insured credit risk and no other kind of risk—also played a significant role in the modern credit system by insuring against the default of CDOs, MBSs, and related assets. The guarantee typically took the form of a CDS. CDSs were also used to construct various bets on housing prices. The investor John Paulson was able to bet on a housing price collapse by buying CDSs on mortgage-backed securities derived from mortgages that he thought were vulnerable. He and his counterparties paid money into a fund, which paid the counterparties as long as the securities traded above a stipulated price, but ultimately paid Paulson when the prices fell.

These and related securities made shadow banking possible. In shadow banking, a nearly equivalent version of the bank deposit was engineered outside of the banking system. It worked roughly like this. A pension fund, insurance company, sovereign wealth fund, money market mutual fund, or other large institution makes a one- or two-day loan to an investment bank or other large borrower. The loan is secured by a very safe security like a short-term Treasury bond. If the borrower defaults, the lender keeps the bond and (with very high probability) is made whole. The parties can make a tiny risk even tinier by applying a haircut to the collateral, so that even if its value declines a bit, the lender would be made whole when it sells it. In practice, the loans are rolled over. If a lender needs its funds back, it declines to roll over the loan. Functionally, the repo transaction (as it was called) and the deposit were the same. The short-term loan was akin to a demand deposit, while not-rolling-over was akin to a withdrawal. The major difference was that the repo transaction was not insured but was protected by collateral, and the borrower was not formally a "depository institution," thus not a "bank," thus not subject to strict bank regulation, which based on the old model assumed that banks alone were vulnerable to runs, or at least runs that could lead to a system-wide panic.

In the old system, bank depositors—ordinary people and businesses—made short-term loans to banks in the form of deposits. In the shadow system, short-term loans come from big institutions that seek a highly secure, liquid investment that pays a tiny rate of interest but still a higher rate than banks pay on deposits. In the old system, the bank pooled the deposits and lent them out, keeping the loans on their books. In the shadow system, the shadow bank intermediary pools the investments to purchase loans from agents who find and screen borrowers but do not actually incur credit risk (or only a small portion of it).

This transformation did not take place in one day. Shadow bank institutions existed centuries ago. And regular banking never disappeared. During the relevant period, from the 1990s to the financial crisis, bank deposits and lending grew, which may be why regulators continued to assume that banking was the backbone of the financial system. The shadow banking system was seen as a useful supplement but not the heart of the system of financial intermediation. But during the same period, shadow banking grew exponentially, from next to nothing to a magnitude that exceeded that of the banking system.

The shadow banking system functioned effectively for years, and it was easy to see why. It was a cheap, secure way to lend money and make a little interest, and to borrow money. Only with hindsight did economists identify its problems. One was that the parties started to substitute in other forms of collateral for Treasuries—including mortgage-derived securities like CDOs—using bigger haircuts to address their additional riskiness. This might not have been a problem except that the risks of the mortgage-derived securities were more sensitive to housing prices than people thought, and housing prices were more volatile than people thought. House prices collapsed in 2006 and 2007; the price of mortgage-derived securities plunged; lenders in the repo market demanded larger haircuts and then stopped accepting them altogether. Borrowers raised cash by selling off those securities, which sent their prices even lower. Only after the crisis ended did economists start writing about how shadow banking was a form of regulatory arbitrage—a way of evading regulations that were intended to minimize risk.[5]

People who constructed, bought, and sold mortgage-related instruments priced them using mathematical models. The models told them that the safe tranches were indeed safe. Ratings agencies believed the models as well. Yet the AAA-related securities defaulted at a high rate, and rating agencies were forced to downgrade their ratings. Why was everyone wrong? The models were based on historical data about housing prices; the data showed that while regional downturns had occurred, national downturns had not. This gave the impression that a nationwide downturn was extremely unlikely.[6] Data about the subprime mortgage market was even more scarce because subprime lending was of more recent vintage (Brunnermeier 2009). Based on the limited data, investors concluded that the risk of default was negligible. It may also have been the case that even very sophisticated investors ignored "tail risk"—the very small risk of very bad events—either because of cognitive limits or practical constraints on data analysis.

But the problem was actually deeper. The fragility of the banking system derived from the fundamental role of banks, which was maturity transformation. Banks can avoid runs only as long as depositors' withdrawals are uncorrelated. The shadow banking system also engaged in maturity transformation, but its source of fragility lay elsewhere. To ensure that their loans were secure, the repo lenders demanded collateral. When they ran out of Treasuries, they had to rely on artificially constructed assets like CDOs. But the CDOs themselves depended on housing values being uncorrelated or sufficiently so. When that assumption was violated, the system collapsed.

The Nature of the Crisis: Liquidity versus Solvency

The financial crisis is often blamed on the housing bubble, but the housing bubble did not by itself cause the crisis. Many officials—including Ben Bernanke—acknowledged long before the crisis that housing prices seemed too high. So did many commentators. But no one—not even people who understood the problems in the housing market—anticipated the financial crisis.

The prices of houses and other assets, like stocks and bonds, are set by the laws of supply and demand. Restrictive zoning laws have been blamed for skyrocketing house prices in places like San Francisco. House prices might also increase because more people—such as immigrants or people rising into the middle class—want to buy houses. But if these were the only sources of housing price variation, a bubble could not form. The prices would perform their normal function of telling builders to build more houses (if prices rise) or fewer (if prices fall).

These fundamental or "real" sources of house price variation can be contrasted with purely psychological factors that cause price movements. Even sophisticated investors can make mistakes and think that housing prices will rise more than they do. Sophisticated investors might think, for example, that immigration will increase housing prices when in fact a new wave of immigrants double up in the homes of relatives who already live in the United States. Miscalculations, if widely shared, could cause prices to deviate from fundamental values. But probably not for very long. During the crisis, many people seemed to be susceptible to a kind of mania, as a result of which they thought that the rules had changed, and prices would keep rising regardless of real factors.[7] Some of these people were new investors who lacked any understanding of markets. "Flippers" bought houses, held them for a few months, and then sold them, gambling that the price would rise instead of stagnate or fall, based on no other reason than that prices had risen in the past. Some of them were sophisticated investors who believed that there had been a fundamental shift in the demand for housing. Other sophisticated investors joined in the fun—not because they believed that housing prices would rise forever, but because they thought that enough other people held this belief, and would continue to hold it long enough, that the sophisticated investors could make money by timing their investments.

Why did the housing bubble lead to the financial crisis? The dot-com bubble had inflated and collapsed in the 1990s, and the value lost then was also many trillions of dollars. Yet no financial crisis occurred then. Why not?

To understand why, imagine that most dot-com stocks were owned by pensions, 401(k) plans, and sovereign wealth funds. These plans and institutions also owned many other assets—including bonds and other stocks. When the dot-com stocks lost their value, many middle-class and wealthy people saw their retirement plans lose value, but—in most cases—not by enough to make them change their behavior. If you are 50 years old and your retirement plan falls from $1.5 million to $1.4 million, you are not going to do anything different from what you used to do. Of course, many speculators and investors—including employees of dot-coms and dot-com speculators—lost a lot more money, but these people constituted a small part of the economy.

When the housing bubble burst, many people could no longer afford their mortgages and started defaulting. This by itself would not have caused the crisis. The key problem was that investors realized that the mathematical models that were used to construct and value the mortgage-related bonds assumed that housing prices could not fall as rapidly or broadly as they did. The models were based on historical data, and the bubble was historically unprecedented. Moreover, the investors who bought mortgage-derived bonds assumed that the underlying mortgages complied with the underwriting standards identified in the prospectuses that accompanied those assets. However, investors gradually realized that this assumption was false. Mortgage brokers helped home buyers misrepresent their financial positions; mortgage packagers may have been complicit in this fraud as well. As this information became widely known, firms stopped buying and selling the mortgage-derived bonds. No one could value them so no one wanted to buy them. Many owners were the investment banks that created the bonds and possessed private information about their value. A massive adverse selection problem arose as the investment banks were reluctant to sell bonds whose hold-to-maturity value they considered high while the market suspected that they would unload only those bonds that were recklessly designed.[8] When sales did occur, they were at very low prices, reflecting buyers' aversion to buying assets they did not understand, as well as their suspicion that sellers would seek to unload their most toxic assets first.

This feedback loop in asset prices is characteristic of any financial crisis. In the old-fashioned version, depositors run on banks; the banks frantically raise cash by selling mortgages; the value of the mortgages fall as all or most banks try to sell their mortgages simultaneously and accordingly find few buyers; the value of the banks' portfolios therefore fall as well, causing even sophisticated creditors to withdraw deposits or stop lending; and the banks must sell still more mortgages to raise still more cash. In the recent financial crisis, this feedback loop existed in different forms. Once it became clear that there were problems in the subprime market, people stopped trading subprime-related assets. Their prices plummeted. This meant that firms that held these assets in great numbers were required either to acknowledge that they were insolvent or claim that the assets were undervalued, as they were permitted to do under the principles of fair value accounting. But in either event, creditors lost confidence in them and stopped lending to them, forcing them to sell the subprime-related assets at fire-sale prices, further driving down their prices and driving themselves deeper into insolvency and otherwise apparently solvent firms to the precipice.

Cash-strapped firms also sold off other assets—causing the feedback loop to spread. In the repo market, creditors demanded increasingly large haircuts on loans secured by mortgage-related assets and then stopped lending altogether.[9] Borrowers were then forced to sell these assets into the falling market, further reducing their value. Firms that were heavily exposed to mortgage-related assets—Lehman, for example—collapsed. When these firms went bankrupt, their creditors took a hit. It turned out that money market mutual funds had heavily invested in the debt of investment banks. As they lost money, a run began on the funds, forcing the funds to unload assets, whose prices also plummeted. And so on.

The feedback loop created a wedge between the "real" value of assets and the prices at which they sold. As everyone tried to sell mortgage-related bonds, and the debt of firms invested in mortgage-related bonds, and derivatives tied to mortgage-related bonds and the firms invested in mortgage related bonds, the prices of these assets fell below the discounted stream of principal and interest payments that they would very likely have generated. The prices of some highly rated mortgage-related bonds implied that nearly every homeowner would default *and* that the foreclosed-upon house would sell at 20 to 30 percent of its value, something that had never happened before and, even at the height of the crisis, was inconceivable. A study of subprime bonds found that their pricing implied, under normal assumptions about recovery rates and mortgage prepayments, default rates on the underlying loans of 100 percent or even higher (Stanton and Wallace, 2011, 3253)! Yet subprime default rates—while extremely high by historical standards—never went much above 20 to 30 percent, nor did housing prices go down to zero, although they fell precipitously in many areas. In normal times, investors would borrow money from banks and buy up these undervalued assets. But banks did not want to lend—hardly anyone wanted to lend. Financial institutions, concerned about their own ability to repay their debts, hoarded cash.

The firms that faced trouble in the initial stage of the crisis were overexposed to subprime and real estate generally, but they also suffered from another problem: excessive leverage. Because investment banks believed that borrowing in the repo market was super-safe, they borrowed a lot, leaving only a small capital cushion to absorb losses. When the assets that served as collateral stopped trading, the firms could not borrow. To pay their bills, the firms sold the collateral at fire-sale prices. The small equity cushions could not absorb the loss, sending the firms into insolvency.

The panic spread through other channels as well. While the big commercial banks—banks like Bank of America, Barclays, Citigroup, Deutsche Bank, and JP Morgan—faced weaker funding pressures than investment banks and hedge funds because they relied on insured deposits, they also funded themselves from repo, uninsured eurodollar accounts, interbank lending, and other sources that were not insured. Their liquidity-starved customers drew down credit lines, and many banks or the companies that held them absorbed the losses of the trusts that they had created to package mortgages and other assets into securities or facilitate investments in those securities. Finding it increasingly hard to borrow in these markets, the big banks also cut down on lending. They radically cut back on interbank lending—that is, lending to each other, unsecured, overnight.

Because they publicly reported the interest rates that they paid on interbank borrowing—via the British Bankers Association, which maintained
the LIBOR benchmark[10]—their own creditors got wind of their funding
problems. The banks that made the highest LIBOR submissions attracted
the attention of the press, which speculated that those outlier banks were
insolvent or on the verge of insolvency—creating the classic self-fulfilling
prophecy as risk-averse creditors responded by withdrawing credit from
the outlier banks.

As the banks' struggles with interbank borrowing became known, their
customers took their money elsewhere. The banks served as prime brokers
to hedge funds and other big financial institutions—managing their accounts, offering credit lines, holding their assets, and facilitating trades.
These customers closed accounts, withdrawing assets that the banks were
permitted to use as collateral for loans and thus drying up another source
of funds. The banks shut down other services In normal times, they helped
corporations raise capital by underwriting securities issuances. And they
matched buyers and sellers of securities by holding vast quantities of securities for sale along with standing offers to buy. They sold (and bought)
interest rate swaps, credit default swaps, and currency swaps. Funding
troubles interfered with all of these activities.

As this sketch should make clear, the key to the financial crisis was
not the popping of the housing bubble alone, but the interaction between
the housing bubble and financial activity. If the mortgage-derived bonds
had sat in the vaults of sovereign wealth funds and pension funds, the
crisis would not have occurred. But because they were used as collateral in
countless financial transactions, and contributed to the net worth of financial institutions whose credit was relied on by the entire credit market, the
collapse of housing prices froze the entire financial system.

Financial economists are divided as to whether financial panics are
caused by pure liquidity problems—solvent firms that cannot borrow—or
also require insolvency.[11] It is, of course, possible for a financial crisis to
flare up because banks have made bad loans. If the loans are not repaid,
a bank can become insolvent, causing a run as depositors rush to remove
their funds, and harming other banks and other lenders. The S&L crisis of
the 1980s was due to such bad loans. Because high interest rates increased
the cost of funds for S&Ls, they were driven to make riskier loans for
which they could charge high rates themselves (White 1992). Deregulation allowed them to branch into areas of lending of which they had little

experience. Overinvestment in commercial building created a price bubble, which destroyed the S&Ls when it burst.

Most financial crises are likely a combination of liquidity and solvency problems. In the 2007–8 crisis, for example, many financial institutions failed simply because they issued too many subprime mortgages that defaulted and bought too many mortgage-related securities that lost value because of those defaults. These firms were highly leveraged and overexposed to the real estate market. The defaults indicated that the fundamental value of the assets was low, in aggregate lower than the value of the firms' liabilities. These firms were economically insolvent. However, many of the firms that suffered from withdrawal of credit were well managed, not excessively leveraged, and not excessively exposed to real estate. Lenders stopped lending to them because the lenders needed to hoard cash to protect themselves from runs, not because the lenders believed that the firms were insolvent. While the temporary decline in the market price of the assets caused by the withdrawal of liquidity made the firms appear insolvent, they were solvent in the fundamental-value or economic sense.

The recent financial crisis is best understood as a liquidity crisis, not merely a matter of insolvency.[12] While the banks and mortgage originators that concentrated on subprime lending were surely insolvent in 2007 and 2008, subprime lending was a small part of the credit market. The panic spread from subprime to healthy parts of the credit market, and the panic-driven runs threatened healthy firms. The fact that large, solvent, heavily regulated banks would not lend to each other—or would lend to each other only at historically unprecedented interest rate premiums—and not lend to each other even overnight, was persuasive evidence, universally accepted by policymakers, that the crisis was essentially one of illiquidity.

Financial crises are extreme events. They almost always lead to significant recessions (Reinhart and Rogoff 2010). The leading explanation is that banks and other financial institutions add value through the relationships they develop with borrowers; when the lenders collapse, the relationship-specific information is lost (Bernanke 1983; Chodorow-Reich 2014). Another explanation is that the sudden withdrawal of credit from the "real" economy forces businesses to lay off workers, sell inventories at fire-sale prices, and so on, leading to further downward spirals that disrupt existing commercial relationships.[13] Meanwhile, households had borrowed excessively and when housing prices collapsed, homeowners could not refinance their mortgages and cut back on spending (Mian and Sufi 2014).

The financial crisis of 2007–8 caused the Great Recession of 2007–9, in which all of these disruptions were visible.

OTHER CULPRITS

While the transformation of the financial system was the major cause of the crisis, other events and factors contributed as well. We survey them briefly.

Housing policy. As discussed above, the housing bubble and the relatively undiversified exposure of financial institutions to house prices as a result of the transformation of the financial system were the proximate causes of the financial crisis. It is natural to look for deeper causes in the laws and institutions that govern housing and the credit market. We start with housing.

The United States has subsidized housing since the Great Depression. The Depression badly hurt homeowners, who defaulted on mortgages after they lost their jobs, and banks, which absorbed those losses. Defaults, foreclosures, and the collapse of housing prices deepened the crisis. Congress created numerous institutions to help restart the mortgage market; many of them long outlasted the purpose for which they were created. Congress also created tax subsidies for housing. The idea that everyone should own a home became entrenched in the American psyche; the significant financial risks of homeownership, even to the middle class, were disregarded.

In 1977, Congress passed the Community Reinvestment Act (CRA),[14] which encouraged banks to provide services to low-income and minority neighborhoods. The law did not establish strict numerical requirements, but regulators could block banks from merging or entering new lines of business unless they opened branches and made loans in underserved areas. The law probably made little difference in its first two decades. The loans that banks made pursuant to the CRA were a tiny portion of total credit. But starting in the 1990s, the government increased the pressure on banks. CRA commitments soared from $43 billion in 1992 to $4.6 trillion in 2007 (Calomiris and Haber 2014, 217). In 1992, Congress passed a law requiring Fannie and Freddie to expand their loan repurchase business so that a substantial portion of it was devoted to mortgages to low-income home buyers. Inevitably, Fannie and Freddie lowered the underwriting standards for the mortgages they bought and borrowed more aggressively so as to lower their own costs. While there is little evidence that Fannie's and Freddie's actions directly contributed to the financial crisis,[15] the weakening of underwriting standards—made necessary if loans to low-income home buyers were to be made—spread to the prime credit market, which enabled middle-class home buyers to buy more expensive houses and to increase borrowing against their houses, further inflating the amount of credit in the system. Many homeowners during this period (like me) were surprised to learn that they could obtain a mortgage with a down payment of 10 percent, 5 percent, or even 0 percent, when historically the requirement was 20 percent. Adjustable-rate mortgages became more widely available as well, and so were exotic mortgages—at higher-risk levels—that enabled people to make hardly any payments at all during the initial years of the loan. Riskier, highly leveraged mortgages inevitably default at greater rates than safer mortgages do—and their ubiquity by 2007 helped cause the crash in housing prices.[16]

While underwriting standards declined in the prime as well as the subprime market, the shenanigans in the subprime market have since become legendary. Because low-income home buyers do not typically have savings, they cannot make a down payment. Because their income is low, they often cannot pay regular mortgage rates either. And because they sometimes work on the margins of the economy or are self-employed, they often cannot document whatever income they receive. However, banks realized that none of this mattered—*as long as housing prices continued to appreciate.* If a home buyer cannot pay her mortgage, but the house's value has increased, she can refinance her mortgage using equity from the house; sell her house and pocket the profit; or default on the mortgage, allowing the bank to foreclose on the house and sell it, with the proceeds covering any amount that was due on the mortgage. And even if (as it was still possible to admit) the price of the house declined and the lender lost money, the losses would be spread among investors in the securities into which the mortgage was transformed rather than absorbed by the mortgage-originating bank. A high interest rate compensated the bank and the investors for the risk they took on.

To create subprime mortgages, banks needed to use some creativity. To address the subprime borrower's lack of savings, it was easy enough to make a second loan to cover the down payment. To address the lack of income, the banks backloaded the mortgage payments: low "teaser" rates were used for the first few years, and then the rates would shoot up later. To address the lack of documentation, the banks simply waived the requirement. They may also have hinted to borrowers that they should exaggerate their incomes and financial health. The banks also reduced the risk borne by investors (and transferred it to the home buyers) by offering adjustable-rate mortgages and mortgages with prepayment and other penalties. When housing prices collapsed, subprime mortgages defaulted in vast numbers. Prime mortgages defaulted as well, but not as frequently.

Did housing policy—and specifically, housing policy that encouraged mortgage lending to low-income groups[17]—cause the financial crisis? Some conservatives put the blame on housing policy (Wallison 2015), while most liberals deny that housing policy mattered at all. The debate between them reflects a larger philosophical dispute about whether government intervention in the market caused the financial crisis. It is unlikely that housing policy was the sole cause or even a major cause of the financial crisis. Subsidies for the middle class and poor go back many decades; they do not coincide with the crisis. Moreover, only a small portion of subprime lending can be traced to government policy.

The subprime versus prime issue is a distraction from the major problem: the excessive amount of debt that ordinary people took on to buy houses they could not afford or to indulge in an orgy of overconsumption. Laufer (2013), for example, attributes 30 percent of the mortgage defaults in Los Angeles to second mortgages and other forms of equity extraction that were based on the assumption that housing prices would continue to rise. Mian and Sufi (2014) show that mortgage debt was vastly greater than what could be sustained by people's income. Home buyers frequently misunderstand the risks that they take on; government policy, which in previous eras limited this sort of behavior, contributed to these mistakes. Whether or not government policy encouraged excessive subprime lending, it certainly *allowed* excessive mortgage-based consumer debt, indeed excessive consumer debt of all kinds.

Financial innovation and derivatives. Financial innovation is as old as the financial system. Every innovation has raised the same questions: does it reduce the cost of credit, or does it provide new opportunities for speculation that may bring down the system? And the answer is always the same—both. The modern era dates back to the development of currency swaps in the 1940s and 1950s (Mehrling 2011). In the Bretton Woods era of capital controls, the currency swap enabled a firm to finance its foreign subsidiaries by trading positions with a foreign firm that sought to finance a subsidiary in the first firm's home country. A US company seeks to lend money to a subsidiary located in France. Capital controls prevent it from buying francs with dollars and sending the francs to the sub. Instead, it finds a French company that would like to lend money to a US-domiciled subsidiary. The French company wants to buy dollars with francs and send the dollars to the sub, but capital controls also frustrate its plans. The companies make a deal: the US company lends dollars to the US-domiciled French sub, and the French company lends francs, of equivalent economic value, to the France-domiciled US sub. To simplify the transaction, a multinational bank serves as intermediary. Each company pays its home currency to the bank and receives the foreign currency for its sub. The bank hedges its position by matching transactions, which means that the counterparties do not need to find and deal with each other. Currency swaps enabled firms to finance expansion across borders—which generated economic gains—and to avoid the regulatory restrictions on the international flow of capital.

Interest rate swaps and credit default swaps, which were developed in the last decades of the twentieth century, followed this pattern. An interest rate swap enabled a borrower to rid itself of the risky obligation to pay variable interest rates—which might at any time skyrocket. A credit default swap allowed a creditor to shed the risk that its borrower will default. The counterparties that took on these risks were thought to be large and diversified enough to survive them—and indeed could hedge them away, spreading and atomizing the risks across the market. But investors were not required to hedge away their risks, and many didn't. The party with the floating leg of an interest rate swap acts a lot like a bank—it bears the risk that interest rates will rise, and if they do, it needs to come up with the money to pay its counterparty—yet it is not regulated like a bank (Mehrling 2011, 82). Moreover, because these instruments were so powerful, they could be put to work spreading the risk of ever-riskier transactions, like subprime lending.

As noted above, the collapse of housing prices and the increase in mortgage defaults probably would not have caused the financial crisis by themselves. Subprime lending—where the highest default rates occurred—accounted for a small portion of the mortgages that existed on the eve of the crisis; securities derived from subprime mortgages accounted for a miniscule fraction, less than 0.01 percent, of the securities that traded globally (Dwyer and Tkac 2009). The real problem was that once the models were shown to be wrong, people could no longer determine the value of the securities, and so stopped trading them, which led to the liquidity crisis. Moreover, as a result of financial innovation, the exposure of firms to housing-price risk was concentrated rather than spread. Large firms could be exposed in numerous ways—they owned or lent against CDOs and MBSs, they wrote CDSs, they originated mortgages, and so on. Many firms, including the firms that held subprime loans on their books while packaging them into MBSs, thought that because they bought CDSs, their risk was limited. They didn't realize that since only a few firms issued CDSs, the risk was converted into highly concentrated counterparty risk.[18] Nor did the market realize that CDS insurance against default led issuers and investors to disregard the decline in underwriting standards as mortgage originators searched out riskier borrowers to sate the demand for mortgages (Arentsen et al. 2015).

In some cases, financial innovation should have set off alarms. The fragility introduced into the system through the construction of the CDO-squared, for example, which recombined the low-ranked tranches of CDOs so as to produce new high-quality securities, was just a matter of math (Coval, Jurek, and Stafford 2009). But economists and investors did not realize that financial innovation posed a threat to the financial system. They thought the opposite—that financial innovation enhanced the stability and efficiency of the financial system. Their view was not unreasonable. Banks are inherently unstable institutions. The benign-seeming S&L of old, which took deposits from consumers and made 30-year fixed-rate mortgages, was vulnerable to interest rate risk. If interest rates spiked, then the S&L either lost depositors or was required to pay more for credit, driving it into bankruptcy. This, in fact, is what led to the S&L crisis of the 1980s. Financial innovation seemed like a godsend. An S&L or bank could now protect itself from a spike in interest rates by entering into interest rate swaps; offload the risky mortgages to investments banks, which securitized them; protect themselves from credit risk by buying CDSs; and so on. While everyone understood that homeowners could default on mortgages in great numbers, the harm from the defaults would be limited by the value of the collateral; and even if housing prices fell, the investment losses on the mortgages would be spread among millions of people all across the world. This should have made financial crises rarer rather than more common.

Perhaps financial institutions were excessively confident and bought more mortgage-related assets than was prudent. The more one buys protection against risk, the greater will be the temptation to make riskier investments. Clues about the dangers posed by derivatives appeared as early as the 1990s. But it is hard to tell people to avoid relying on financial innovations just because they are new. Investors could not see what was going on throughout the whole system until it was too late. Moreover, the fragility of the system did not result from the investing activities of any particular bank or the invention of any specific derivative. The fragility resulted from the configuration of connections among institutions and the type of financial activities they engaged in—but these connections and activities were mostly invisible to everyone, even regulators; and even if they had been visible, no one would have understood them. Even today, the way in which financial interconnections within a network produce fragility or robustness is very poorly understood. It turns out that interconnected financial networks are, to use a tellingly oxymoronic term, "robust-yet-fragile," meaning that the system can absorb shocks over a range of (mostly unobservable) parameters while turning on a dime to become unstable once those parameters exceed (an unknown) threshold (Acemoglu, Ozdaglar, and Tahbaz-Salehi 2015, 566). In a financial network with *too many* connections, the failure of one bank propagates to many others, making a crisis more likely; but in a network with *too few* connections, any individual bank is vulnerable to shocks, again making a crisis likely (Elliott, Golub, and Jackson 2014). Again, the thresholds are unknown: therefore, no one—not even an ideal regulator with perfect information about the network—could possibly know whether the network is robust or fragile except in extreme cases.[19]

Mismanagement of financial institutions. Some financial institutions failed; others did not. A natural explanation lies in management. Ellul and Yerramilli (2013) examined the risk management practices of bank holding companies (BHCs) (a type of large financial institution) before the crisis and found that BHCs with better risk management practices had fewer nonperforming loans and higher profits during the financial crisis than other BHCs.[20] The worse-managed BHCs apparently did not recognize the extent of their exposure to subprime mortgages and so were caught off guard when the crisis struck. It does not appear that they deliberately gambled on subprime exposure while expecting to be rescued if their gambles failed. Mismanagement can be blamed for a litany of other sins: fraudulent underwriting and securities issuance, excessive reliance on credit-rating agencies, manipulation of marks, failures to renegotiate mortgages, reliance on compensation packages that encouraged excessive risk taking by employees,[21] and failure to monitor and constrain risk-taking mortgage originators.[22] But while all these activities took place and received a great deal of attention during the crisis, they are at best second-order factors. Their effects were mostly minor or ambiguous relative to the size of the financial system and the magnitude of the crisis, which took down the well and poorly managed firms alike.

Ellul and Yerramilli's findings just push the question back. Why did some BHCs practice risk management more effectively than others? They were all regulated by the same agency—the Fed—which applied common regulatory standards to all its charges. Before the crisis, managers faced the question how much to invest in risk management systems, and this question did not have an obvious answer. We don't really know which managers acted most responsibly because we don't know what the net present value of risk management investments was prior to the crisis.

There is other evidence that executives did not deliberately gamble on housing prices, expecting to be rescued by the government. In an amusing paper, Cheng, Raina, and Xiong (2014) test this hypothesis by comparing how Wall Street employees treat the assets with which they are entrusted and their personal finances. They compared a group of "securitization agents"—including both high-level executives and ordinary employees involved in mortgage securitization at major financial institutions—with control groups consisting of S&P 500 equity analysts and lawyers. The securitization agents did not show any more investment savvy than the people in the control groups. The securitization agents bought vacation homes at the height of the market rather than delaying purchasing. Moreover, the agents showed no awareness in their consumption decisions that their high rate of compensation—which was driven by the housing bubble—was temporary.

Attention has also focused on credit-ratings agencies, which played a significant role in the crisis. Credit-rating agencies gave AAA ratings to prime MBSs and the highest tranches of the CDOs; these ratings turned out to be spectacularly inaccurate. The leading hypothesis is that investment banks pressured the rating agencies to give AAA ratings to CDOs by threatening to take their business elsewhere if they did not. There was a race to the bottom among the ratings agencies as each sought to protect its market share. The problem was exacerbated by the opacity of the

CDO structures and the ability of the investment banks to redesign them as necessary to make them incrementally safer but not sufficiently safe when rating agencies withheld the AAA certification. Agency employees were either intellectually outmatched by their investment bank counterparts, or they conspired with them to obtain fees. Finally, numerous large investors—pension funds, banks, insurance companies—relied on the AAA ratings when they bought CDOs. But sophisticated investors distrusted the ratings and priced the risk that large CDO issuers pressured the agencies for favorable ratings (He, Qian, and Strahan 2012). While less sophisticated investors were fooled, the problem seems to be less one of mismanagement than of reasonable error. Rating agencies had built up a reputation for accuracy based on their ratings of corporate bonds; their customers reasonably believed that the rating agencies would maintain their standards for structured bonds.[23]

Deregulation. In 1999, President Clinton signed the Gramm-Leach-Bliley Act,[24] which eliminated some restrictions on the power of banks to affiliate with nonbank financial institutions like insurance companies and investment banks. Some people say that Gramm-Leach-Bliley repealed the Glass-Steagall Act,[25] which is said to have created a "wall" between commercial and investment banking, and that the elimination of this wall caused the financial crisis eight years later. This view is confused—it creates the false impression that there was a sharp break between an Edenic period of safe banking and a wild ride of casino finance—but it conveys an element of the truth as well. You can think of Gramm-Leach-Bliley as a metaphor for deregulation of the financial industry—a much more complicated series of events that extends back many decades—which *did* contribute to the financial crisis.

Deregulation took many different forms. Rules that blocked banks from operating outside of localities and across state lines were relaxed. So were artificial constraints that divided the banking industry into consumer-oriented thrifts and business-oriented banks. Banks were gradually allowed to enter new lines of business. While commercial banks were never allowed to enter the core markets of investment banks or insurance companies, they were allowed to sell themselves to holding companies that owned different types of financial institutions. But restrictions on subsidiaries' interactions with each other were retained.

Even at the height of deregulation, which occurred in the late 1990s and early 2000s, banks remained subject to strict regulations. These regulations limited how banks loaned money—to whom and on what terms. They restricted the lines of business of banks; how they were managed and operated; the types of investments they could make; how much risk they could take on. Regulators routinely inspected the books of banks, and demanded changes in management, in capital structure, and in their business practices. Bank operations did not resemble a "free market." And no one of any importance advocated a free market in banking. No one forgot that banks are fragile because of their role as credit intermediaries, and that the collapse of one bank can cause a liquidity crisis via contagion. Deposit insurance and the LLR served as backstops against this risk; all of the regulation on bank operations was necessitated by it.

Gramm-Leach-Bliley did not change any of this. The law allowed investors to create holding companies that could simultaneously own a commercial bank, an investment bank, an insurance company, and other financial subsidiaries. But the commercial bank remained subject to strict regulation and supervision, as did the insurance company. Their interactions with the investment bank were restricted. It is possible that the Act facilitated financial contagion during the crisis. If the holding companies spent resources propping up structured investment vehicles, proprietary trading desks, and other subsidiaries exposed to housing prices, they had fewer resources to support bank subsidiaries that were subject to runs. But if so, this was a relatively minor problem.

The real problem was the failure to see the transformation of finance—the rise of shadow banking—and to create new regulations that addressed this transformation. Regulators, like investors and financial institutions, did not understand the changes that had taken place in how financial markets operated. In 1998, Brooksley Born, the chair of the Commodity Futures Trading Commission, warned that the derivatives market was opaque. Regulators could not regulate effectively unless they could see whether any problems existed. At a minimum, derivatives traders should be required to disclose their positions to the government. Her argument was foolishly brushed aside by Fed chair Alan Greenspan and other top economic officials in the Clinton administration. They believed that financial innovation improved financial stability and feared that greater regulation of the derivatives market would reverse these gains.

Moreover, regulators blundered by allowing the capital cushions of banks and other financial institutions to erode. The central element of the regulatory framework of financial institutions is a set of rules that require all such institutions to maintain a surplus of capital—known as capital adequacy rules or capital requirements. The capital requirements imposed on banks and insurance companies have always been larger than the capital requirements imposed on other financial institutions like investment banks, dealers, brokers, and traders. With the benefit of hindsight (Posner 2015), we know that the capital requirements imposed on all of these institutions were too low. Bank regulators did not maintain sufficiently strict capital regulations for commercial banks, while the Securities and Exchange Commission (SEC) loosened capital requirements for broker-dealers in 2004. Most of the major financial institutions were in compliance with the relevant capital regulations and related rules until the day of their collapse—unlike the S&Ls back in the 1980s.[26]

Still, while higher capital requirements would have reduced the damage caused by the financial crisis, they would not have prevented it. The crisis-driven collapse in prices was so extreme that if these prices were taken at face value, even the most well-capitalized firms were insolvent. And capital requirements cannot address the problem of liquidity. A well-capitalized firm that is forced to sell off assets at fire-sale prices to raise cash will quickly become insolvent. The problem was not that the regulators failed to enforce the rules, or even that they relaxed the rules. The problem was that they did not see how the rules needed to be changed to address the new risks created by the transformation of the financial system.

Mistakes by the Fed and other failures in crisis response. For a long time, economists blamed the Great Depression on speculation in the stock market. The story was that investors borrowed from banks to buy stocks, driving stocks far above their fundamental value. When stock prices collapsed, investors could not repay the banks and the banks failed, which resulted in contagion and an economy-wide loss of liquidity.

In 1963, Milton Friedman and Anna Schwartz wrote an important book that placed the blame on the Fed's shoulders (Friedman and Schwartz 1963). The financial crisis that began in 1929 would have been a run-of-the-mill crisis—of the sort that had occurred frequently in the previous century—but for the Fed's inexplicable failure to increase the money supply to offset the contraction. Various other blunders by the government deepened and prolonged the Depression.

Friedman and Schwartz's view became accepted economic wisdom. In a famous speech in 2002, Bernanke (2002) facetiously apologized to them on behalf of the Fed and promised not to repeat the mistake. But years later the theory that government blundering caused the financial crisis of 2007–8 would echo Friedman and Schwartz's diagnosis.

The economist John Taylor (2009) has argued that the Fed created the bubble by pursuing an inflationary monetary policy. The Fed kept interest rates low in the decade leading up to the financial crisis—as a result of the 9/11 attacks and other events the Fed saw as confidence-damaging shocks. Taylor argues that the Fed deviated from sound monetary policy. The artificial reduction in interest rates encouraged people to seek out investments with greater payoffs. They ended up investing in housing and housing-related securities; the risky activity of financial institutions was an effect of the loose monetary policy rather than a cause of the crisis. The bubble was the unintended consequence of the Fed's lax monetary policy.

Taylor's argument is not widely accepted, but criticisms of the Fed's actions after the crisis started are more common. The Fed's single biggest error was its failure to rescue Lehman in September 2008. The collapse of Lehman sparked a run on money market mutual funds and caused disruption elsewhere in the financial system. Lehman played a significant role in the financial system; when Lehman entered bankruptcy, its counterparties were deprived of expected revenue streams and, so in turn, were thrown into distress or forced to stop lending. Moreover, the failure to rescue Lehman signaled—or seemed to signal—that the Fed would not issue emergency loans to other firms or would do so only under limited conditions. If the Fed were to abandon its role as LLR in the midst of a crisis, it would repeat its errors of the 1930s.

We will return to the Lehman debacle in chapters 2 and 3. As for Taylor, in truth his argument, even if correct, is of little practical importance. We do not know whether optimal macroeconomic policy by the Fed could—as Taylor implies—prevent financial crises from ever occurring, but it seems unlikely. Financial crises occur as a result of poorly understood and unpredictable financial behavior in private markets. A central bank that could anticipate and block such behavior would need preternatural wisdom and political freedom. Nor is there any evidence that a simple, rule-bound response to crises like lowering interest rates would be sufficient for restoring confidence. The Fed reduced interest rates to nearly zero, but the actions that ultimately broke the crisis appear to have been the accumulation of lending and investment programs, along with the stress tests of large financial organizations in the spring of 2009.

Government officials will always make errors. They will ignore the advice of economists, especially when economists can't agree among themselves—and the crisis left the theories of economists in shambles. Even if financial markets are not inherently prone to crisis, the involvement of fallible government officials in the financial system—which will not change anytime in the foreseeable future—means that bailouts will be needed. And that means that bailout policy needs to be formulated and embodied in law.

Capitalism and globalization. Finally, we should mention a culprit that received a lot of attention in the wake of the crisis: capitalism itself. Capitalism is the economic system in which capital is owned by private individuals and firms, who may invest it however they want. It can be contrasted with socialism, where capital is owned and invested by the government. Socialism was never a viable system of economic organization: because governments lack the expertise and incentives to invest capital wisely, socialism leads to massive misallocations of resources. This harm greatly outweighed one modest advantage of socialism—which is that since the government allocates capital, financial crises—at least, financial crises resulting from private-sector activity—cannot occur.[27] Capitalism allocates resources more efficiently. But capitalism has long been thought to be inherently unstable, in part because of recurrent financial crises in capitalist countries, which have caused great hardship and political instability.

Capitalism survived the great critiques of the nineteenth century not just because of the failures of its major rival, but also because governments learned to temper its edges. Financial crises cannot be prevented, but governments have figured out ways to reduce their frequency and severity— mainly through regulation, deposit insurance, and emergency lending. Countercyclical macroeconomic policy, welfare, unemployment insurance, minimum wages, progressive taxation, and other elements of the social safety net also seem to reduce opposition toward capitalism among those who do worst by it.

These approaches do not fully restore stability to the system. Debtors and creditors have a strong joint interest: to keep credit flowing despite government regulation. They have done this in three major ways. First, they sometimes just break the law and conceal their transactions from the government. During the financial crisis, many banks and mortgage originators violated underwriting standards, often with the complicity of the debtors themselves. Second, they pressure the government to deregulate. Third, and probably most important, the credit industry innovates. Much of the innovation is pure regulatory arbitrage—standard credit transactions are structured as if they were leases, insurance policies, derivatives, or other transactions that do not fall under the relevant financial regulators' sway. For example, banks could avoid restrictions on the amount of money they could borrow to fund loans by creating off-balance sheet entities that borrowed to make loans or buy MBSs—while the bank would offer a credit line to reassure investors in those entities. The credit line exposed the banks to risk, but normal regulations did not apply.[28] Regulators will usually catch on to this type of behavior, but they have trouble with innovative financial practices that plausibly reduce costs and risks, at least on the margin.[29] Securitization, for example, helped firms spread risks when they wanted to, but also turned out to concentrate risks in ways that regulators did not understand until the crisis struck. Moreover, regulators must contend with the ever-present fear that if they overregulate, capital will flow overseas. These pressures ensure that instability will always be a feature of a financial system (as famously argued by Minsky (1994)). It is for that reason that emergency measures, like the LLR function, must be put in the hands of government officials.

Here is another irony exposed by the crisis. Developing countries sought protection from currency crises by buying up liquid assets denominated in US dollars, which they would be able to sell quickly to shore up their currency. The surge in demand for safe, liquid assets fed the growth of mortgage-derived securities that would eventually cause the financial crisis of 2007–8. Rajan (2010) makes the "fault lines" between rich and poor countries (as well as between the rich and poor within countries) the central factor in his diagnosis of the events leading up to the financial crisis. But the fault lines are no one's fault; they cannot be removed. Financial instability will plague us for a long time to come.

Did Anyone Predict the Financial Crisis?

No. The standard forward-looking measures used to evaluate bank risk raised no alarms until the crisis was underway. Virtually no expert commentators predicted the financial crisis.[30] An earnest, sophisticated effort to measure financial stability published in 2007, sponsored by the European Central Bank, was very good at showing that past periods of financial volatility could have been predicted by the proposed measure while failing to notice the financial crisis just around the corner (Nelson and Perli 2007). The Fed did not predict the crisis; it recognized the systemic collapse of the credit markets only as it was taking place—in the wake of the BNP Paribas redemptions in August 2007 (Judge 2016, 879). As the crisis unfolded, virtually everyone, including Wall Street professionals, was surprised by nearly everything that happened—the collapse or near-collapse of all the major investment banks, the disappearance of even super-safe overnight lending between big banks, the run on highly regulated money market mutual funds, the collapse of repo.[31] This failure is worth dwelling on. It plays an important role in the legal analysis that will follow in subsequent chapters.

Not everyone was equally ignorant. The Yale economist Robert Shiller correctly identified the distortion in housing prices and predicted that the bubble would burst. Shiller deserves credit because his predictions were based on a careful analysis of the housing market. But he was hardly the only Cassandra. Numerous investors bet against housing. Many of them lost money because they placed their short bets too soon. It is costly to short an asset like housing, and those investors could not maintain their positions long enough to reap the windfall from the collapse of the economy. The journalist Michael Lewis, in his book *The Big Short*, celebrates a group of investors who shorted the housing market and won. These investors were shrewd but also exceptionally lucky that they did not place their bets too early—they were shrewd, but not as shrewd as the shorts who *lost* money.

There is a difference between predicting that the price of an asset will decline and that the financial system will blow up. The first type of prediction is undertaken every day, and people who are smart or lucky make lots of money when they bet correctly. Housing is just another asset, although a very important one. Investors who predicted that housing prices would collapse did not predict the collapse of the financial system.

We can make this statement with a high degree of confidence even though most investors do not reveal their bets. The reason is that if you predict that the financial system will collapse, the last thing that you want to do is place a bet with a highly leveraged investment bank, which is exactly what Lewis's shorts did. While it is possible that the bank will be rescued by the government (Bear), it's also possible that it will not be (Lehman). If you predict that the financial system will collapse, you should hoard cash or buy gold or very safe securities like Treasuries, not buy synthetic collateralized debt obligations that entitle you to a payoff from a financial institution that no longer exists.

Some economists made public predictions that the bursting of the housing bubble would cause significant economic pain. Shiller himself said that a recession was a serious risk. Nouriel Roubini predicted as early as 2005 that a collapse of housing prices would cause difficulties for financial institutions engaged in mortgage-lending and a major recession. Dean Baker made a similar prediction. Raghuram Rajan pointed out in 2005 that financial innovation—and specifically, the movement of financial intermediation outside the regulated banking system—might enhance risk in the financial system rather than (as thought at the time) reduce it.[32] But none of these economists predicted the financial crisis. Behavioral economists claimed to be vindicated by the crisis—which showed that many people acted irrationally—but they did not predict the crisis either. No one did. Not only did no economist predict the financial crisis in the years leading up to it; no economist predicted the financial crisis as late as the summer of 2007, shortly before it began. Indeed, it appears that the profession did not even think a financial crisis in the United States was possible (Gorton 2012, viii).

Wall Street also did not believe that a financial crisis could or would take place. Or it believed that if a financial crisis began, the Fed would end it by serving as the liquidity-providing LLR. These beliefs may have been self-serving, but they were reasonable beliefs. Is it self-serving for a homeowner to believe that he does not need to buy weapons and barricades because the government has effectively prevented civil unrest for many decades? A financial crisis had not occurred in the United States since the 1930s. The modern regulatory environment was, even after years of deregulation, far stricter than financial regulation in 1929. At the same time, the financial system was more flexible and vastly more sophisticated. And in a few instances where the collapse of a financial institution might have started a crisis—including Continental Illinois in 1984 and Long-Term Capital Management in 1998—the government intervened swiftly to restore confidence in the financial system before panic could spread.

If no one predicted the financial crisis, can regulators and bankers be blamed for thinking that the existing regulatory system was adequate? It is one thing to blame the managers of Bear and Lehman for putting their firms at risk by borrowing excessively and overinvesting in real estate–linked assets at the height of a bubble. Even without the financial crisis, their firms may have failed, causing a great deal of pain to shareholders and counterparties. But it does not seem right to blame them for causing or contributing to the financial crisis, and hence to the Great Recession, through their carelessness if that is what it was. They had every reason to believe that the regulators would take care of systemic risk.

2 Crisis

Every banker knows that if he has to *prove* he is worthy of
credit, however good may be his arguments, in fact his credit
is gone.

WALTER BAGEHOT (1873, 64)

HOUSE PRICES PEAKED IN 2006. AS PRICES BEGAN THEIR DECLINE,
the market for subprime mortgages—which, remember, was driven in part
by the expectation of ever-higher house prices—dried up. Homeowners
with mortgage payments they could not afford could not refinance and
lost their houses to foreclosure. In the early months of 2007, subprime
mortgage lenders filed for bankruptcy or shut down operations, and rating
agencies began downgrading mortgage-backed securities (MBSs). The defaults, foreclosures, and downgrades drove down the price of MBSs and
similar securities like collateralized debt obligations (CDOs). In April,
New Century Financial, which was one of the largest subprime lenders,
filed for bankruptcy. Bear Stearns owned two hedge funds that made
money by borrowing from creditors and investing in CDOs. As the value
of the CDOs declined, the creditors demanded additional cash collateral
on their loans, forcing the funds to sell off CDOs to raise the cash, forcing
their prices down further—in a downward spiral that we will see again and
again. In July 2007, Bear liquidated the funds.

While in retrospect we can date the crisis to the collapse of these funds,
even as late as mid-2007 the market did not perceive a *systemic* crisis—
a crisis affecting all credit markets. While the asset-backed commercial
paper market collapsed in July, other forms of commercial paper were only
modestly affected, indicating that the market saw a problem with MBSs,
but not with credit in general (Brunnermeier 2009, 84). The slack was

taken up by repo lending and interbank lending. The stock market continued to rise in July, and the fund collapse did not set off a contagion. It was not until August that it became clear that something was wrong. On August 9, the French bank BNP Paribas stopped withdrawal from three funds that had invested in subprime (but highly rated) mortgage-related securities. The bank reported that trading had shut down in the subprime securities, and so it could not value them. This was the first public sign of the breakdown in financial markets. And while one might have thought the problem was confined to subprime mortgages,[1] the cost of interbank lending—as measured by the LIBOR-OIS spread—rose beyond the historical norm, indicating that the largest banks were losing confidence in each other. Beginning in August, the Fed began cutting the discount rate and buying government securities, hoping to push down market interest rates so that banks would continue to lend to each other and to the public. In the same month, Countrywide—the country's largest mortgage lender—was hit by a run by depositors and other creditors. It was stabilized by an investment from Bank of America, which later bought it.

Countrywide's difficulties exposed to regulators the vulnerabilities of the financial system after the transformation (Geithner 2014, 122–28). While Countrywide owned a thrift that took deposits, most of its mortgage operations took place in nonbank subsidiaries that were funded from the repo and commercial paper markets. In the repo market, money market funds and other institutions lent money to Countrywide overnight against mostly high-quality collateral—Treasury securities and securities issued by government-sponsored entities (GSE) like Fannie Mae and Freddie Mac—but also some more questionable MBSs. When the lenders learned of Countrywide's business difficulties, they became reluctant to roll over the loans. They didn't want to end up with the MBSs, which were losing value; they didn't even want the Treasuries. Money market funds also didn't want to roll over Countrywide's commercial paper, which would lose value if Countrywide went bankrupt. If Countrywide collapsed, money market mutual funds might have themselves lost so much value that their own customers would run on *them*. The funds would be forced to sell off the mortgage-related assets, sending their prices even lower. To avoid the risk of a run, the funds were tempted to stop lending—but if they had done that, Countrywide would have collapsed even more quickly, bringing down the funds and other investors who had not withdrawn credit quickly enough.

It is usual to point out that in a liquidity crisis, everyone hoards money—people withdraw money from banks or other financial institutions and put it under the mattress. But this is not quite right. Mattresses don't pay interest; borrowers do. Instead of withdrawing all money from all banks, investors withdraw their money from the weakest banks and put it in stronger banks. Of course, after the weakest banks collapse, the next-weakest banks become the weakest, and become the target of withdrawal as well. That is why a liquidity crisis is an unraveling over time rather than an implosion that instantly destroys the financial system.

Financial institutions go to great lengths to avoid being stigmatized as the weakest. The Fed offers emergency loans to banks, but banks are reluctant to take them because they believe that the depositors infer that any bank that takes an emergency loan must be weak and withdraw their money from it, destroying it despite the emergency liquidity. To address this problem, in December 2007 the Fed opened the Term Auction Facility (TAF), which made loans to banks for an interest rate determined by an auction. This "facility," like the ones that would follow, just meant that the Fed would make loans to banks on terms different from—more flexible and generous than—the terms of the discount-window loans. An auction could drive down the interest rate so that a loan was less stigmatizing; and the loans could be made for longer terms and based on different kinds of collateral, including MBSs. Finally, the TAF took place through biweekly auctions in which groups of banks participated, further reducing the stigma that would otherwise attach to a bank that approached the discount window by itself. The TAF worked just as advertised, lending out at its peak almost $500 billion.

While the TAF created some breathing room and the markets seemed to settle down, another wave of downgrades of MBSs and write-downs by financial institutions created worries about the monoline insurers that insured the MBSs. If they were downgraded, then so would be the bonds that they insured. (While many monolines were downgraded, none would need a federal bailout.) In March 2008, the Fed opened another facility—the Term Securities Lending Facility (TSLF), through which it loaned Treasury securities to primary dealers—including the major investment banks—who were allowed to post highly rated securities, including MBSs, as collateral. In the same month, the Fed facilitated JP Morgan's takeover of Bear Stearns. Now the repo market was in jeopardy. Bear had bet heavily on housing prices and did not realize its errors until too late. Immediately after the bailout, the Fed opened a new facility, called the Primary Dealer Credit Facility (PDCF), through which it loaned funds (rather than just securities) to the primary dealers. The Fed was expanding its rescue operations from ordinary commercial banks to an important chunk of the financial system that existed outside the heavily regulated commercial banks.

In July, the crisis spread to the commercial banking system. IndyMac, a large savings and loan that specialized in risky mortgages, collapsed. The FDIC took it over and paid off depositors. Problems then became evident in the finances of Fannie Mae and Freddie Mac. These two institutions were hybrid public-private institutions that played major roles in the prime mortgage market by buying up mortgages and packaging them as securities. Their exposure to the subprime market was minimal. But the collapse of housing prices was affecting the prime market and—although this was little understood at the time—the collapse of the subprime market would hamper other types of financial transactions that were remote from that market. The Treasury Department, under Hank Paulson, persuaded Congress to pass the Housing and Economic Recovery Act,[2] which enhanced the government's powers to rescue Fannie and Freddie. This was Paulson's (2010, xvii) famous bazooka. "If you've got a bazooka, and people know you've got it, you may not have to take it out." (Wall Street Journal 2008). He meant that if Fannie and Freddie's creditors understood that the government would rescue Fannie and Freddie if they had trouble, those creditors would not run. This prediction turned out to be wrong.

The Height of the Crisis: Fall 2008 to Winter 2009

The crisis unfolded in slow motion until the fall of 2008. In September, the dominoes fell one after another. On September 6, the government took over Fannie Mae and Freddie Mac. On September 14, the government helped arrange a takeover of Merrill Lynch—a great and storied investment bank—by Bank of America. Lehman's bankruptcy filing on September 15 greatly intensified the panic. The next day, the Reserve Primary Fund—a major money market mutual fund—"broke the buck," announcing that it could not redeem shares at par and setting off a run on money market mutual funds. The Reserve Primary Fund owned millions of dollars of Lehman debt, which was now worthless or close to it. Later that week the Fed arranged an $85 billion loan to AIG, and Treasury issued a guarantee of the deposits of money market mutual funds while the Fed opened credit lines to them. On September 22, the next two dominoes— Morgan Stanley and Goldman Sachs—became bank holding companies. While they already could access credit from the Fed through the PDCF, bank holding company status may have reassured the market that the Fed would continue to stand behind them. Moreover, at the Fed's insistence, they raised capital on the market, which bolstered their stability. On September 25, Washington Mutual—a huge savings and loan—was taken over by the FDIC. The FDIC blundered badly by refusing to pay off creditors not covered by its insurance, which further increased strains in the system. When Wachovia—an even bigger bank—collapsed on September 28, the FDIC engineered a purchase by Citigroup, this time guaranteeing all of Wachovia's creditors based on the systemic importance of the bank. (Wachovia would eventually be sold to Wells Fargo, instead.) Less visibly, financial institutions that had traditionally relied on the big money center banks for funding fled them en masse (Beltran, Bolotnyy, and Klee 2015).

These massive rescue efforts did not calm the markets. Bernanke and Paulson agreed that congressional participation was necessary. The Fed had made trillions of dollars of loans—and FDIC and Treasury had contributed as well—but there were limits to what the Fed could do. It could not, on one view of the law (to be discussed in subsequent chapters), make loans to firms that it knew were insolvent or could not offer adequate collateral. And even if the Fed disregarded the law, it needed political support. Law violations, by themselves, could result in lawsuits, damages, and injunctions, but even if not, they could anger Congress. And independent of the legal issues, the Fed was not willing to risk public support by launching a rescue effort that could cost taxpayers billions of dollars—if the loans were not repaid, and Congress was forced to raise taxes or cut expenditures.

Calling on Congress in an election year was a fraught business. Members of Congress did not understand what was happening, and leaders felt constrained to trust Bernanke and Paulson. But the rank and file revolted. After the initial House bill was voted down—causing markets to plunge— a compromise was enacted and signed by the president on October 3. The Emergency Economic Stabilization Act (EESA)[3] was loaded with pork to compensate unhappy members of Congress, but it also authorized Treasury to spend $700 billion to rescue the financial system, under what was called the Troubled Asset Relief Program (TARP). Treasury was given explicit authority to buy financial assets of all types; it was not subject to the collateral requirements that hampered the Fed. And yet these resources were paltry compared to the credit capacity of the Fed, and even FDIC.

The three agencies worked in tandem throughout the rest of the crisis. In October, the Fed opened the Commercial Paper Funding Facility, which enabled it to buy commercial paper—a type of short-term loan, often unsecured. The FDIC implemented the Temporary Liquidity Guarantee Program, which guaranteed deposits and various forms of bank-issued short-term debt that were not covered by the FDIC insurance program. Treasury announced the Capital Purchase Program, under which it invested $250 billion of TARP money in nine major commercial banks. In November, the agencies put together bailout packages for Citigroup and Bank of America (the latter of which was not implemented). These packages guaranteed a portion of the banks' liabilities. In December, Treasury loaned TARP money to General Motors and Chrysler, the teetering auto giants. Over the winter and spring, Treasury implemented stress tests on the banks, requiring those that failed the tests to raise additional capital from the private market or Treasury itself. It also created a program for supporting private purchases of toxic assets, hoping that cash-rich investors would be willing to gamble that the prices of these assets would eventually rise and in the process remove them from the balance sheets of systemically risky banks and investment banks. Meanwhile, the Fed initiated a program to buy MBSs backed by the GSEs—eventually it would buy more than $1 trillion of them. By spring, the financial crisis was over, but the Great Recession had begun.

Bagehot

Why did the Fed and the other rescuers intervene in the crisis? And how did they decide how to intervene—which companies to save, and on what terms, and which companies to leave alone? Bernanke himself said that he was guided by a fellow named Walter Bagehot.

The principles governing the LLR were most famously articulated by the British journalist Bagehot in his book, *Lombard Street*, which was published in 1873. Although Bagehot was not the first person to identify these principles, he is routinely cited by central bankers, and I will do the same.[4] According to Bagehot (1873, 196–97), during a liquidity crisis, the central bank should (1) lend as widely as possible, (2) against good collateral, (3) at

a high rate of interest.[5] The function of the LLR is to avoid bankruptcy—
and sale of assets at fire-sale prices—of firms that are economically solvent. The LLR is not supposed to rescue insolvent firms, which should be
wound down in bankruptcy and deserve to be liquidated because they were
mismanaged and are worth more in pieces than as going concerns.

The three elements of the Bagehot approach are thought to advance
this goal. First, the LLR should lend freely, that is, to as many solvent
firms as possible, because it needs to replace the withdrawal of credit from
the economy by private creditors. The LLR should not limit itself to large
or "too-big-to-fail" institutions, nor to banks. A liquidity crisis affects
everyone and can lead everyone to sell off assets at fire-sale prices, which
causes spiraling harm. The extension of credit by the LLR allows all firms
to hold assets until maturity or until the credit market recovers. When fire
sales stop and asset values recover, the crisis ends, and the LLR should
withdraw credit.

Second, the LLR should lend against "good collateral" because it cannot afford to lose money. However, the meaning of good collateral is not
entirely clear. In Bagehot's time, it may have meant government securities
and other highly rated, liquid assets of the sort that a central bank routinely accepts as collateral during normal times (Bignon, Flandreau, and
Ugolini 2012, 596–98). The Bank of England was a (quasi-) private institution. If it loaned vast sums of money and then was not repaid, it would go
bankrupt itself. While it was in the Bank of England's interest to rescue
the financial system (so it could continue lending), it was by definition not
in its interest to risk its own existence (Goodhart 1995, 333–35). Modern
central banks are public institutions, but this principle has been preserved
under the theory that central banks should not take risks with taxpayers'
money that is the domain of the fiscal authority—Congress and Treasury.
Today, at a minimum, good collateral consists of assets whose "real" value
(meaning value during ordinary times) exceeds the loan and is not excessively volatile. If central banks do not lend against good collateral and are
not paid back, the taxpayer must bear the loss. The good collateral requirement just means that the credit risk incurred by the central bank should
be as low as possible.

Third, the LLR should charge "a very high rate" of interest, or a
"penalty" rate. The usual explanation for this rule is that a penalty rate
combats perverse incentive created by the LLR's existence.[6] The LLR,
which financial economists unhelpfully call a "liquidity put" because banks

can force it to "sell" cash to them, provides a kind of insurance for financial institutions, and all types of insurance create moral hazard by protecting firms from downside risk. To combat moral hazard, the LLR charges a high interest rate, which means that the firm that receives an emergency loan is not fully insured but only partially insured, much as a person with homeowner or auto insurance must pay a deductible. Partial insurance in all these cases provides the insured entity with an incentive to take care ex ante. The penalty rate also encourages borrowers to return to the private market as soon as it recovers. It is important to understand that the penalty rate is not very high. It must be lower than the high rate of interest that prevails during the crisis; otherwise, it will not solve the liquidity crisis. Typically, a penalty rate might be just a percentage point or so higher than the rate that existed just prior to the crisis.[7]

Central banks have not always followed Bagehot's advice. In the United States, the idea took hold in connection with the bank reforms of the Great Depression that the LLR function should be directed at the banking system but not the entire financial system. The government segregated the financial system into a safe and boring banking system, which would be backed by the LLR and FDIC insurance and subject to strict regulation, and the rest of the system, where (nearly) anything goes. Bagehot did not make this distinction. The law created the Old Model, which hampered the Fed's response to the post-transformation liquidity crisis. While the Fed did eventually extend emergency loans to nonbanks, it initially did so slowly and grudgingly (Wessel 2009, 147–49).

Central banks have also struggled with Bagehot's idea of "good collateral." During a liquidity crisis, assets lose their value because of the withdrawal of liquidity, but they may retain fundamental value. This means that a firm that holds an asset until the crisis ends will be able to sell it for more than the market price during the crisis. To resolve a crisis, the central bank must calculate this "real" value—that is, the value of the discounted stream of payoffs until the maturity of the asset, on the assumption that the credit market eventually revives. However, it is difficult to determine how much of the price decline is attributable to the liquidity shortage and how much is attributable to fundamental economic variables.

Some financial economists are skeptical that the concept of "good collateral" in the sense that Bagehot meant is meaningful. They believe that market values alone determine the value of assets. Fire-sale prices are just the market prices, and it is meaningless to talk about the "real" or "fundamental" value of assets as if the value of an asset could be determined independently of the market.

This argument is not persuasive, though it does contain an important truth. To see what is wrong with it, imagine that the government announced that, henceforth, it would refuse to enforce a specific type of financial contract. Assets constructed from that type of contract would lose their value and, if the market believes that the ban will remain in place, "trade" at a market price of zero. Nonetheless, we can meaningfully ask the following question: how would the market price change if the government on the following day announced that it had changed its mind and would start enforcing the contracts again? We might imagine that the price would rise, and predict accordingly. If we are confident that the government will not change its mind yet again, then we predict that the market price will rise back to its original level. This also means that during the day on which the contract is banned, the asset nonetheless had a "real" value roughly equal to its earlier market value multiplied by the probability that the government would retract its decision.

Provision of liquidity by the Fed is, conceptually, no different from the government's willingness to enforce contract rights. The Fed could achieve the same result as a government ban on financial contracts simply by raising interest rates by an arbitrarily large magnitude and removing all liquidity from the system. When the Fed decides to provide liquidity during a crisis by making loans against "good collateral," it moves in the opposite direction, restarting the market by replacing liquidity that has dried up because of a crisis of confidence. It is the government discretion to act or not act that creates the wedge between market value and "real" value.

If we do not like the semantic distinction between "real" and "market" values, we can eliminate all reference to "real" values without changing our conclusions by redescribing the Fed's behavior. When the Fed lends against collateral that is trading at a low price because of a liquidity crisis, it makes a prediction about how much the price will rise as a result of the Fed's efforts to end the liquidity crisis—including, of course, this very loan. Suppose that the Fed lends $100 against collateral trading at $80. The Fed believes that as a result of its efforts to end the crisis, the collateral will eventually be worth $120. If a purist would insist that the Fed is technically undersecured, the response is that the proper approach of the Fed is not to be "secured" in the normal sense, but to make loans that have a high probability of being repaid. A $100 loan against collateral trading at $80 has a high probability of being repaid only if the Fed can credibly argue that its rescue efforts will cause the price of the collateral to rise well above $100 (or that the borrower is otherwise highly likely to repay). On this approach, we do not need to distinguish between market and "fundamental" (or "real") values. The market value is the price at which assets trade during the crisis; the Fed makes undersecured loans against them; and the Fed is justified to the extent that it credibly and in good faith believes that its rescue efforts will create a high probability that it will be repaid and that a reasonable interest rate fully compensates it for credit risk. But as a practical matter, the two approaches are identical.

The objections of financial economists are best understood as practical and empirical arguments rather than conceptual arguments. Predictions about future price movements in the midst of a liquidity crisis will always be exceedingly difficult to make. In many cases, a liquidity shortage may result in an asset trading below its "real" value, but it does not follow that the asset's "real" value is par or above. The asset may be otherwise impaired. For example, during the 2007–9 crisis, AAA CDOs from the 2005 vintage (which mostly did not include subprime mortgages) lost considerable value—as much as 70 or 80 percent—and after the crisis were trading about 5 to 10 percent below par value (Stanton and Wallace 2011, 3255 fig. 1). This suggests that a part of the crisis-era price decline could be attributed to fundamental problems, that is, defaults that were not anticipated at the time that the CDOs were constructed. But while the Fed ended up accepting collateral that could not be considered "good" under normal definitions, it believed, based on standard financial analysis, that the collateral was valuable enough to protect it from defaults. As Geithner (2014, 156) puts it, in connection with the Bear rescue:

> Larry Fink of BlackRock assured me that if we held on to the assets for a few years, we could probably break even, with at most a few billion dollars in losses; I made him repeat that on a call with Ben [Bernanke] and Hank [Paulson]. I told Ben I thought that met the legal test under 13(3) that we be "secured to our satisfaction," and he agreed.

Finally, central banks have deviated from Bagehot's advice by forgoing penalty rates during a financial crisis because of the stigma problem (Hoggarth and Soussa 2001, 174–75). Moreover, it is not even clear that the LLR does create moral hazard.[8] According to Bignon, Flandreau, and Ugolini (2012), there is no historical evidence that the introduction of the LLR function in Britain and France in the nineteenth century created moral hazard. The central banks countered moral hazard by tightening prudential standards. Financial crises are rare and unpredictable events. A firm that mismanages its liquidity will not be rescued by the LLR unless it happens to fail at the same time that a crisis takes place; but because crises are rare, a firm can hardly depend on such "luck." To protect itself from a crisis, a financial institution must keep a great deal of cash on hand or raise capital through long-term debt or equity, but this would defeat one of the major purposes of the financial system, which is to transform short-term loans to long-term loans. Policymakers do not want to protect us from financial crises by blocking financial firms from engaging in finance!

I have dwelled on Bagehot because he gives us an important clue for understanding the wedge between the Fed's actions and the law during the financial crisis. The Fed was psychologically and institutionally committed to the Bagehot tradition as modified by the Old Model. Lowering the discount rate required no psychological adjustment; lending to an investment bank (like Bear) or an insurance company (like AIG) did—even though these institutions were functionally no different from the banks. The bank focus, the concerns about "good" collateral, and the penalty idea help explain the initial concentration on discount-window lending and rate cuts, the attempt to minimize shareholder returns in the Bear sale, the failure to rescue Lehman, the harsh treatment of the GSEs and AIG, the turn to Congress for EESA. Fortunately, the Fed was able to improvise as well—and, doubly fortunately, Congress came through with money. With the help of Congress and Treasury, the Fed was able to transform itself from the LLR into an asset buyer and insurer of last resort. It (or Treasury) bought assets and held them to maturity rather than loaned money to the owners of those assets so that they could hold them to maturity; and the agencies (including FDIC) issued guarantees left and right—fortunately, in time to save the financial system.

Aftermath

There is a popular view that the government lost money on the emergency loans that it made in 2008 and 2009, that the loans were a taxpayer subsidy for Wall Street that rewarded it for the reckless behavior of bankers.[9] This view is not only incorrect, but it fundamentally misunderstands the nature of the LLR function.

The government made rather than lost money on the loans—one estimate is $75.8 billion as of March 2017.[10] But whether it made or lost money is not the issue. The point of the LLR is to resolve financial crises, not to make money for the government or for taxpayers. As we will see, it is possible that the LLR could lose money on loans and investments that benefit taxpayers because they stimulate the economy. Still, the government's returns on investment provide a useful starting point for thinking about the standards for evaluating the bailout.

Why did the government make money? It could have been luck, but it is in the nature of the LLR that it should make money. When a liquidity crisis strikes, private lenders stop or greatly reduce lending, threatening the solvency of firms that depend on short-term borrowing, as most financial firms do. The LLR has a unique advantage over private lenders: it can make loans without raising capital. Of course, if the LLR is never paid back, it could, in theory, go bankrupt itself—in the sense of being unable to cover its operating expenses. But governments depend on the central bank, and the government would rescue it by using its coercive powers to raise taxes.

The unique position of the LLR gives it a quasi-monopoly over credit during liquidity crises. This means that it can charge a high price for its credit. This power was most clearly on display when the Fed demanded 79.9 percent of AIG's equity in return for an $85 billion loan. But even when the Fed charged ordinary interest, it could demand interest at rates high enough to ensure a hefty profit, if it so wished.[11]

The Fed is a like a fire department that charges people for putting out fires. A fire department is needed because the free market fails to produce private fire-fighting firms. While governments supply fire fighting for free, they could in theory charge a price, as they do for other services like public parking. If they did, they could—in principle—allow the fire department to charge whatever the market will bear, which would mean monopoly prices, as high as the value of the house to be saved. A fire department with such power would make a lot of money. But governments do not allow fire department to charge above a flat rate of $0 because the government's goal is not to make money but to save houses.

The Fed and the other LLR agencies put out the fire in late 2008 by reducing interest rates, lending broadly, lending narrowly, guaranteeing liabilities, buying toxic assets, and much else. While controversy will forever rage over which of these particular actions were needed, there is little doubt that the aggressive intervention did the trick, just as theory and historical practice would have predicted.[12] Yet the Fed was widely criticized and was to endure various slaps on the wrist from Congress over the ensuing years. Why were people so unhappy? The major objection was that the Fed has encouraged recklessness, which will sooner or later lead to another financial crisis. The argument is that if creditors know that the Fed stands ready to rescue firms that cannot pay their debts, then creditors will lend to borrowers even if they believe that there is a good chance that the borrowers will fail to repay on their own. More technically, creditors will demand an interest rate that does not fully compensate them for the credit risk that they undertake. This will lead to excessive lending, bad loans, and eventually another crisis.

The argument contains grains of truth, but the reality is far more complicated. Most financial institutions cannot depend on a government bailout if they face normal financial difficulties. An ordinary investment bank—say, a Drexel Burnham Lambert, which was one of the largest in the country when it entered bankruptcy in 1990—will go out of business, and creditors will suffer as they should. They can expect government help only in the case of a systemic crisis. But a systemic crisis is not something that financial institutions can prepare for. Consider again the plight of homeowners. They might take precautions against fire because they know that the fire department may come too late to save the house. But they are not going to take precautions against the risk of a citywide conflagration that overwhelms the fire department and requires the national guard to be called in. Because of the remote probability of a catastrophe, precautions are not cost-justified; and because of the massiveness of the catastrophe, precautions would not have an effect in any event. This is the ideal setting for government intervention.

A small number of financial institutions can depend on a government rescue. These are the too-big-to-fail institutions: they are so interconnected with the financial system that the government cannot afford to let them fail. Because of the likelihood of government intervention, their creditors will accept below-market rates in return for credit. Congress addressed this problem in the Dodd-Frank Act[13] by authorizing government agencies to identify systemically important financial institutions and subjecting them to an additional layer of regulation. It is too soon to tell whether the response has been adequate, but a perhaps telling sign of their effectiveness is that institutions fight designation as systemically important, presumably because the cost of the additional regulation exceeds any benefits in terms of lower borrowing costs.[14] The widely peddled view that the too-big-to-fail designation benefits firms by promising a bailout and hence reducing their cost of credit appears to be false.

3 The Lawfulness of the Rescue

> Some find it inconceivable that policymakers could be
> confronted with a situation in which there was no legal
> and viable course of action to avoid financial catastrophe.
> In this case, that is what happened.
>
> FCIC (2011, 435)

THE GOVERNMENT SOUGHT TO USE AGGRESSIVE MEASURES TO UN-
freeze the credit markets, but found itself repeatedly blocked by the law.
Officials reacted to their legal problems in different ways. After the collapse of Lehman, Fed officials claimed that they could not have made an
emergency loan because of legal hurdles. However, in the cases of Bear and
AIG, the Fed violated the law or interpreted it in an extremely narrow way,
rather than refrain from the emergency actions that events called for. The
Fed and Treasury relied on additional questionable legal interpretations for
the numerous credit facilities that they established, and in the bailouts of
Freddie Mae, Freddie Mac, General Motors, and Chrysler. In many cases,
the agencies evaded the law by engaging in elaborate legal maneuvers that
obfuscated their actions.

It is possible to argue that the law makes little difference. The agencies and their leaders did not pay a price for their legal violations during
the crisis; next time around, they may disregard the law again (Posner and
Vermeule 2010).[1] But it is clearly better if the Fed acts lawfully than if it
acts illegally. The legal restrictions were not costless. They caused the Fed
to act more cautiously than it should have and allowed officials to blame
their costly failure to rescue Lehman Brothers in September 2008 on legal
constraints and hence to deflect criticism of their judgment. The law also
forced the Fed and Treasury to structure straightforward transactions—
loans and asset purchases—in complex ways, which reduced transparency,
increased cost, and produced unintended consequences. The law was also

responsible for the division of authority between different agencies—the
Fed, Treasury, the FDIC, the SEC, and others—and their disagreements
during the crisis led to delay and coordination failures. Finally, the government's legal violations have generated expensive and time-consuming litigation, which may ultimately force the government to pay tens of billions
of dollars to shareholders (Zaring 2014).

The Law of the LLR

While the Fed is usually identified as the Lender of Last Resort (LLR)
in the United States, the LLR function is actually shared by the Fed and
FDIC. Before the Dodd-Frank Act,[2] the Fed was understood to be the
LLR for solvent banks and nonbanks. The FDIC possessed the authority
to wind down insolvent banks; as part of its power to do so, it was allowed to make LLR-like loans to counterparties in exigent circumstances.
There was no similar authority for lending to counterparties of insolvent
nonbanks, which necessitated creative actions by the Fed and the FDIC
during the 2007–9 financial crisis, and the enactment of the Emergency
Economic Stabilization Act (EESA)[3] in October 2008. The Dodd-Frank
Act corrects this omission by providing for an orderly resolution process
for insolvent financial institutions of all types.

The Fed's authority to make emergency loans to banks is located in section 10B of the Federal Reserve Act.[4] The Fed can make short-term loans;
the loans must be secured by high-quality collateral; and various procedural requirements and limits must be respected, especially if the bank
is undercapitalized. Under current regulations, the Fed charges a penalty
of 50 basis points above the federal funds rate for banks in "generally
sound financial condition," and an additional 50 basis points for weaker
banks (Federal Reserve 2016d). This type of lending is known as discount-
window lending.

The Fed may make loans to nonbanks under section 13(3).[5] This section requires the Fed to jump some significant procedural hurdles. It must
determine that "unusual and exigent circumstances" exist, and the Board
of Governors must hold a vote with approval of a supermajority of five
members. The loan must be "secured to the satisfaction of the Federal Reserve bank," and the borrowers must be "unable to secure adequate credit
accommodations from other banking institutions." Dodd-Frank added an
additional requirement that loans be made through a "program or facility

with broad-based eligibility," meaning that the Fed must set out eligibility requirements rather than pick and choose among borrowers.

Together, these two sections were thought to implement Bagehot's dictum. The Fed can lend broadly—to banks and nonbanks—in an emergency and must be fully secured. The statutes leave the Fed discretion as to how much interest to charge, allowing it to charge a penalty rate if it wants to.

The FDIC is given the power to wind down banks that are undercapitalized or have failed. In normal cases, the FDIC pays off insured depositors from its insurance fund, but otherwise creditors are not protected; they share in the proceeds of the sale of the bank's assets according to priority, and pro rata, as in a normal bankruptcy. In such cases, the FDIC is required to minimize the cost to the insurance fund—which means paying only those creditors (mainly, depositors) covered by it.[6] However, the law makes an exception where a bank's failure "would have serious adverse effects on economic conditions or financial stability."[7] With the concurrence of the secretary of the Treasury, a two-thirds majority of the Federal Reserve Board, and a two-thirds majority of the FDIC's board of directors, the FDIC may pay off creditors of the bank in question. The FDIC's role as LLR thus has two components: the routine payoff of insured bank depositors and the power to compensate other bank creditors in emergency circumstances.

This leaves a significant gap: large nonbank financial institutions that face solvency (rather than merely liquidity) problems. Before Dodd-Frank, the FDIC had no jurisdiction over nonbanks, while the Fed could lend to them only if they had collateral. During the crisis, the Fed and the FDIC engaged in significant legal maneuvering to address these types of institution, as we will now discuss.

The Fed's Struggles with the Law during the Financial Crisis

ACTING WITHIN ITS AUTHORITY

The Fed's initial responses to the financial crisis occurred after the BNP Paribas announcement, and in this initial phase, the Fed used traditional instruments that were well within its statutory powers. On August 17, 2007, the Fed lowered the interest rate for discount-window loans and extended the term of those loans, relying on section 10B of the Federal Reserve Act.[8] In September 2007, the Fed lowered its target federal funds rate from 5.25 to 4.75 percent. The Fed continued lowering the interest rate during the crisis, reaching 0 to 0.25 percent in December 2008. The Fed's authority to adjust the target federal funds rate by trading securities on the open market is codified in section 14 of the Federal Reserve Act.[9] No one questioned the Fed's legal authority to engage in these actions.[10]

In December 2007, the Fed tried to mitigate the stigma effect of discount-window lending by auctioning off the emergency loans rather than setting an arbitrarily high price for them. The Term Auction Facility (TAF), as the program was called (Anderson and Rieder 2008), resulted in an additional 4,214 loans, totaling more than $3 trillion (Berger et al. 2015). While these programs did increase bank lending (Berger et al. 2015), they did not unfreeze the credit market. Indeed, major banks preferred to increase their liquidity by borrowing from Federal Home Loan Banks—whose emergency lending powers were apparently off the radar screen—and attracting insured deposits (Ashcraft, Bech, and Frame 2010). While all of this lending was legal, it was insufficient.[11]

The lowering of interest rates also failed to end the crisis. In theory, by lowering rates the Fed reduces the cost of funds for banks and increases their incentive to lend. Home buyers can take advantage of low interest rates to obtain affordable mortgages, and existing homeowners can refinance their mortgages, providing them with additional cash to buy goods and services. However, the mechanism through which lower rates kindle greater lending had broken down. Banks and other financial institutions stopped lending because they could not determine the value of mortgage-related assets offered as collateral and the credit risk of borrowers who owned great quantities of mortgage-related assets. The modestly increased incentive, if any, to make loans encouraged by the interest rate cuts could not offset these massive risks. Moreover, as creditors realized that they could have trouble borrowing money, they hoarded cash rather than lent it out, so that they could repay *their* creditors or pay their expenses if further credit was not forthcoming. Home buyers and homeowners could not take advantage of low interest rates because creditors stopped lending (Gorton 2012, 186–94).

The more fundamental problem was that the source of the crisis lay outside traditional bank activities, in the shadow banking system. Most banks did not suffer from runs; deposit insurance and perhaps the discount window and related sources of support from the Fed reassured depositors (Bair 2012, 292–93). Runs occurred in the repo market, affecting investment banks, pensions, insurance companies, hedge funds, and

other nonbank institutions; and against prime brokers, also usually investment banks, which offered various credit-related services to their clients.
To address the problems in the shadow banking system, the Fed was
forced to draw on its authority under section 13(3) of the Federal Reserve
Act.[12] On March 11, 2008, the Fed created the Term Securities Lending Facility (TSLF), through which the Fed loaned Treasury securities to
primary dealers (major investment banks) that posted collateral, including mortgage-derived securities (Federal Reserve 2010b). By this time, it
was clear that "unusual and exigent circumstances" existed—a major collapse of the credit markets. The loans were made against collateral already
used in the repo market, including investment-grade corporate bonds and
MBSs. In the initial stages of the TSLF, the collateral was highly rated, almost certainly qualifying as "good collateral."[13] On March 17, the Fed supplemented the TSLF with the Primary Dealer Credit Facility (PDCF),
through which primary dealers could obtain short-term cash loans by
posting the same types of collateral Federal Reserve (2016e). The PDCF
was also legally straightforward—although as we will discuss in the next
section, some questions arise as to the quality of the collateral that the Fed
accepted. However, while firms borrowed huge sums through the TSLF
and PDCF, the facilities failed to resolve the crisis.[14]

STRETCHING THE LIMITS OF ITS AUTHORITY
AND VIOLATING THE LAW

On March 13, Bear warned Fed officials that it would file for bankruptcy
the next day unless the Fed loaned it money.[15] Fearing a systemic failure, the Fed authorized a $12.9 billion bridge loan to JP Morgan, which
JP Morgan would then lend to Bear Stearns, using as collateral $13.8 bil-
lion in securities owned by Bear.[16] The loan was originally directed at JP
Morgan so as to avoid having to rely on section 13(3). But this bit of legal
legerdemain, crafted by the general counsel of the Federal Reserve Bank
of New York (FRBNY), was nixed by the Federal Reserve Board's general counsel (Bernanke 2015, 214). The Fed ended up citing 13(3). The loan
bought time, which Bear used to find a purchaser. Merger negotiations
between JP Morgan and Bear commenced. In the final transaction, which
was consummated on March 24, the Fed created a special-purpose vehicle
(SPV) called Maiden Lane, which was financed from a $28.82 billion loan
from the Fed and a $1.15 billion subordinated loan from JP Morgan. The
Fed was given the "residual interest," meaning the equity, in the assets.

Maiden Lane purchased toxic assets from Bear, including agency MBSs, commercial and residential loans, nonagency residential MBSs, and other derivatives.

Under these terms, JP Morgan and the Fed shared the downside. If the value of the assets declined by up to $1.15 billion, JP Morgan would absorb the entire loss; if it declined more, then the Fed would absorb the residual loss up to $28.82 billion. The Fed alone benefited from the upside. If the assets were sold for more than $30 billion, then JP Morgan and the Fed would be paid off in full, and the Fed would receive the residual. As it turned out, the assets appreciated, and the Fed earned a profit.

The Fed invoked section 13(3) for this transaction with little explanation. The theory was apparently that the transaction was secured to the Fed's satisfaction and that the loan was directed to a nonbank in unusual and exigent circumstances, as 13(3) permitted. This argument could certainly be used to justify the initial bridge loan—assuming that Bear's collateral actually was adequate, for which there is no evidence one way or the other.[17] However, the Maiden Lane transaction was less clearly lawful.

The Fed lacks the authority to buy assets other than Treasury securities and a few other types of assets used in open-market operations.[18] If the Fed had simply purchased MBSs and the other toxic assets for $30 billion, it would have violated the law. The transaction was structured to avoid this type of blatant illegality. Instead of buying assets, the Fed made a secured loan to Maiden Lane, which then paid the Fed back. A secured loan falls more comfortably into the Fed's 13(3) authority.

The problem with this approach is that the transaction provided that the value of the Fed's interest would be tightly connected to the value of the underlying assets. If the assets fell in value by as little as 4 percent, the Fed would lose money. If the assets rose in value, the Fed would receive the entire gain. By contrast, in a secured loan—and especially a loan secured by "good," that is, high-quality collateral, in Bagehot's sense—the lender bears very little to no risk from the fluctuation of asset values. Functionally, the Maiden Lane transaction was a sale of assets, not a secured loan.[19]

The PDCF itself raises legal questions. Section 13(3) allows the Fed to make secured loans, but the loans must be "secured to the satisfaction" of the Fed. The PDCF accepted CCC-rated and other low-rated collateral and indeed collateral that was not rated at all, including equity interests that were not traded and exceedingly difficult to value.[20]

The Fed might argue that "secured to its satisfaction" means that complete discretion is vested in the Fed. But if this were true, then the Fed could issue unsecured loans based on collateral with no value. The statute limits the Fed to secured loans, and the Fed must make a good-faith determination that the collateral adequately secures it. For example, the Fed would be justified in arguing that collateral trading at a low market value adequately secures it because crisis conditions suppress the price. But the Fed would not be justified in taking as collateral assets whose fundamental value is minimal. Because the Fed has not disclosed its analysis of the collateral, we do not know whether it acted lawfully. But we are not required to take its word for it, and the large quantity of unrated and low-rated assets that it accepted as collateral in the PDCF provides grounds for skepticism.

The Fed's rescue of AIG in September 2008 faced similar obstacles, forcing the Fed to evade the law yet again. It created two new SPVs—Maiden Lane II, which purchased MBSs and related assets from AIG's insurance subsidiaries, and Maiden Lane III, which purchased CDOs from AIG's counterparties. In both cases, the Fed shared the downside with AIG and was given a major share of the profits—that is, equity. These two transactions were legally dubious in the same way that the Maiden Lane I transaction was—they were, for all intents and purposes, purchases of assets rather than loans.

Another aspect of the AIG rescue was legally questionable. In the initial transaction, the Fed loaned $85 billion to AIG secured by virtually all its assets; and, in addition to charging interest and fees, the Fed took nearly 80 percent of AIG's equity. The equity was put into a trust whose beneficiary was Treasury. A court later held that the transaction violated the law because section 13(3) does not give the Fed the authority to take equity in return for a loan.[21]

Later in the fall of 2008, the Fed opened additional credit facilities. To stop a run on money market mutual funds, the Fed opened the Asset-Backed Commercial Paper Money Market Mutual Fund Liquidity Facility (AMLF) and the Money Market Investor Funding Facility (MMIFF) (Federal Reserve 2010a; 2016a). It also opened the Commercial Paper Funding Facility (CPFF) and the Term Asset-Backed Securities Loan Facility (TALF) (Federal Reserve 2016c; GAO 2011, app. XII). All of these facilities formally made "loans," consistent with section 13(3) and the Fed's other authorities. But, other than TALF,[22] they all raised legal problems.

Through the AMLF, the Fed made nonrecourse loans to banks, which in turn used the money to buy asset-backed commercial paper from money market mutual funds (GAO 2011, 28–29, app. II). The banks used the asset-backed commercial paper as collateral for the Fed loans. Thus, formally the Fed made secured loans to banks, though, perhaps in recognition that the ultimate beneficiaries were nonbanks, the Fed cited its section 13(3) authority. Functionally, the banks were used as conduits through which the Fed purchased the asset-backed commercial paper. If commercial paper dropped in value, the Fed would be left holding the collateral, with no recourse against the banks. So, just like in a purchase, the Fed bore the risk of the decline of asset values. Unlike a purchase, the Fed did not have a share of the upside but would be required to return the collateral to the banks if they repaid the loans. The MMIFF complemented the AMLF by enabling money market mutual funds to sell other types of short-term debt instruments, including unsecured commercial paper (GAO 2011, app. X). A more complicated structure, involving SPVs, protected the Fed from more of the downside but did not cure the legal infirmities.

In the case of the CPFF, the veil was dropped. The Fed set up a SPV called CPFF LLC, which purchased commercial paper, both secured and unsecured, directly from issuers (GAO 2011, app. VII). The Fed's loans to CPFF LLC were secured by the commercial paper that CPFF LLC purchased from the issuers. Where that commercial paper was unsecured, the collateral for the Fed's loan did not protect the Fed from credit risk. The risk of any variation in asset values—up or down—would be borne by the Fed. The transaction could thus be viewed simply as a purchase of assets (the commercial paper) or, indirectly, an unsecured loan to the issuers, in either case in violation of the law, which does not authorize asset purchases and requires all loans to be secured (Mehra 2010, 244–45; Wallach 2015, 94–96).

The Fed's legal division made two arguments that the CPFF was lawful (Federal Reserve 2009). First, it argued that the recipient of the loan was CPFF LLC and that the loan was secured by the commercial paper owned by CPFF LLC. Accordingly, the transaction was a loan secured to the satisfaction of the Fed. However, this argument is specious as it would allow the Fed to make an unsecured loan to anyone simply by creating an SPV. Imagine, for example, that the Fed would like to make an unsecured loan to Joe Shmo, who has no assets. Following the legal division's advice, the

Fed could create an SPV called Shmo LLC. Shmo LLC would then lend money to Joe and, in return, receive an unsecured note from him, that is, an IOU. Shmo LLC would get its money from the Fed, which would make a section 13(3) loan to Shmo LLC secured by Shmo's note. Functionally, this is an unsecured loan to Shmo. If he defaults on the loan from Shmo LLC, Shmo LLC would have no money to repay the Fed, and the collateral—Shmo's note—would be worthless.

One could argue that the relevant language in section 13(3), "secured to the satisfaction of the Federal Reserve bank," just means that the Fed must jump through the legal hoops of filing notice of a security interest, and can take a security interest in whatever it wants, such as the cash it advances to the borrower, and the proceeds (if any) from the borrower's use of that cash. The Fed has never made this argument, as I far as I know. The reason is most likely that the Fed, Congress, and all other relevant actors have always understood section 13(3) to implement Bagehot, which requires "real" security—in the sense of collateral that would render the loan riskless or close to that, based on (good-faith) predictions of post-crisis collateral values. Note that if the Fed did believe that it could make unsecured loans, its claim that a Lehman rescue was illegal would be impossible to defend.

The Fed's legal division made a second argument in defense of the CPFF. It argued that that Fed could deem the loan "secured to its satisfaction" because in these cases the issuer was charged an "insurance fee" of 100 basis points (Federal Reserve 2009, 7). The insurance fee was in essence a premium, which, multiplied by the number of borrowers, created an "insurance fund" that could be used to pay the Fed if borrowers defaulted.

This argument is also unsound. The legal division simply redescribes an unsecured loan as a secured loan. To see why, note that *every* unsecured loan—in private markets as well as Fed loans—carries with it an interest rate that it is higher than the interest rate of a secured loan, all else equal. This "premium" can be described as an insurance fee if you want: the point of it is to compensate the lender for the extra risk that results from the absence of collateral. A private bank makes hundreds of unsecured loans; it can certainly claim, if the Fed's reasoning is correct, that the high interest rate is a "premium" and so goes into an "insurance fund" that can be used to compensate the bank if borrowers default. If this logic is accepted, every

unsecured loan is actually a secured loan. Try telling that to your bank ex-
aminer (who may well be the Fed itself)! David Wessel (2009, 228) reports
that "Fed lawyers swallowed hard" when asked to approve the CPFF.

WAS THE FED SECURED TO ITS SATISFACTION?

Section 13(3) says that the Fed can make emergency loans only when it is
"secured to the satisfaction of the Federal Reserve bank" that makes the
loan. The Fed repeatedly faced challenging questions raised by this provision. But what does the provision mean?

One possible argument is that the Fed can make any kind of loan that
it wants. As we saw above, the Fed's lawyers argued that even an unsecured
loan could be "secured to the satisfaction" of the Fed. The lawyers argued
that fees charged on the loan created an insurance fund that created the
necessary security. But why stop there? Suppose Lehman's boss, Richard
Fuld Jr., offered a donut to the Fed as security for a $10 billion rescue loan.
Could the Fed deem itself secured to its satisfaction?

In law, phrases that seem to open up infinite discretion for a person or
agency are rarely interpreted in such a way. "Secured to the satisfaction"
must be given a narrower interpretation. There are two interpretations that
are worth considering.

On the first interpretation, the Fed must be fully secured. It must, hon-
estly and in good faith, believe that the value of the collateral is greater
than the loan. However, the Fed, like any private financial institution, cannot always rely on market prices when valuing collateral; instead, models
based on historical data can be used to project future sale prices under a
range of assumptions. The Fed did, in fact, rely on such models—in many
cases, contracting out to private financial advisers who ran their own tests.
During the crisis, the Fed reasonably believed that mortgage-related assets were trading at a discount from their true value and was justified in
lending against them at prices reflecting estimates of their true value. This
is a reasonable, conservative interpretation of 13(3). It tracks the principles
of fair value accounting, which allow firms to rely on models when market
prices are unreliable.

On the second interpretation, the Fed need not be fully secured in
the sense above. Instead, it merely needs to believe that there is a high
probability that it will be paid back—high enough that the interest rate it
charges compensates it for credit risk. One often gets the sense from Bernanke's memoir that this is how he thought of the 13(3) security require-

ment. And, as I argue in chapter 8, there may be good reason to believe that the Fed should be allowed to make unsecured loans if it believes that the credit risk it faces is not too high. But this interpretation of the law is not a good one. The problem is that the word "secured" has a clear and definite meaning in financial transactions—it means that the creditor is entitled to collateral if the debtor defaults on the loan. The Fed itself, as far as I know, has made secured loans only during its normal and emergency operations, up until the recent financial crisis.[23] And the Fed's lawyers have not claimed that 13(3) permits the Fed to make unsecured loans.

When we evaluate the legality of the Fed's emergency lending, we need to rely on the first interpretation. And we know that the Fed did in fact determine "fundamental" values of the assets that it lent against, or at least some of them. Moreover, post-crisis work by financial economists validate the Fed's judgment that the assets were significantly undervalued by the market[24]—and we know that the value of the assets recovered enough so that the Fed did not lose money on its loans in aggregate. However, no one, to my knowledge, has tried to look at the loans case by case to see whether they were adequately secured. On September 15, 2008, the Fed made a $28 billion loan to Lehman through the PDCF against collateral worth $32.9 billion.[25] As much as $12 billion of this collateral consisted of securities with credit ratings of BBB or lower (including $1.3 billion of collateral that was CCC or lower) or unrated securities or equity. A case can be made that the Fed was adequately secured, but we may well doubt that it was.

PREVENTED FROM TAKING NECESSARY ACTIONS

Despite their elastic interpretations of the law, government officials—including Bernanke, Paulson, and Geithner—claimed that legal restrictions prevented the Fed from rescuing Lehman (Bernanke 2015, 252; Paulson 2010, 183; Geithner 2014, 180). They argue that Lehman, unlike Bear and other institutions, was insolvent and accordingly could not be saved under section 13(3).

This claim has engendered great controversy. First, section 13(3) does not require that the borrower be solvent; it requires that loans be secured. Up until Lehman's bankruptcy, the Fed made loans to Lehman through the PDCF, including the $28 billion loan on September 15.[26] The loans were lawful if they were sufficiently backed by Lehman's collateral. The Fed evidently felt that even highly dubious collateral—C rated and unrated securities—could secure the PDCF loans.[27] If the Fed was correct, it could have lawfully continued lending to Lehman, enabling the investment bank to pay off its counterparties. The Fed could also have purchased the securities using the SPV mechanism developed for the Bear rescue.

Moreover, the *New York Times* (Stewart and Eavis 2014) reported that lower-level officials in FRBNY believed that Lehman was solvent. A subsequent FDIC report found that Lehman was insolvent, but only barely (FDIC 2011). And a careful academic study finds that Lehman was economically solvent until the first week of September 2008, when it started unloading its assets at crisis-driven prices (Kapur 2015).[28] While FRBNY might have believed that it would lose money on a loan to Lehman in September, it could very likely have made fully secured loans to Lehman earlier in 2008, before Lehman's assets lost value, to a greater extent than it did. Because a rescue at an earlier date would have made Lehman's fire sales unnecessary, Lehman would not have been driven into (or near) insolvency by those sales.

Second, contemporary evidence indicates that the major reasons for letting Lehman fail were political and operational rather than legal. Paulson wanted to avoid being labeled "Mr. Bailout"—for political, and possibly ideological reasons, he wanted to avoid another Bear-style bailout. Paulson and others also worried that a Lehman bailout would create moral hazard (Paulson 2010, 109–10; Wessel 2009, 174–75). At the same time, the Fed was prepared to provide financial assistance if Barclays agreed to purchase Lehman, as everyone hoped (Wessel 2009, 21). It is hard to believe that Bernanke and the others would have facilitated a purchase if they believed that Lehman was deeply insolvent since such a purchase would have damaged Barclays, one of the largest banks in the world and an even more important institution than Lehman. Finally, Bernanke seemed more concerned that the Fed would lose money on a bailout than that the bailout was illegal. As I will discuss below, a risky loan, even if legal, might have angered Congress and posed a threat to the Fed's independence.

All that said, the questionable legality of a Lehman rescue provided a convenient excuse to government officials whose economic, political, and operational judgments were under heavy scrutiny. Moreover, some combination of legal and political norms must have led Bernanke to advise Paulson in September that the Fed's limits had been reached and that Congress must be approached (Bernanke 2015, 299). Bernanke may have believed that the financial crisis required the government to buy toxic assets, make equity investments in banks, make unsecured loans, and engage in other transactions that either the Fed could not engage in or could engage in only to a limited extent. These considerations could have taken different forms. Perhaps marginal violations of the law were permissible, but wholesale violations were not. Or perhaps the Fed lacked the institutional capacity to rescue the entire financial system—it just did not have enough staff, experience, and resources. Or perhaps the Fed sought to force Congress to share the political blame for the unpopular bailouts.

Congress passed the EESA on October 3, 2008. However, the legislative response was not ideal. In its first attempt, the House of Representatives voted down the bill, with nearly catastrophic consequences for the financial system. The Dow Jones index fell 7 percent. A later bill, overloaded with pork, did pass. There is little evidence that members of the House or Senate understood what was at stake; they deferred to the expertise of the agency heads. Hearings were expedited; witnesses who disagreed with the bills under considerations were not permitted to testify (Samples 2010, 4–9; Calomiris and Khan 2015, 55 n.2). Rather than resolve any of the policy debates, Congress gave enormous discretion to Treasury to spend hundreds of billions of dollars as it saw fit, subject to very loose supervision.

How can we summarize the relationship between the law and the Fed's actions? The overall picture is complex. The Fed arguably violated the law on several occasions and flagrantly violated the law on a few occasions, but it also acted as though the law put limits on what it could accomplish. In particular, the Fed felt constrained, on some (but not all) occasions, by legal prohibitions on asset purchases, equity investments, and unsecured lending.

Treasury's Lawbreaking

The Fed was not the only government agency that violated the law during the financial crisis. Treasury and the FDIC did as well.

During the run on money market mutual funds in September 2008, Treasury supplemented the Fed's rescue efforts by creating an insurance program for money market mutual funds. In return for a fee, a fund would receive a Treasury guarantee for its investors (US Treasury 2008). The purpose of this program was to restore confidence in money market mutual funds. The Treasury made available $50 billion for this program from the Exchange Stabilization Fund (ESF).

The ESF was created by Congress in 1934 for the purpose of stabilizing foreign exchange rates, as the name implies.[29] The law empowered Treasury to do so by giving it the authority to buy treasury securities, gold, foreign exchange, "and other instruments of credit and securities the Secretary considers necessary."[30] While this language is vague, in context it clearly means that if the secretary believes that Treasury must purchase or sell some other security to maintain the value of the dollar in terms of gold or foreign currencies, it may do so.

As far as I know, neither Treasury nor anyone else has offered a legal argument that the use of ESF to guarantee money market mutual funds was lawful. Guaranteeing the funds was not designed to affect the value of the US dollar.[31] Guaranteeing funds is not the same thing as dealing in securities; nor is there any other language in the statute that implies power to guarantee money market mutual funds or any other institutions. Nothing in the law authorized Treasury to require premiums in return for the guarantee.

Treasury's lack of legal power to address the financial crisis led to the enactment of EESA. This law put immense resources at Treasury's disposal, subject to exceptionally broad limits. The statute authorizes Treasury "to purchase . . . troubled assets from any financial institution."[32] "Troubled assets" are mortgages, mortgage-related securities, and "any other financial instrument that the Secretary . . . determines the purchase of which is necessary to promote financial market stability."[33] A "financial institution" "means any institution, including, but not limited to, any bank, savings association," etc.—with a list of other standard financial institutions.[34]

Treasury violated these limits in two programs. First, in the Home Affordable Modification Program (HAMP), Treasury attempted to pay loan servicers, investors, and homeowners to renegotiate mortgages. Paying a loan servicer to renegotiate a loan is not the same thing as buying a financial instrument. Although the latter term is not defined in EESA, definitions can be found in other areas of the law. For example, the Uniform Commercial Code provides:

> "Instrument" means a negotiable instrument or any other writing that evidences a right to the payment of a monetary obligation, is not itself

a security agreement or lease, and is of a type that in ordinary course of business is transferred by delivery with any necessary indorsement or assignment. The term does not include (i) investment property, (ii) letters of credit, or (iii) writings that evidence a right to payment arising out of the use of a credit or charge card or information contained on or for use with the card.[35]

Courts distill this definition into two elements: (1) a writing that evidences a right to the payment of a monetary obligation, (2) of a type that in ordinary course of business is transferred by delivery with any necessary endorsement or assignment.[36]

Treasury set up HAMP by creating a model contract entitled, no doubt with the language of EESA in mind, the Commitment to Purchase Financial Instrument and Servicer Participation Agreement (US Treasury 2009a). Fannie Mae, as financial agent of the United States, was authorized to enter this contract with any loan servicer eligible to participate in the program. Under the contract, Fannie Mae pays loan servicers to modify mortgage contracts in favor of homeowners, using funds made available to Treasury under EESA. In addition, Fannie Mae channels money through the loan servicer to homeowners who stay current with HAMP-modified loans and investors whose contractual rights are modified.

The contract modification is embodied in a writing, but it does not evidence a right to the payment of a monetary obligation. Instead, it evidences a right to the modification of mortgages held by others. Someone who possesses the financial instrument, whether Fannie Mae or a transferee, would have no right to obtain money from anyone. In addition, writings evidencing rights to loan modifications are not transferred by delivery in the ordinary course of business. Such rights may be assigned as part of a contract, but their value is not embodied in a piece of paper that is routinely transferred as a way of conveying value, as is the case for checks, securities, and other conventional financial instruments.

The other violation took place during the automaker bailout. In the fall of 2008 and the first half of 2009, Treasury used funds from the Troubled Asset Relief Program (TARP) to advance loans to General Motors and Chrysler, which ultimately entered bankruptcy and reemerged with stripped-down operations and modified capital structures. GM and Chrysler are not financial institutions but ordinary businesses, and hence beyond the scope of Treasury's authority under EESA. Treasury argued that GM and Chrysler are financial institutions because they owned financial subsidiaries, which advanced funds to car buyers, but Treasury could have made loans to those subsidiaries without also making loans to the holding companies. Treasury also argued that the automakers were interconnected with the financial institutions. If Chrysler collapsed, then Chrysler Financial would collapse as well—it would not have Chrysler customers to lend to—and the collapse of Chrysler Financial would reverberate throughout the financial system, exacerbating the liquidity crisis.[37]

As far as I am aware, the government never attempted to demonstrate that collapse of Chrysler Financial or GM Financial would have caused a systemic failure. By the time of the bankruptcies in the late spring of 2009, the immediate threat to the financial system had been resolved. If the secretary's say-so was entitled to deference, as one court concluded,[38] then the restriction to financial institutions in the statute would have been meaningless since all businesses are connected to the financial system.[39] In bankruptcy, the government used its power as debtor-in-possession financer to manipulate payoffs, ensuring that lower-priority but politically connected groups like autoworkers were paid more than secured creditors and equal-priority unsecured creditors. While courts ultimately approved the bankruptcy outcomes (with some litigation pending[40]), scholars have persuasively argued that the wealth transfers that took place through the bankruptcy process violated bankruptcy law (Roe and Skeel 2010; Baird (2012). We return to this issue in chapter 6.

The FDIC's Lawbreaking

During the crisis, the FDIC went well beyond its normal role of providing insurance to bank depositors. In October 2008, it created the Temporary Liquidity Guarantee Program (TLGP) (GAO 2010). The TLGP was composed of two pieces: a Debt Guarantee Program (DGP) and a Transaction Account Guarantee (TAG). Under the DGP, banks paid a fee to the FDIC fund in return for guarantees of new unsecured debt. Under the TAG, banks could pay for the extension of deposit insurance to non-interest-bearing accounts greater than $250,000, that is, beyond the then-existing limit of deposit insurance (which had been raised from $100,000 by EESA on October 3, 2008) (FDIC 2008). TAG was designed to deter large depositors like businesses from withdrawing funds from demand deposit accounts, while DGP enabled banks to raise more funds if withdrawals nonetheless occurred.[41] The programs were made available not only to insured banks but also to bank holding companies and bank affiliates that are not entitled to ordinary FDIC deposit insurance.

FDIC claimed authority for TLGP under section 13(c) of the Federal Deposit Insurance Act (GAO 2010, app. II). The law authorizes the FDIC "to make loans to, to make deposits in, to purchase the assets or securities of, to assume the liabilities of, or to make contributions to, *any insured depository institution*" to prevent it from defaulting; to restore it to normal operation; or to prevent it from taking down other banks, "when severe financial conditions exist," if the collapse of those other banks would threaten the FDIC fund.[42] Other provisions dictate that the FDIC must satisfy "least-cost" requirements, meaning that it must use the least costly method of helping a bank, and should not benefit uninsured creditors, shareholders, and affiliates of the bank in question.[43]

These provisions, by themselves, do not authorize TLGP. Under the quoted provisions, the FDIC can offer these services to banks—depository institutions—that receive FDIC insurance. But it offered TLGP to other financial institutions, including bank holding companies and bank affiliates, as noted above. Moreover, the law authorizes the FDIC to render assistance to a bank that is in trouble. But TLGP was made available to financial institutions that were not in immediate danger of default or undercapitalization. The program was aimed at the financial system as a whole, not at individual troubled banks.

The FDIC based its argument on a key provision in section 13(c), which creates new powers in the case of systemic risk. If various procedural hurdles are satisfied and Treasury (in consultation with the president) determines that compliance with the least-cost requirements "would have serious adverse effects on economic conditions or financial stability," then the FDIC "*may take other action* or *provide assistance under this section* . . . as necessary to avoid or mitigate such effects."[44] The italicized language is key. The most natural reading is that the FDIC may (1) take other action *under this section*, or (2) provide assistance *under this section*. The FDIC can use only the powers it has under the section—to lend, to buy assets, to monitor, and so on—but it can use them, when systemic risk exists, to help banks and counterparties who would otherwise be denied help because they do not have the FDIC insurance.

The FDIC's position, as summarized by the GAO, is that when the systemic risk exception is triggered, the FDIC's power to "take other action or provide assistance under this section as necessary to avoid or mitigate such effects" permits it to engage in *any* action—whether or not listed in the statute—as long as the action would mitigate systemic risk. The FDIC reads the language to create two powers: "to take other action" *of any type*, and "to provide assistance *under this section*." If systemic risk exists, the FDIC may invoke its statutory powers ("provide assistance under this section") *or*—do anything (GAO 2010, 50).

This is a stretch. The interpretation renders the phrase "provide assistance under this section" meaningless because it is fully encompassed by "other action." The language "under this section" refers back to both "other action" and "provide assistance," confining the action/assistance powers to those that the FDIC already possesses under the statute or closely related to them—the only purpose of the section being to eliminate the least-cost requirements when the entire banking system is at risk. As the GAO notes, "the practical effect of a systemic risk determination under the agencies' reading is to authorize any type of assistance to any type of entity, provided the aid is deemed necessary to avoid or mitigate systemic risk." (GAO 2010, 53). The FDIC's interpretation converts the FDIC into a general LLR that can rescue any company, not just a bank—duplicating the Fed's powers.

This is plainly wrong. Congress saw the FDIC as foremost a preserver of the deposit insurance fund and supervisor of banks and, in 1991, added language to the FDIC's authorizing statute to encourage it to spend as little money rescuing banks as possible (GAO 2010). If a systemic crisis occurs, the FDIC may rescue a bank in the non-least-cost-way—for example, by paying off creditors who are not covered by deposit insurance or keeping a bank temporarily alive when it is insolvent—when nonpayment of creditors or the bank's failure would threaten the system. By contrast, under the TLGP, the FDIC offered insurance beyond the regular FDIC insurance program to banks that were not under threat of collapse and that were not determined to be systemically important, and to nonbanks as well.[45]

The FDIC also violated the law through its participation in the public-private investment program, a Treasury initiative that enabled private entities and Treasury to jointly buy toxic loans and toxic securities from banks (US Treasury 2009b; 2009c). The FDIC supported this program by insuring the debt issued by Public-Private Investment Funds (PPIFs), which were supplied by equity capital from Treasury and private investors. PPIFs would buy undervalued mortgages and mortgage securities from banks and either hold them to maturity or sell them after their prices recovered. The debt, secured by the mortgages or securities, would be paid off first, with the balance going to the investors, as usual. The FDIC relied on the systemic-risk trigger in its statute. Under its interpretation, the PPIF guarantees certainly qualified as "other actions," and other actions that plausibility mitigate systemic risk. Under the more plausible interpretation of the statute, the PPIF guarantees were illegal because they were not issued to banks. They were issued to funds or trusts, which were effectively hedge funds, not depository institutions.[46]

Gaps in the Rescue Agencies' Authority

The crisis response was hampered by gaps in the government's powers. While EESA closed some of these gaps, the involvement of Congress in the midst of a crisis created problems of its own. There was not enough time for members of Congress to educate themselves about the crisis and to deliberate about it. Election-year politics also interfered with deliberation; experts outside the government, whose testimony would have normally been sought, were excluded from participation by Democrats who, according to a pair of authors, wanted to ensure that the public would associate the crisis response with the Bush administration (Calomiris and Khan 2015). Congress was little more than a rubber stamp.

In sum, the agencies were hampered by their lack of authority to

- buy assets, including equity;
- make unsecured loans to nonbank financial institutions;
- control nonbank financial institutions to which the Fed made loans, to force them to pay off counterparties, lend money, and so on;
- wind up insolvent nonbank financial institutions, including the lack of authority to lend to them or counterparties to ensure an orderly liquidation;
- force nonbank financial institutions to raise capital;
- dictate terms of transactions, control the behavior of firms (for example, forcing them to lend), or acquire them where necessary.

It turns out that the financial system needs not just a LLR, but also a "dealer of last resort" (Mehrling 2011) or "market-maker of last resort" (Tucker 2014).[47] Congress had never given the Fed the powers it needed to discharge *this* function because—before the transformation of the financial system—no one knew that it needed those powers.

In the absence of these authorities, the agencies improvised. In some cases, the agencies simply violated the law. In others, the agencies used both veiled threats to force financial institutions to act in ways that would, in the government's view, restore financial stability, and "regulated by deal" (Davidoff and Zaring 2009)—effectively, bribing financial institutions to act in those ways. As an illustration of both these points, consider the Capital Purchase Program (CPP). To persuade banks to participate in this program, Treasury both offered favorable terms and issued a veiled threat ("regulatory consequences") that things would go poorly for banks that did not participate (Geithner 2014, 238; Wessel 2009, 24)). Neither of these strategies is good from a public policy standpoint. As Veronesi and Zingales (2010) show, to induce the banks to participate in the CPP, the government offered terms that in the end gave the banks a subsidy from taxpayers worth between $21 and $44 billion. In theory, the government could have offered less generous terms; but the government officials weren't willing to take the risk that the banks would turn them down. At the same time, threats—veiled or otherwise—present their own set of problems. To threaten the banks, the regulators must credibly be able to impose costs on them or deprive them of benefits. But the regulators are supposed to impose costs on banks only if they violate regulations. If they don't, then courts will block the sanctions. Thus, only a threat to deny benefits—like approval of future merger applications—is credible. But even here, if a merger benefits a bank and hence its customers, the regulator will be hard pressed to refuse approval. Judicial review as well as the regulator's own interest in approving bank mergers that enhance stability will further deprive the threat of credibility. Treasury officials would later claim that they could not use threats to force AIG's Maiden Lane III counterparties to accept haircuts, as we will see in chapter 4.

In the next three chapters, I examine the consequences of the LLR's lawbreaking in more detail.

4

The Trial of AIG

We forced losses on shareholders proportionate
to the mistakes of the firm.
TIMOTHY GEITHNER[1]

AIG WAS A HUGE CONGLOMERATE THAT OWNED NUMEROUS INSUR-
ance companies. The vast majority of AIG's activities were unconnected to
traditional finance. AIG offered life, home, and other kinds of insurance.
It was a highly regarded, well-managed firm that had a credit rating of
AAA until 2005, when its credit rating was reduced to a (still high) AA+
as a result of an accounting scandal. The insurance subsidiaries were all
financially healthy and closely regulated by the insurance commissions of
the states and of foreign countries.

An AIG subsidiary called AIG Financial Products (AIG FP) was the
major source of AIG's woes during the financial crisis. AIG FP wrote
credit default swaps (CDSs) on many of the collateralized debt obligations
(CDOs) that lost their value or stopped trading during the crisis. Many of
AIG's insurance subsidiaries also invested in mortgage-backed securities
(MBSs). FP stopped writing CDSs in 2005 when FP executives realized
that FP had become overexposed to real estate and that the quality of the
CDOs had degraded as issuers packaged increasingly dubious mortgages
into them. However, AIG either could not, or would not, exit from or
hedge its existing CDS deals. And the insurance subsidiaries continued
investing in MBSs. When the financial crisis struck, AIG was forced to
post collateral on its CDS transactions; meanwhile, its securities lending
counterparties demanded their collateral back. When its creditors stopped
lending to it, AIG faced bankruptcy.

The Fed made an emergency loan to AIG, which enabled it to post collateral and settle its CDS transactions. In return, AIG was required to give the US government 79.9 percent of its equity. Additional funds from the Troubled Asset Relief Program (TARP) kept AIG alive until the financial crisis ended and AIG was able to access private financial markets. The government turned a $22.7 billion profit on its investment in AIG.

In 2011, Starr International, which was AIG's largest shareholder at the time of the rescue, brought lawsuits against the Federal Reserve Bank of New York (FRBNY) and the US government. Starr argued that the FRBNY violated its fiduciary duty to minority shareholders by causing AIG to transfer funds to counterparties, and that the 79.9 percent equity transfer was a taking in violation of the US Constitution, as it left AIG shareholders with only 20 percent of the value of their equity. The government responded that "twenty percent of something [is] better than 100 percent of nothing."[2] But for the government's intervention, shareholders would have received nothing. This chapter evaluates Starr's argument and the government's response.

AIG before the Crisis

AIG was (and is) a gigantic insurance company, one of the largest in the world. Its current market capitalization is about $60 billion on more than $500 billion in assets. Most of its growth occurred under the leadership of Maurice (Hank) Greenberg, who became CEO in 1968. Greenberg purchased insurance companies around the world and expanded their operations.

AIG's Role in Financial Markets

AIG's financial difficulties in 2008 derived from two sources. First was its involvement in the CDS market. FP sold insurance on CDOs and other debt instruments, offering to pay the par value of the bonds if they defaulted, in return for a small premium. FP, like most other market participants, believed that the risk of default on the highly rated tranches of the CDOs was miniscule. A highly rated CDO tranche is given preference over the streams of payments generated from numerous mortgages. If a homeowner misses a payment, or even a lot of homeowners miss their payments, the payoffs to holders of AAA tranches will not be affected because they receive payments from those who do not miss payments, while lower-rated tranches take the hit. And because the mortgages are diversified—they come from different regions and involve different types of people—the probability that many or most homeowners would all simultaneously miss payments was small. And even then, holders of AAA tranches would be entitled to payments from the foreclosure and sale of their houses. That meant default could take place only if there was a nationwide collapse in housing prices of a type that had not occurred since the Great Depression. Accordingly, FP—and other CDS writers—charged very low prices to insure AAA-rated CDOs.

FP insured a vast number of such CDOs, but it left the market in late 2005. It was then that FP executives realized that FP was overexposed to them and that the quality of CDOs was declining as banks increasingly created them from subprime (rather than prime) mortgages. Under the terms of the contracts, the institutions that managed the CDOs were allowed to replace expiring prime mortgages with new subprime mortgages, which further degraded the quality of the instruments. AIG exited the CDS market, while other companies stayed in it. These other companies insured the new subprime-based CDOs that AIG wouldn't touch. But AIG did not attempt to unwind or hedge its deals. At the end of 2007, AIG's exposure to CDOs amounted to $78 billion (McDonald and Paulson 2015).

Under its contracts with counterparties, AIG was required to post cash collateral on the CDSs. Before the crisis, the collateral requirements were minimal. Indeed, senior officials at AIG apparently did not even know about these requirements (Boyd 2011). But the contracts stipulated that AIG would be required to post additional collateral if AIG's credit rating declined or the market value or credit ratings of the CDOs declined. In 2008, credit rating agencies began to reduce the credit ratings on the underlying securities, and their prices fell. As AIG posted additional collateral, its financial position became more precarious—as it needed to post cash and had only so much. As its position entered a critical phase, AIG had posted $15 billion in collateral and was rapidly running out of money. AIG faced a rating downgrade, which would have further increased its collateral obligations to a level that it could not afford.

Second, AIG's insurance subsidiaries had bought numerous residential MBSs using the proceeds from their securities-lending business. Insurance regulations require insurance companies to invest their assets in safe securities like corporate bonds. Under the securities-lending program, AIG lent these securities out to hedge funds and other financial institutions in return for interest. The counterparties posted cash collateral with AIG, which invested it in mortgage-backed securities as well as other instruments. In 2007, AIG's life insurance subsidiaries collectively lent out 19 percent of their assets, securities worth $364.5 billion (McDonald and Paulson 2015, 90). AIG believed that these transactions were safe because the MBSs were highly rated and liquid. If counterparties returned the securities to AIG and demanded their cash collateral back, AIG could raise the cash by selling the MBSs. When the crisis struck, however, the MBS market froze up. AIG could not sell the MBSs in its portfolio at par value. When counterparties demanded their collateral back, AIG was forced to sell assets at a loss.

These two activities exposed AIG to fluctuations in housing prices to a considerable degree. McDonald and Paulson (2015, 101, online app.) calculate that AIG's real estate exposure was $380 billion in 2007, compared to equity of only $95.8 billion and reported assets of $1.06 trillion. This put AIG in the company of other highly exposed financial institutions like Citigroup and MetLife. AIG's CDS business lost $28.6 billion in 2008, and its securities-lending business lost about $21 billion.

AIG's exposure to real estate came as a surprise to government officials. AIG was an insurance company, and insurance companies are supposed to be conservatively run. The public debate about the bailouts in the fall of 2008 assumed that AIG and other companies had behaved "recklessly" and the government was doing them a favor by bailing them out. Bernanke told Congress that AIG's collapse angered him more than any other event during the crisis. But the actual nature and degree of AIG's culpability is more complicated than it first appears.

Many companies acted badly in the years leading up to the crisis. First on the list were the banks and other mortgage originators that issued subprime loans that violated underwriting standards, and the commercial and investment banks that packaged these mortgages into CDOs. The SEC brought enforcement actions against 198 entities or individuals for wrongdoing arising from the financial crisis—including nearly all the major banks and nonbank financial institutions (SEC 2016).[3] Many of these companies not only acted recklessly but violated the law, and were duly punished. Bank of America coughed up $16 billion in just one settlement with the Department of Justice. In all, the major banks paid more than $100 billion in settlements related to federal investigations into their mortgage practices, and this doesn't include billions more paid to plaintiffs in private litigation (Rexrode and Grossman 2014). The ratings agencies, which assigned high ratings to the CDOs based on faulty models, were also blameworthy and paid fines to the government. AIG was not among this group of companies. It did not issue or package mortgages, nor was it charged or prosecuted or sued by the government. Its major mistake was believing the AAA ratings of the ratings agencies and accepting the representations of the underwriters and packagers. It also took on excessive exposure to real estate.

So what went wrong? AIG fell through significant regulatory cracks in the crazy-quilt system of regulation that prevailed (and still prevails) in the United States. AIG's subsidiaries were regulated by state insurance commissions, which ensured that the subsidiaries themselves were adequately capitalized and conservatively managed. The state regulators were aware of the securities-lending business but unconcerned because the loans were collateralized, and this business practice was longstanding and considered safe. The regulators did not know that FP was insuring mortgages, and so could not have known that the holding company might fail at precisely the moment that the securities-lending business dried up. Not that they might have done anything even if they had known about FP's activities; because the subsidiaries were independently regulated and subject to significant capital requirements, the agencies might have regarded FP's activities as irrelevant.[4] Meanwhile, the hapless Office of Thrift Supervision (OTS) oversaw the holding company—AIG owned a thrift—and thus could have ordered AIG to curtail FP's investments if they posed a risk to the company. But OTS did not appreciate the risks posed by FP to the business as a whole.[5]

AIG's troubles began in the summer of 2007. That was when Goldman issued the first of the collateral calls that would eventually deplete AIG of liquidity. In July, Goldman issued a collateral call for $1.8 billion. To justify the collateral call, Goldman argued that the relevant CDOs traded well below par value. Indeed, the CDOs hardly traded at all. Other firms were able to avoid marking down the CDOs in their portfolio because they refused to trade them. But it was precisely this refusal to trade at anywhere near par value that confirmed Goldman's calculations. At the same time, the absence of trading also made it possible for AIG to dispute the collateral call. With so little trading, no one knew how much the CDOs were worth. If the CDOs could not be valued, then the collateral requirement—which was a function of the difference between the par value and the market values of the CDOs—could not be calculated. For this reason, AIG refused to post the full amount of collateral that Goldman demanded, and instead eventually posted a significantly smaller amount. Goldman continued to make collateral calls over the ensuing months, and AIG continued to dispute them. In the summer of 2008, other firms joined in. As the collapse of the market value of CDOs became inescapable at the start of fall, AIG was forced to submit to the collateral calls in full, and that was what led to the rescue.

As recounted by Boyd (2011), Goldman prided itself in its rigorous approach to marking the value of assets in its portfolio. As long as it used objective market values, its traders could not engage in wishful thinking. But marking-to-market makes sense only during normal financial times. In a crisis, the fundamental value of assets deviates from their market value. That is why principles of fair value accounting allow firms to deviate from market values during a financial crisis.[6] AIG was confident in its portfolio until the bitter end because it believed that mortgage payments and the proceeds from foreclosures would generate enough cash to pay off the AAA-rated tranches of CDOs that AIG had insured, or at least enough not to wipe out AIG's equity. The problem was that the liquidity crisis caused the market value of the CDOs to collapse, which generated the collateral calls.

Figure 4.1 shows the effect of the liquidity crisis on the market price of a selection of AAA-rated subprime mortgages packaged in 2006 (after AIG had left the market). The market prices of the CDOs were temporarily suppressed at 60 to 80 percent of their par value during the financial crisis, but have since moved above 90 percent. While these CDOs hardly deserved their AAA rating, they were not nearly as bad investments as they appeared during the liquidity crisis.

This was why AIG invested so heavily in the CDS market in the first place, why it charged such low premiums, and why it was slow to realize that it was vulnerable to a downturn in housing prices. In a world in which AIG was not required to meet collateral calls, it would have survived the crisis. While AIG's investments lost a huge amount of money, the losses in the "inherent value" of its assets (i.e., their value if AIG could have held them to maturity) were never large enough to threaten AIG's equity cushion.[7]

As AIG's problems mounted during the summer of 2008, it sought

FIGURE 4.1. Subprime RMBS prices (based on Markit's ABX.HE.AAA.06-1 Index)

help from the Fed but was refused. After the Fed failed to rescue Lehman in September 2008 and the credit market collapsed, AIG could no longer find creditors willing to lend to it and made plans to file for bankruptcy.

The Rescue

The Fed rescued AIG because it worried that if AIG failed, the financial crisis would worsen significantly.[8] Lehman had collapsed just a few days before, and the credit market was in turmoil. AIG's short-term liabilities exceeded $70 billion, far more than Lehman's. AIG's CDS counterparties included numerous major financial institutions. AIG also provided insurance in many different industries, and it seemed likely that if AIG collapsed, disruption would result. Moreover, no one knew how AIG's insurance subsidiaries would fare in bankruptcy. But the Fed told AIG that it would let AIG fail unless the company accepted the terms of a take-it-or-leave-it offer. The offer was partly based on an abandoned proposal by a number of private banks, which had considered making a loan to AIG. But the bank proposal was extremely unfavorable because the banks themselves faced liquidity demands (Geithner 2014, 192); it was not a suitable basis for a proposal from the government, which faced no such problem. Starr also accused the government of unilaterally changing the terms of the offer after AIG agreed to it. In the initial offer, the government was to be given warrants, which it would be able to exercise only by paying billions of dollars; in the final deal, the warrants were eliminated and the government was given equity.

Under the Credit Agreement, the Fed opened an $85 billion credit facility for AIG, which was secured by AIG's assets, including its insurance companies. In return AIG agreed to pay an interest rate of 14.5 percent (later reduced) and to give the government preferred stock (denoted "Series C shares"), which was convertible into 79.9 percent of AIG's common stock—worth, at the time, $23 billion. The Series C shares were put into a Trust, whose only beneficiary was the US government. AIG's CEO, Robert Willumstad, stepped down, and Ed Liddy took his place. A month later, the government extended an additional $37.8 billion of credit to AIG, also secured by AIG's assets.

The credit extension did not satisfy the CDS counterparties, who renewed their demands for collateral based on the low market value of the CDOs. To address this problem, the Fed established a special-purpose vehicle called Maiden Lane III. Maiden Lane III was financed with an equity investment of $5 billion from AIG and a $24.3 billion loan from the Fed; the agency used this money, together with AIG's already posted collateral, to buy the underlying CDOs that AIG had insured. This led to a transfer of $62 billion in cash to the counterparties. This transaction raised eyebrows because AIG was not legally required to buy the CDOs, let alone to pay par value for them. It could have kept posting collateral, paying only if default of the CDOs actually took place. Because the counterparties were desperate for cash, AIG could probably have negotiated haircuts. The government's failure to demand haircuts on behalf of AIG was called a "backdoor bailout" by critics, who accused the government of manipulating AIG to conceal politically unpopular bailouts of other financial institutions from the public.[9]

The Fed created another facility called Maiden Lane II, which paid AIG's insurance subsidiaries $21 billion for MBSs with par value of $39.3 billion. The Fed loaned almost $20 billion to Maiden Lane II to finance these purchases (McDonald and Paulson 2015, 87), while AIG put in $1 billion. Later, Treasury invested TARP money in AIG. Other transactions and various restructurings ensued, but none of them of relevance here. In all, the government pumped about $126 billion into AIG (Sjostrom 2015, 797).

The Aftermath of the Rescue

In March 2009, the Series C preferred stock was transferred to the trust. The three trustees had ties to the Fed—one had been an employee of the FRBNY for more than three decades, the second had been a member of the board of the FRBNY, and the third was the chair of the board of directors at a branch of the Federal Reserve Bank of Dallas. The trust agreement directed the trustees to manage the trust so as to ensure AIG's repayment of the loans, and "in a manner that will not disrupt financial market conditions." The Series C stock gave the trust 79.9 percent of the voting power in AIG.

AIG's charter did not allow it to issue enough shares of common stock to the government to give it 79.9 percent of the total. To enable the trust to convert its Series C stock into common stock, AIG needed to amend its charter so as to increase the number of issuable shares of common stock. Under Delaware law, such an amendment required the votes of a majority of common shareholders. AIG—now under the control of the trustees—dutifully asked its common shareholders to approve the creation of additional common stock, and they voted down the proposal. But at the same meeting, AIG also proposed a 20 : 1 reverse stock split of AIG's issued common stock. The reverse stock split would have reduced the total number of issued shares of common stock from about 3 billion to 150 million. This, by itself, would not have hurt common stockholders because the price of their stock would have increased by twenty times. However, the reverse stock split did not apply to 2 billion shares of authorized but unissued stock. In other words, the issued stock—owned by shareholders—was to be reduced from 3 billion shares to 150 million shares, while the unissued stock, which was controlled by AIG, would remain at 2 billion shares.

The reverse stock split was put up to vote and passed. It passed not because the common shareholders supported it but because the trust was allowed under the charter to use its 79.9 percent voting power to dictate the outcome. The result was that AIG could use some of the unissued 2 billion shares of common stock to give the trust its 79.9 percent share of the common stock. Starr argued that the reverse stock split was a subterfuge for circumventing Delaware protections for shareholders, while the Fed argued that it was needed to prevent AIG stock from being delisted from the New York Stock Exchange.[10]

In 2011, AIG repaid the outstanding balance of the loan and transferred 562,868,096 shares of common stock to the trust in return for the Series C shares. The trust transferred the common stock to the US Treasury, which eventually sold it off. The Fed was also paid back by Maiden Lane II and Maiden Lane III. The Fed and Treasury jointly earned a profit of $22.7 billion on the rescue transactions (Sjostrom 2015, 796). According to calculations by McDonald and Paulson (2015, 97–100), the agencies obtained a return of 13 percent on the Maiden Lane II assets and 35 percent on the Maiden Lane III assets, for an overall return of just under 17 percent. As of October 2014, the Maiden Lane II assets had been written down 5.1 percent and the Maiden Lane III assets 12 percent. (These figures do not include the return on the initial loans, including the 79.9 percent equity stake.) As McDonald and Paulson (2015, 82) point out, these outcomes show that AIG executives were wrong to claim that the assets were "money good," that is, having essentially no credit risk. However, these numbers are also consistent with the plaintiffs' argument that AIG was never insolvent in an economic sense. It had made bad investments, but the investments were not bad enough to destroy AIG's equity. In a normal market, AIG could have survived by borrowing against these assets. During a liquidity crisis, it could not.

The New York Lawsuit

Starr brought separate lawsuits against the FRBNY and the US government because of the ambiguity about who exactly was responsible for the rescue. The FRBNY issued the loan in September 2008, but it acted under the authority of the Federal Reserve Board and created a trust whose beneficiary was Treasury. As a nominally independent entity, the FRBNY could not be sued in the Court of Federal Claims in Washington, DC, which is where one brings claims against the government. So a suit against the US government was brought in the Court of Federal Claims in Washington, DC, while the suit against FRBNY was brought in the Southern District of New York. The suits were also based on different theories. In New York, Starr argued that FRBNY had violated Delaware law by taking control of AIG and pumping its funds into the US Treasury and to favored counterparty financial institutions like Goldman Sachs at the expense of AIG's minority shareholders. In Washington, it argued that the US government, acting through the Fed and Treasury, violated the takings clause and the due process clause of the Constitution by expropriating 79.9 percent of AIG's equity and other assets, in the process harming AIG's shareholders.

In the New York lawsuit, Starr focused on the Maiden Lane III transaction in November 2008, the reverse stock split in June 2009, and the exchange of Series C preferred stock for AIG common stock in January 2011. The Maiden Lane III transaction resulted in a transfer of billions of dollars from AIG's coffers to AIG's counterparties, while the reverse stock split prevented common stockholders from blocking the transfer of equity from AIG to the government. If Starr was right that these transactions were not justified by business necessity and were simply transfers from AIG's shareholders to counterparties and taxpayers, then whoever controlled AIG violated their fiduciary duties toward the shareholders.

The court rejected Starr's argument on two grounds. First, it rejected the allegation that FRBNY controlled AIG and so could be held responsible for these transactions, even if they were wrongful. FRBNY did not control AIG at the time of the credit agreement but negotiated with its CEO and board. FRBNY did not control AIG during the Maiden Lane transaction, which took place before the trust received the Series C stock. Even after the stock was transferred, it was the trust, not FRBNY, that controlled AIG, and Starr failed to persuade the court that FRBNY controlled the trust.

Second, the court held that even if FRBNY did control AIG, FRBNY was a federal instrumentality, and so federal law—which authorized it to rescue financial institutions during financial crises—preempted state law.[11] Normally, because AIG is a Delaware corporation, Delaware law would regulate how its shareholders and others with control may manage the firm. FRBNY is set up as a bank, but it possesses significant federal powers, including the power to regulate commercial banks and the power to make emergency loans during financial crises. It would make little sense to permit Delaware to regulate the FRBNY.

Still, federal courts recognize that federal instrumentalities must be given some duties, and so they frequently incorporate state law into federal common law, which effectively means that state law governs after all. Courts import fiduciary duties unless they would interfere with the federal law that the instrumentality is supposed to enforce. The question boiled down to whether the fiduciary duties to which Starr believes that the FRBNY should have been held would have interfered with its lawful power to make an emergency loan under section 13(3) of the Federal Reserve Act.[12]

The court said that they would have. Section 13(3) gives the FRBNY, acting with the approval of the board of governors of the Federal Reserve, the power to issue emergency loans in crisis conditions to nonbank institutions like AIG. It also gives the FRBNY unspecified "incidental powers," presumably those powers that are necessary or useful for implementing the emergency lending power. The September Credit Agreement was an exercise of 13(3) emergency powers. Maiden Lane III involved another emergency loan as well as credit left over from the initial loan. The reverse stock split was necessary to ensure that the terms of the Credit Agreement were complied with. And the eventual exchange of Series C shares for common equity was the consummation of the agreement.

Consider, for example, Starr's argument that the FRBNY violated its fiduciary duties by compelling AIG to buy its counterparties' CDOs at par value through the Maiden Lane III facility. Starr argued that deliberately overpaying counterparties was wrongful. The court replied:

> But while driving a hard bargain with the counterparties might have saved AIG and its shareholders money, FRBNY could reasonably conclude that its statutory mission of stabilizing the economy made speed and closure a top priority. It could reasonably conclude that it was time for the cycle of collateral calls and mammoth rescue loans to end; that the stability of the U.S. economy required decisively terminating AIG's exposure to counterparties; and that paying par value—as opposed to opening up a bazaar of uncertain and maybe protracted negotiations with counterparties—was the best means to attain such closure.[13]

Yet the court pulled back from the logical implication of its argument, which is that the FRBNY could have done anything at all, including expropriating AIG's assets for the benefit of itself or others. During oral argument, the court asked FRBNY's lawyer whether Starr would have had a claim if the FRBNY caused AIG to pay a Utah bank $1 billion for a copy machine to stabilize that bank. The FRBNY counsel replied that "a cause of action might lie then against the United States, under the Tucker Act."[14] If so, then AIG's only problem was its choice of forum, not its substantive argument—and it could look forward to prevailing in the Court of

Federal Claims. The court instead argued that the Maiden Lane III transaction was distinguishable from the hypothetical transaction because AIG paid par value rather than a sum vastly exceeding a fair value, and that the transaction benefited AIG. But of course, if AIG needed a photocopier, then the Utah transaction would have benefited it as well. And if the fundamental value of the CDOs was less than the par value—which was the premise of the government's intervention—then the par value is irrelevant. If AIG paid the new-copier list price for a used photocopier worth far less, then the transaction was unfair.

Clues about the court's concerns can be found in another area of the opinion that addressed the limits on tort liability for government officials acting within the scope of their duties. Starr did not sue Timothy Geithner in tort, but the court considered these cases persuasive authority. The court cited cases that gave immunity or qualified immunity to emergency responders—including a Coast Guard crew that ended up damaging a ship it tried to save and police officials who failed to put down a riot—and denied recovery from the US Treasury as well. In the Coast Guard case, for example, the court said:

> [T]he instinct of self-preservation would inevitably function even under the pressures of life or death crises which so often arise in rescue operations when members of the Coast Guard are called upon to make decisions. *If men are to be brought to an abrupt halt in the midst of crisis—to think first that if they err in their performance they may expose their Government to financial loss and themselves to disciplinary measures or loss of existing status, and then to pause and deliberate and weigh the chances of success or failure in alternate rescue procedures, the delay may often prove fatal to the distressed who urgently require their immediate aid.*[15]

One might read the SDNY opinion as an expression of deference to the government at a time of emergency. The court could not bring itself to rule that the government could never be liable for expropriating property during an emergency. But it believed that under the circumstances described in the complaint, any abuse, if it occurred, was justified by emergency conditions.[16]

The DC Lawsuit

Starr's lawsuit in the Court of Federal Claims was based on a different theory. The defendant in that case was the US government (which alone can be sued in the Court of Federal Claims for damages), not the FRBNY. Starr argued that the US government, acting through Treasury, the Federal Reserve Board, and the FRBNY, expropriated property from the shareholders of AIG in violation of the takings and the due process clauses of the US Constitution.

The takings clause forbids the government to take "private property . . . for public use, without just compensation." It requires the government to pay people if it wants to seize their houses, land, or other property for government purposes, for example, to clear a way for a road. Shares of a corporation are also property. While the government did not seize Starr's shares of AIG, it did reduce their value by causing AIG to issue hundreds of millions of shares to the government. A corporation is just an asset that sloughs off cash in the form of dividends. If the government diverts a portion of those dividends to itself, it has taken money from shareholders. The due process clause prohibits the government from taking property "without due process of law," which has been interpreted to forbid regulatory agencies from taking property without congressional authorization.

According to Starr, the government's wrongful actions took place over several years. The September 2008 Credit Agreement gave the government a contractual right to the 79.9 percent share of equity, initially embodied in the Series C preferred stock.[17] The reverse stock split of June 2009 deprived the shareholders of their voting power, making it impossible for them to block the eventual conversion of Series C preferred stock into common equity in January 2011. Moreover, the Maiden Lane III transaction of November 2008 also constituted an expropriation of AIG assets, which were used to pay off counterparties at par value.

The government's major defense is that it provided a benefit to shareholders and that the Credit Agreement was a voluntary transaction. Most takings involve expropriations—coercive transfers from citizen to government, as when the government seizes houses in the way of a planned road. If the government offers to buy someone's house and the owner agrees, no taking has taken place, no matter how bad the deal. AIG was in difficult circumstances, but the government did not force it to take a loan.

Starr's claim takes several different forms. The first two invoke the takings clause; the third relies on the due process clause. First, Starr argues that government officials "took" the shareholders' property through coercion: it coerced AIG—that is, AIG's directors—to consent to the Credit Agreement by showering them with threats and lies (an allegation denied by the government). Once the government took control of AIG—which Starr argues took place at the time of the Credit Agreement—it imposed the Maiden Lane III transaction and the reverse stock split on the (now) minority shareholders against their will.

Second, Starr argues that the government violated the unconstitutional conditions doctrine by conditioning an emergency liquidity loan on the transfer of equity. The Fed was given the power but not the obligation to provide a benefit in the form of credit. Starr acknowledges that the Fed was not legally required to give a loan to AIG. But the Supreme Court has held that the government cannot require people to give up constitutional rights to obtain discretionary benefits unless there is a "nexus" between the government interest and the waiver.[18] A city agency that possesses the discretion to grant or withhold a license to develop a plot of land may refuse the license because it believes that development would cause harm. It could also grant the license on the condition that the property owner takes steps to minimize the harm that development might bring. But it could not grant the license on the condition that the owner give some other piece of property to the city or makes the original property accessible to the public. In these cases, there is no "nexus" between the government's interest (developing land in a way that serves the public interest) and the condition (giving some other land to the government or access to people).

Unconstitutional conditions cases are tricky because the transaction is voluntary in the sense that the owner wants the license or other benefit badly enough that it agrees to the deal. In the example, the owner believes itself better off than if it did not enter the transaction in the first place— which is why the owner agrees to the deal. But the transactions are also coercive in the larger context of the legal scheme. If a local government can ban unlicensed development without any reason while selectively permitting people to develop if they pay a fee, this is equivalent to selective expropriation of property, a circumvention of the takings clause. The unconstitutional conditions doctrine blocks this type of evasion.

Starr argues that the Fed's behavior ran afoul of this constitutional principle. The Fed could have denied the loan just as a development commission could deny a license. But conditioning the loan on consent to a large equity transfer forced AIG (and hence its shareholders) to give up their right to just compensation. Starr's argument rests on the further claim that there was no "nexus" between the loan and the equity transfer because the loan was fully secured. The nexus argument boils down to the question whether the Fed could offer a reasonable policy justification for demanding equity on top of interest on a fully secured loan.

Third, Starr argues that because the Fed lacked the authority to obtain equity in return for its loan, the equity transfer was a violation of the due process clause. Section 13(3) of the Federal Reserve Act authorizes the Fed to make emergency loans to nonbanks like AIG. The law requires that the loan be "secured to the satisfaction of the Federal Reserve bank" and, by cross-reference to section 14(d), authorizes the Fed to charge an interest rate "which shall be fixed with a view of accommodating commerce and business."[19] The statute thus allows the Fed to charge an interest rate— and an interest rate that is reasonable rather than, say, an interest rate that would maximize the Fed's return. Nowhere does the statute give the Fed any explicit authority to take equity as consideration for the loan. The government points out that the Fed enjoys unspecified "incidental powers" and argues that taking equity in return for a loan falls under those powers. However, the Fed had never before taken equity in a corporation in return for a loan or for any other purpose. The "incidental powers" provision mirrors a similar provision in the National Bank Act,[20] but national banks also are prohibited from taking equity as consideration for a loan, or owning equity, except under limited conditions not relevant here.

If the Fed does not enjoy authority to take or own equity, then the transfer of equity is "an illegal exaction." Illegal exaction cases typically arise when an agency (like the Fed) enters into a transaction with a party in which the agency gives something to that party (such as a license) in return for money, goods, or services that the agency has no authority to ask for. In a series of cases after World War II, courts held that a maritime agency had acted unlawfully by requiring US ship owners to pay money into the US Treasury in return for a license to sell ships to foreigners.[21] Because Congress had not authorized the agency to charge a fee, the owners were entitled to restitution, even though they had voluntarily agreed to pay it.

At the time of the Credit Agreement, the Fed was worried about whether it possessed the authority to take equity. Rather than take the equity itself, it established the trust, which was (at least formally) independent of the Fed and Treasury. The legal question then becomes one whether the trust was just a subterfuge or, even if it wasn't, whether the Fed could have authority to enter a transaction that resulted in the transfer of equity even if the Fed itself never received it.

The government filed a motion to dismiss. The Court of Federal Claims dismissed the unconstitutional conditions claim but allowed the others to go to trial.[22] The court rejected the unconstitutional conditions claim on the ground that it was available only in land use cases. But while it is true that no court had applied the "nexus" test outside land restrictions, the unconstitutional conditions doctrine applies broadly, to all kinds of constitutional rights, not just property rights. The court also argued that in land use cases, the owner cannot use her land without government approval, while AIG was not subject to any restrictions on its operations that it was seeking to be released from. The response to this argument is complex, and we will return to it below.

The Merits: Preliminaries

At first sight, one might think that the differences among these legal claims matter. They probably do not. The three claims are legal pigeonholes for the same theory: that the Fed acted wrongfully by extracting equity in return for its emergency loan and using Maiden Lane III to transfer assets to counterparties. To prevail on the coercion claim, Starr argues that the setting was inherently coercive because of the government's position as credit monopolist: only the Fed could make a loan to AIG. The government, Starr argues, bullied AIG's board into approving the transaction, lying to the board members by telling them that the government would not lend to AIG after it had resolved to do so, and threatening them with infamy if they resisted. The government then picked AIG's CEO and dictated his behavior. Whether or not these allegations fairly capture events, coercion is a slippery concept, and so the real question becomes whether the Credit Agreement was reasonable or fair. If the government had good reason to demand equity, then the board had good reason to accept the demand.

Similarly, on the illegal exaction issue, incidental or implied powers of the Fed or the FRBNY could be invoked to justify the equity transfer if the equity transfer was a necessary or reasonable incident to the emergency loan. The question then becomes one of whether the terms of the transactions were reasonable. If the court had not dismissed the unconstitutional conditions claim, then the parties would have argued about whether there was a "nexus" between the equity transfer and the loan, or again, whether the equity transfer was a reasonable incident to the loan.

The government tried to short-circuit this inquiry by arguing that Starr would have been worse off if the Fed had never made the emergency loan—whether it was fair or unfair. "Twenty percent of something [is] better than one hundred percent of nothing."[23] A taking that makes the owner better off does not seem like a taking. If the fire department caused water damage to your house in the course of putting out a fire, you would not be able to recover damages from the government. No taking occurred; or, if one occurred, the damages calculation would subtract the offsetting benefit (the portion of the house spared from fire) from the loss (the portion of the house damaged by water).

But suppose that the fire department agreed to put out the fire only if you paid 80 percent of the house's equity into the city treasury. You agree to its offer because you prefer 20 percent of the value of an undamaged house to 100 percent of a pile of embers, and the fire department puts out the fire. It remains true that 20 percent of your house is worth more than nothing, but the fire department acted wrongfully, and you would be entitled to a remedy.

The Fed, like the fire department, is a monopolist of liquidity at a time of crisis. Coercion is not so much a problem as an inherent feature of the relationship between the government and the private party. The policy problem is thus not so much coercion as abuse of discretion. We need to give the government discretion but must prevent the government from abusing that discretion—by charging a monopoly price or demanding harsh terms. So just as a victim of an illegal monopoly can obtain damages from the monopolist even though he is better off with the product than without it, the victim of a government abuse of power can obtain a remedy even though the government gave him something rather than nothing. This is why plaintiffs can recover in illegal exactions and unconstitutional conditions cases where the plaintiff voluntarily entered a transaction to obtain gains relative to the status quo.

The Merits: Was the Equity Transfer Justified?

For this reason, the trial focused on the policy reasons for the transactions. The two sides agreed that the starting point for answering this question can be found in the theories of Bagehot. Fed officials, including Bernanke and Geithner, testified that they were guided by Bagehot's principles.

Bagehot argued that during a financial crisis the central bank should lend widely, "to this man and that man," against good collateral, at a rate of interest greater than the market price during normal (noncrisis) times. The Federal Reserve Act does not mention Bagehot or his principles. It says that the Fed can make loans only to banks during normal times, but under section 13(3) it can lend to anyone during emergencies. The loans must be collateralized, and the Fed must charge a reasonable interest rate. The Act does not require the Fed to make loans to everyone who can offer collateral—that would be logistically impossible. Nor does it dictate how transactions should be structured. It is widely agreed that the Fed enjoys discretion over these matters. And yet still its mission is to stop financial crises, and so its discretion must be used to that end.

Starr argued that while the Fed can decide who to make loans to, it must use that discretion consistently with Bagehot's principles. The interest rate must be reasonable. The goal is to restart the credit market, not to use monopoly power over the credit market to make as much money as possible. The equity provision did not advance that goal. It merely resulted in a transfer of private wealth to the government.[24] The government responded that the equity transfer was necessary and well within the Fed's discretion.

The Court of Federal Claims held for Starr on its third argument—that the Fed lacked the authority to take equity and therefore engaged in an illegal exaction. The court observed that the Federal Reserve Act does not explicitly authorize the Fed to own equity in a firm. While the statute also does not rule out loans in return for equity, banks as a general matter are not allowed to own equity, and the Fed is—sort of—a bank. Moreover, a statute provides that government agencies are not allowed to own corporations without explicit congressional authorization—and no such authorization can be found in the Act.[25] The government noted that the Office of the Comptroller of the Currency has permitted banks to take "equity kickers" in return for loans. In these loans, the bank is paid some equity in addition to interest. Further, in the AIG transaction, the government was merely adopting the plan arranged by the private consortium of banks— in which the banks demanded equity in return for their loan to AIG. But equity kickers usually involve a small amount of equity, not 79.9 percent, and do not allow commercial banks to control the firm in question, which is strictly prohibited.

The court's ruling is not hard to understand. It would have surprised any of the Congresses that enacted the Federal Reserve Act and its amendments that they had authorized the Fed to own companies. But I am less interested in this argument than in the policy arguments that feed into the claims, which the court did not resolve. These arguments fall under several headings.

MORAL HAZARD

Paulson and Geithner argued that AIG needed to be punished for engaging in reckless behavior. (Bernanke testified that he made no such judgment.) AIG was supposed to be an insurance company, not a hedge fund, yet it took on enormous credit risk by selling CDSs on poorly constructed CDOs. The equity transfer, by punishing AIG for its reckless behavior, would deter insurance companies and other financial firms from acting similarly in the future.

As noted earlier, however, there was no reason to single out AIG's shareholders for punishment. AIG did not act more recklessly than other firms; it acted more prudently than most of the major financial institutions that were caught up in the crisis—the mortgage originators, the CDO packagers, the monoline insurers, and the rating agencies. Singling out AIG could not have contributed to general deterrence. Indeed, the AIG rescue mainly benefited counterparties who were not penalized at all and, in many cases, acted more recklessly than AIG did. AIG exited the CDS market in 2005 when CDOs were still constructed from prime mortgages. There is no evidence that AIG ever believed that the underlying mortgages were risky; indeed, AIG charged extremely low prices on the CDSs because it believed they were safe. In this, AIG's view was congruent with that of the rest of the market. AIG's insurance subsidiaries did invest in MBSs up until the financial crisis, but again they acted like nearly everyone else in the market. By contrast, a number of banks and mortgage origination companies engaged in fraudulent underwriting practices and were later fined or forced to settle with the government for huge amounts of money. Other financial institutions continued issuing CDSs or self-insured during the years after AIG left the market and the quality of CDOs had degraded. An important but little-recognized aspect of the government's behavior is that it did not ascertain that AIG had acted recklessly before it entered the credit agreement, so it could not have known or reasonably believed that AIG had acted more recklessly than other institutions.

McDonald and Paulson (2015) argue that AIG was overexposed to the real estate market—that is, insufficiently diversified—and overleveraged. But as they also point out, AIG's exposure to the real estate market and their leverage levels were comparable to other firms, including Bank of America and Citigroup, which were offered rescues on generous terms. In some ways, AIG was operated more safely than these other institutions (it was less dependent on short-term liabilities); in other ways, less safely (it did not establish a liquidity risk committee until 2007). Nothing about these differences justified the vastly different treatment in the rescue packages.

In any event, the "penalty rate" attributed to Bagehot was never understood to be confiscatory—that would defeat its purpose. The Lender of Last Resort (LLR) must charge a rate considerably lower than the market rate prevailing in a liquidity crisis—at which no one lends or borrows. The usual benchmark is the rate that prevailed before the crisis or a percentage point or so above it; in practice, central banks charge even lower rates. During the crisis, the Fed charged interest rates less than 4 percent and as low as 0.5 percent to banks, investment banks, and other financial institutions. It did not require them to give it equity. AIG alone was required to pay a high interest rate—initially 12 percent (a "loan shark" rate, in the words of a FRBNY lawyer), later reduced to 5.5 percent, plus, of course, the 79.9 percent equity stake, which was worth tens of billions of dollars.

COMPENSATING THE GOVERNMENT FOR CREDIT RISK

The government argues that AIG was a credit risk, and it needed the equity transfer to compensate it for taking on that risk. The loan to AIG was huge. The Fed and other national regulators did not possess much information about AIG's finances. (The Office of Thrift Supervision was AIG's supervisor because AIG owned a thrift, but the OTS did not possess the expertise to evaluate AIG's derivative positions.) Geithner testified that AIG's collateral was harder to value than the collateral offered by other firms.

The problem with this argument is that during the crisis, the government said—and apparently believed—that AIG's assets fully secured the loan. The government determined the fundamental value of the assets, subjected them to significant haircuts, and used them as collateral for loans. The government believed that it faced little credit risk, as it was required to under the law. A reasonable interest rate should have been sufficient to cover any residual credit risk.

The government could possibly take the position that it believed in good faith both that the loan was fully secured by AIG's assets, including its well-regarded insurance companies, and that the collateral was intrinsically difficult to value. In the midst of a financial crisis, anything could happen. Perhaps people would stop buying life, house, and automobile insurance. In the face of such risk, the government was entitled to substantial compensation for the loan. Because AIG would not be able to pay a high interest rate, the compensation took the form of an equity transfer.

There is, however, no evidence that the Fed believed that it was undersecured or taking on massive credit risk in September 2008. The 79.9 percent figure was not based on a calculation of the probability that the collateral would lose its value, but was apparently taken from the abandoned proposal of the private banks. Fed officials realized that the insurance companies could collapse as a result of an economic downturn, but this was true as well for all the other firms to which it made low-interest loans without demanding equity. The crisis conditions that made AIG so difficult to value also made all the other collateral that the Fed accepted difficult to value. Indeed, to the extent that AIG's value derived from its CDS portfolio, the valuation difficulties were the same.

CREDIT RATIONING

A central bank cannot literally lend to "this man and that man." Millions of people want to borrow money at any given time. In principle, central banks could lend only to banks with the expectation that banks would then relend the money to the market. But during the financial crisis, banks refused to lend money. Section 13(3) anticipates this possibility by authorizing the Fed to lend to nonbanks. The Fed should lend to the largest and most important financial institutions, those that play a key role in the lending market. During the financial crisis, the Fed did just that.

The government argued that the Fed needed to charge AIG more than anyone else to discourage companies like AIG—insurance companies—from applying to the Fed for loans. Bernanke testified that he worried about extending credit to insurance companies. But this argument too was a rationalization. The Fed was capable of denying loan applications from firms that did not need credit. It refused AIG's initial request for an emergency loan in the summer of 2008. In the fall, the Fed was lending as widely as possible not because it could not turn down loan applications but because it did not want to.

AVOIDING A WINDFALL

Bernanke also argued that the equity transfer was justified because otherwise AIG would have received a "windfall." He did not explain what he meant other than to say that the other recipients of emergency loans received windfalls as well but that it was not practical to deprive them of those windfalls.

AIG did receive an enormous loan from the government without which it would probably have gone bankrupt. So AIG's shareholders benefited from the loan. But the word "windfall" implies an illegitimate benefit, and it is this idea that Bernanke does not explain. Any firm that enters a contract with the government makes money. This is true of defense contractors, highway construction firms, and Internet service providers. It is also true of the banks that buy insurance from the FDIC and pay interest for emergency loans. If they did not profit from these contracts, they would not enter into them.

Bernanke's argument could be construed as a claim that in any transaction between the government and a private party, the government should earn the entire surplus from that transaction, or as large a portion of that surplus as possible. By happenstance, it could not extract the surplus from most financial institutions because if it charged high interest rates or demanded equity, those institutions would hold off borrowing from the government, perhaps until too late. In the case of AIG, however, bankruptcy was imminent, so AIG had no choice but to accept the terms that the Fed offered it.

This is not how the government normally operates. The government frequently enjoys monopoly power as the only entity that can offer certain benefits like licenses. Congress requires agencies to charge reasonable fees; it does not direct agencies to charge the maximum amount that anyone would pay. The government should not charge monopoly prices for the same reason that private parties should not—it causes deadweight losses to the economy. Licensing programs are not designed to raise money—they are not tax systems—but to advance the public interest. A license for developing property, for example, is used to ensure that the development does not harm others, not to extract cash from the property owner. If the maximum price were charged, as an indirect form of confiscatory taxation, then land development would be stifled. Similarly, a policy of charging maximal prices for emergency loans would undermine their purpose, which is to resolve a financial crisis.

EMERGENCY CONDITIONS

The financial crisis was the greatest financial emergency that the US government has faced since the Great Depression. The SDNY court felt that emergency conditions justified a posture of judicial deference to the government. The court believed that it is unfair for courts to second-guess the actions of officials during emergencies and that the fear of hindsight bias by courts might cause officials to act too cautiously.

Yet this argument raises a paradox. Section 13(3) was designed for emergencies but, at the same time, subjected the Fed to numerous constraints. The FRBNY could not make an emergency loan without first obtaining consent, by supermajority approval, of the board of governors. It was not permitted to make unsecured loans. It was required to set reasonable terms.

Perhaps for this reason, the government did not argue, except in passing, that the terms of the AIG loan, or the Maiden Lane III transaction, were justified by emergency conditions. Such an argument would have raised the inevitable question of what limits, if any, the government would be subject to—a question that would be difficult to answer, as illustrated by the Utah bank hypothetical.

POLITICS

Henry Paulson testified at trial that AIG "certainly was a scapegoat— for Wall Street and all the bad practices that people were angry about." (Sorkin 2014). Paulson "believed that it was important to be seen as being harsh and punitive to the AIG shareholders in order to quell possible political opposition to TARP and other further financial assistance."[26] To pave the way for funds from the Emergency Economic Stabilization Act[27] and TARP, the government would need to demonstrate that it was punishing those responsible for the crisis.

This account echoes Paulson's approach to the Bear Stearns rescue earlier in the year. JP Morgan originally proposed to buy Bear for $8 to $12 per share, later reduced to $4. As the Fed became more deeply involved in the deal, Paulson "pressured Dimon to keep the price low, to avoid the perception that we [the Fed] were subsidizing a windfall for Bear's share-holders. So the offer was just $2 a share." (Geithner 2014, 155).[28] Bear was forced to accept the offer because the alternative was bankruptcy. How-ever, the savings—hundreds of millions of dollars—would accrue not to taxpayers but to JP Morgan's shareholders. This transfer of wealth was undertaken to manage public opinion.[29]

Paulson's testimony raises the problem of emergency policy in acute form. His argument is both troubling and easy to understand. He admits that the public and Congress did not understand the financial crisis, and that Congress was willing to defer to the executive branch, but only if the executive branch appeased public outrage. The problem of public psychol-ogy would recur later when people demanded that the government refuse to honor AIG's contractual commitments to pay bonuses to its employees, although this time the government resisted. We will return to this issue in chapter 7.

The Merits: Maiden Lane III

Starr argues that Maiden Lane III was used as a vehicle by the govern-ment to redistribute AIG's assets to other financial institutions. It is im-portant to see that the Maiden Lane III transaction was separate from the Credit Agreement with the 79.9 percent equity transfer. Starr argues that even after AIG's original shareholders were diluted, they were now—as a minority—forced to cough up additional value as AIG's assets were given away.

As noted earlier, the chief threat to AIG's liquidity came from the collateral calls from its CDS counterparties. These firms had the right to demand that AIG post additional collateral as the value or ratings of the underlying CDOs declined. Because the cash flows generated by the mortgages in the CDOs sufficed to pay the AAA tranches that AIG in-sured, there had not been a default event that would have required AIG to pay out. The problem was that the market anticipated that eventually such a default would happen, and so the CDOs traded at a discount—as much as 50 percent—when they traded at all.

FRBNY loaned $24.4 billion and AIG made a $5 billion equity con-tribution to Maiden Lane III. Maiden Lane III used most of this money to settle AIG's CDSs. Specifically, Maiden Lane III paid the money to AIG's CDS counterparties, who transferred the underlying CDOs to Maiden Lane III and tore up the CDSs. The counterparties also kept the cash collateral that AIG had posted—approximately $37 billion. In sum, the counterparties received about $70 billion in cash from AIG and Maiden Lane III in return for CDOs with an equivalent par value but a market value of about half that.[30] As a result, the counterparties gained about $30 billion more than they would have if AIG had been unable to pay on the CDSs.

By 2012, Maiden Lane III had sold off its portfolio. Under the terms of the agreement, FRBNY was paid back its loan with interest; and the balance was divided 67 percent to FRBNY and 33 percent to AIG. Since FRBNY reported earning $6 billion, we can infer that the market value of the CDOs increased by about $10 billion.

Thus, both the FRBNY and the counterparties earned billions of dollars from the Maiden Lane III transaction. The FRBNY's gain raises questions similar to those surrounding the 79.9 percent equity transfer. FRBNY's loan of $24.3 billion was fully secured by the CDOs and thus oversecured by $5 billion. The loan was accordingly low-risk, or at least no more risky than any of the other loans that FRBNY made during the financial crisis. Yet it was entitled to two-thirds of the appreciation, effectively a 67 percent equity interest in the portfolio.

But at least the FRBNY's profits were returned to the taxpayers. The purchase of the CDOs from the counterparties at par sparked a public outcry. Before AIG was taken over by the government, it fought against the collateral calls. It disputed Goldman's marks, which were based on Goldman's model and on whatever data Goldman thought appropriate. Other firms that made collateral calls on AIG did not rely on marks as aggressive as Goldman's. AIG and its counterparties could have gone to court to resolve their disputes. In the shadow of litigation, AIG and its counterparties negotiated and occasionally compromised.

Even if AIG had accepted its counterparties' marks, once it received liquidity support from the government, it could have continued posting collateral rather than buying the underlying CDOs at par value. The distinction is important. If AIG had continued posting collateral, it would have transferred cash to its counterparties in amounts considerably less than the par value of the CDOs. If it had a government guarantee, that amount could have been as low as zero. This means that the counterparties would have received a cash infusion of much less than $60 to $70 billion. And AIG would not have overpaid for CDOs worth less than par value. If the counterparties wanted cash (and they did), they would have been willing to sell their CDOs to AIG for less than par value.

Geithner testified that the Fed did not have the time or resources to negotiate haircuts with the counterparties. He also worried that haircuts would spook creditors at a time that they needed reassurance.[31] From the Fed's perspective, what mattered was spewing liquidity into the market. How the gains were distributed was less important. The genius of the Maiden Lane III transaction from this standpoint is that it removed the CDOs from the portfolios of numerous financial institutions and tucked them safely in Maiden Lane III—effectively, a "bad bank"—where they could be held until maturity, if necessary, or sold off when the market recovered, as they were. In the meantime, the financial institutions would no longer be burdened by the hard-to-value assets that rendered opaque the financial health of their owners. If private lenders therefore regained confidence, government life-support could be removed. But be that as it may, the transaction came at the expense of AIG.

Lessons

From the standpoint of policy, the equity transfer and the Maiden Lane III transaction are hard to justify. The consensus approach to emergency lending flowing from Bagehot's theory is that the central bank should lend freely to major financial institutions on a secured basis. While Bagehot advocated penalty rates, that requirement has been abandoned by central banks during crises because it causes financial institutions to delay borrowing to avoid stigma, and in any event the penalty rate justification was never understood to encompass most of the borrower's equity.

The major argument against confiscatory penalty rates is that they deter financial institutions from seeking liquidity help until the last moment, which will often be too late. Indeed, even small penalties create stigma that can destroy financial institutions by sparking runs. The government was able to disregard this concern in its dealing with AIG because the run on AIG had already begun by the time the government began negotiations with it. But if the AIG rescue remains a precedent in future financial crises—that is, if financial institutions draw from the rescue the lesson that their equity will be confiscated if they need an emergency loan—this precedent will strengthen the perverse incentive to hide financial problems from the government until the last minute.

The inconsistent treatment of AIG and other borrowers creates additional problems. If the government is permitted to show favoritism to some firms within a pool of similarly situated firms, then rent-seeking is a certain result. Critics of the Maiden Lane III transaction, for example, see Goldman's fingerprints all over it, while noting that numerous Treasury officials (including Paulson himself) had ties to Goldman. Ed Liddy, whom Paulson selected as the CEO of AIG, and who had no prior experience with AIG or the insurance industry, was a Goldman board member. A recent academic paper shows that firms with ties to Geithner all enjoyed abnormal returns when Geithner's nomination to Treasury was announced.[32] That is why strict rules against favoritism are in place in all of the government's dealings with private actors. Procurement rules, for example, prohibit the government from favoring some contractors over others. Similarly, police and fire departments are prohibited from showing favoritism.

The most potent political defense of the terms is that AIG acted recklessly. But while AIG made its share of mistakes, there was nothing it could do to protect itself from a liquidity crisis. No firm has the capacity. That is why the government serves as LLR. Firms that contributed to the financial crisis by violating underwriting standards were subsequently punished by the government. AIG was punished even though it did not violate the law, and it was given no opportunity to defend itself.

But should AIG's shareholders receive damages on account of the government's wrongdoing? The takings argument rests on the implicit premise that the failure to provide liquidity support is akin to the failure to enforce property rights. Both types of action are discretionary behavior on the party of the government. But if the government were to refuse to enforce property rights to reduce the market values of property it seeks to expropriate, a court would certainly block it—by forcing the government to pay the "fundamental value" of the property (the value if the government enforced property rights) rather than the temporary depleted value. The same argument applies to liquidity support. Ultimately, the argument is that we want to deter the government from manipulating the market— whether through selective provision of liquidity support or selective enforcement of legal rights—to reduce the price it must pay when it confiscates property. We will return to this argument in chapter 7.

5 Fannie and Freddie

If you've got a bazooka, and people know you've got it,
you may not have to take it out.
HENRY PAULSON (2010, 151)

THE FEDERAL NATIONAL MORTGAGE ASSOCIATION (FANNIE MAE) AND
the Federal Home Loan Mortgage Corporation (Freddie Mac) played
larger roles in the financial crisis than AIG did. Their contributions were
also different in kind. While AIG is an ordinary corporation, Fannie and
Freddie are so-called government-sponsored enterprises (GSEs). (When
I refer to "GSEs" in the text, I mean to refer only to Fannie and Freddie.)
While AIG's exposure to the mortgage market was $380 billion (McDon-
ald and Paulson 2015, online app.), Fannie and Freddie owned or guaranteed more than $5 trillion in mortgages. They also played a public role, de-
spite being private corporations, and the tension between their public and
private roles contributed to their collapse.

The GSEs made money by buying mortgages, converting them into
securities, and selling the securities to the public. While the companies were expected to profit on these activities—and they did, up until
the crisis—they were understood to serve a public purpose, which was to
facilitate mortgage lending. Policymakers believed that mortgage lending
would be artificially depressed unless banks and other mortgage originators could slough the mortgages they owned off their books. But private
companies did not raise enough capital and could not bear enough risk to
buy them. Or so it was thought. Fannie and Freddie solved this problem
by buying the mortgages and then converting them into securities that private owners would be willing to buy.

The GSEs financed these activities by selling debt to the public on a huge scale. Because the firms both held onto many of the mortgages and guaranteed them against default, they were heavily exposed to real estate prices. When housing prices collapsed and mortgage defaults spiked, Fannie and Freddie lost tens of billions of dollars. As it became clear that they would default on their loans, the government rescued them.

The rescue unfolded over many years. Congress passed a statute in the summer of 2008 that authorized a new government agency called the Federal Housing Finance Agency (FHFA) to operate the GSEs if they became undercapitalized, and Treasury to lend or invest money in them. In September, FHFA placed the GSEs in conservatorships, and Treasury made loans and investments that ultimately amounted to almost $200 billion. In 2012, FHFA and Treasury agreed with Fannie and Freddie that Treasury would forgo the dividends that the GSEs owed it and, in return, the GSEs would give all future profits to Treasury.

As a result, shareholders—both common and preferred—lost all or nearly all of the value of their shares. Dozens of lawsuits were brought and are currently traveling through the courts.[1] It is too soon to tell whether the plaintiffs will prevail, but the nature of their claims are clear. Placing the legal details aside, one can see that their argument is similar to AIG's: that the government used the liquidity crisis to expropriate a company, using suppressed crisis-driven market prices to avoid paying its full value (or indeed any money at all). Some of the plaintiffs also raise questions about the government's good faith—specifically, whether the Bush administration sought to destroy the institutions for political reasons. Whether or not this allegation is true, the bailout of the GSEs illustrates again the risk of government abuse of power during a financial crisis.

Fannie and Freddie: A Little History

Fannie Mae originated in legislation passed in 1938.[2] It was one of a group of agencies that Congress created for the purpose of supporting the depressed housing industry. Fannie's function at that time was to purchase certain government-insured mortgages, in this way supplying liquidity to banks. It was a government agency and was funded through the government. Over the next several decades, it played only a minor role in the mortgage market. In 1968, the government converted Fannie into a private company—for the questionable purpose of removing Fannie's debt from the government's books. Fannie would now be—in many but not all ways—a regular corporation with shareholders, private creditors, and so on. In 1970, the government also created Freddie Mac to provide competition to Fannie.

In the 1970s, Fannie and Freddie expanded their business of buying mortgages. They made money by buying the mortgages at a discount and holding them until maturity. To protect them from bad loans and risky investments, Congress required the GSEs to impose strict underwriting standards on the mortgages that they bought. The loans could not be too large (in 1975, no more than $55,000); they could be issued only on single-family houses; the homeowners were required to make down payments; and so on. First Freddie and then Fannie began securitizing some of the mortgages. They would take a number of mortgages, pool the principal and interest streams that arrived over time from the homeowners, and sell portions of these streams as securities to investors. Securitization relieved Freddie and Fannie of the risk of holding huge portfolios of mortgages—whose value could decline rapidly if people started defaulting on loans, housing prices fell, or market interest rates spiked. Much of this risk was dispersed among investors, including pension funds, sovereign wealth funds, and other well-heeled pools of money, who in turn provided cash that Freddie and Fannie could use to purchase additional loans.

The GSEs operated successfully, albeit with a few hiccups, for the next two decades. Their era of dominance began in the 1990s. Their share of the mortgage market—which was itself expanding rapidly at this time—increased from less than 10 percent to almost half from 1980 to 2010. By that time, they owned or guaranteed trillions of dollars in mortgages. It is possible that they owed their success to economies of scale and good management. But most economists believed that Fannie and Freddie benefited from an implicit subsidy from the government. While officially Fannie's and Freddie's debt was private debt like any other, the market apparently believed that the government would bail out Fannie and Freddie if they ever had trouble paying their debt. The reason was partly their historical association with the government, which in the past had provided financial assistance to firms with government connections like theirs, and partly their special status as federally chartered companies that were subject to federal regulation. But the main reason was that Fannie and Freddie had become so big and integrated in the mortgage market that their failure could cause a systemic crisis. With no one to sell their loans to, banks would stop issuing mortgages. And, with government encouragement, banks and

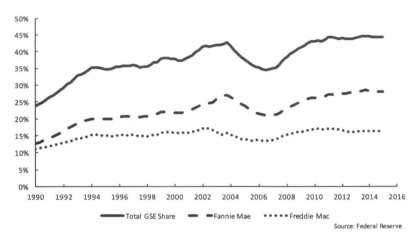

Source: Federal Reserve

FIGURE 5.1. Market share of residential mortgage debt outstanding

other financial institutions had loaded up on Fannie's and Freddie's debt, so their collapse would cause the collapse of countless other financial institutions (as well as annoying foreign countries that had also purchased the debt). Investors believed that the government would not allow the GSEs to fail—that the GSEs were "too big to fail"—and so would therefore pay the GSEs debts if the GSEs could not (see figure 5.1).

Because investors believed that the government, whatever it said, stood behind Fannie and Freddie, they were willing to buy the debt up cheaply, and this demand for their debt gave Fannie and Freddie an insurmountable competitive advantage over investment banks and other private institutions that sought to enter their markets. At the same time, because Fannie and Freddie were not permitted to invest outside of real estate, they were poorly diversified; and as a result of their political influence, they were lightly regulated. There was little evidence that they were needed to support the mortgage market; in many comparable countries without similar GSEs, homeownership was higher than in the United States (Jaffee and Quigley 2011). Indeed, the politically popular view that the government should subsidize homeownership enjoys little support in policy circles. Academics and policymakers understood the GSEs' problems and vulnerabilities long before the financial crisis, but there was no political will to do anything about them.[3]

The GSEs' Contribution to the Crisis

The role of Fannie and Freddie in the crisis has provoked a heated ideological battle (McLean 2015, 46–56). Conservatives assign significant blame to the GSEs and, more broadly, to the government's penchant for meddling in the housing market to redistribute wealth. By contrast, the mainstream view is that while the GSEs probably contributed to the crisis on the margin, the conservative view is an exaggeration. Whoever is right, what should not be forgotten is that GSEs have enjoyed political support from both Democrats and Republicans. Both parties saw advantages in using these institutions to promote homeownership, which (at least until the crisis) benefited low- and middle-income people, home builders, construction workers, and other constituencies. And both parties fell under the influence of the GSEs' well-oiled lobbying machines.

For most of their history, the GSEs were required to subsidize—by buying, securitizing, and guaranteeing—*safe* loans. These were loans to middle-class or wealthy people who bought houses and paid down payments of 20 percent or more. While these *conforming* loans excluded mortgages for very expensive houses, the purchase price could be well above the median in a region. In 1992, Congress passed a law that encouraged the GSEs to buy mortgages that were issued to low- and moderate-income borrowers. At the same time, the GSEs' regulator—at that time, an agency called the Office of Federal Housing Enterprise Oversight—subjected them to light capital regulations, which allowed them to borrow a vast amount of money relative to the value of their assets.

Later regulation, the mandate to help low-income people, and the boom in the housing market during the 1990s combined to spur the GSEs' business. In the 2000s, the GSEs entered the subprime market by allowing homeowners to make smaller down payments and relaxing other underwriting standards. But the share of their business exposed to subprime risk was never very large. Most of the growth of the GSEs was in their prime portfolios. The percentage of loans that they purchased with a down payment of less than 10 percent of the property value more than doubled between 2003 and 2007 but remained low—16 percent for Fannie and 11 percent for Freddie in 2007 (Frame et al. 2015, 31). While this allowed banks to issue some subprime mortgages knowing that they could shed the risk by reselling them to Fannie and Freddie, most of the subprime lending occurred independently of the GSEs.

In 1981, the GSEs issued and guaranteed $20 billion in mortgage-backed securities (MBSs) and owned single-family mortgages worth $50 billion. In 2007, those numbers had increased to $3.4 trillion and $1.1 trillion respectively. Their market share of mortgage debt increased from 7 percent to 40 percent in that period (Frame et al. 2015, 28). It was in that year that the subprime crisis began. Fannie and Freddie began losing money as they were called on to honor their guarantees of defaulting mortgages and as their mortgage holdings lost value in response to the rising defaults. In the second half of 2007, they jointly lost $8.7 billion (Frame et al. 2015, 32). Losses continued in 2008. In the middle of that year, the two firms were still solvent, at least according to the balance sheets they released. Fannie, for example, owned assets worth $885.9 billion and owed $844.5 billion, giving it a capital cushion of $41.2 billion. But that capital cushion looked awfully small considering that Fannie had guaranteed more than $2 trillion in mortgages and that the cushion assumed that the assets reflected their historical value rather than the plunging crisis-driven market value. Even if losses continued at their existing rate rather than worsened, the firms would soon be undercapitalized.

The Rescue of Fannie and Freddie

In the spring of 2008, the Bush administration asked Congress to give it the power to rescue the GSEs if rescue became necessary, and in July 2008 Congress passed the Housing and Economic Recovery Act (HERA).[4] HERA created FHFA, which was authorized to place Fannie and Freddie in a conservatorship or receivership if they became undercapitalized. HERA also provided that Treasury could make emergency loans to, or investments in, the companies. The Bush administration hoped that the promise of federal support would be sufficient to calm markets and enable Fannie and Freddie to raise capital from private investors. "If you've got a bazooka, and people know you've got it, you may not have to take it out," Henry Paulson had explained to the Senate Banking Committee (Wall Street Journal 2008). If creditors believed that the government would rescue the GSEs if they could not pay their debts, then creditors would continue to lend to the GSEs so that they would remain well financed. A run by their creditors would not take place.

But if you start carrying around a bazooka, people are liable to infer that you have reasons to need it. HERA did not calm the markets. The financial positions of the GSEs continued to deteriorate. As their losses swelled, it became apparent that they would not be able to repay their debts on their own. In September, the bazooka was unsheathed. FHFA placed the firms in conservatorship—which meant that it took over the firms and operated them. Treasury committed $100 billion in funding to them, an amount it doubled in May of the following year. In November 2009, Treasury agreed to lend or invest as much as necessary to keep the firms afloat. In all, Treasury invested $187 billion in the firms.

In the September 2008 transaction, Treasury received senior preferred stock in return for its money. The stock agreement entitled Treasury to various dividends, fees, and warrants, and gave it preferential treatment in case of liquidation of the firms. This meant that if the GSEs were liquidated, Treasury would be paid before common shareholders and existing preferred shareholders. Those groups of shareholders would receive money only if Treasury was fully compensated for its investment. The warrants gave Treasury the right to buy 79.9 percent of Fannie's and Freddie's common stock for a nominal price. The dividends equaled 10 percent of the outstanding amount that the GSEs had received from Treasury—and so reached almost $19 billion before the GSEs regained their financial footing and could stop drawing funds from Treasury.

It is worth highlighting that under the terms of the agreements, Treasury's cash contribution would be just enough to ensure that the firms remained solvent. This means that any contribution at all would be possible only if their liabilities exceeded the value of their assets—and the aggregate $187 billion contribution implies that the liabilities of the GSEs eventually exceeded the value of their assets by that amount. But it is unclear whether these numbers reflected the crisis-driven market values of those assets or their fundamental values. If the former, then the GSEs were not economically worthless even if the parties treated them as if they were for the purpose of calculating Treasury's contributions.

For the first few years of the conservatorship, Fannie and Freddie were unable to afford to pay the dividends. As a result, Treasury advanced additional funds to the GSEs so that they could pay the dividends back to Treasury. In August 2012, Treasury and FHFA agreed that the GSEs would pay all their profits to Treasury instead of the various fees and dividends under earlier agreements. This was called the "net worth sweep." Treasury gave up its right to the 10 percent dividends and, in return, received the right to Fannie's and Freddie's net worth—that is, the equivalent of 100 percent of their equity—with the proviso that it would be paid out over a period of years so that Fannie and Freddie could retain revenues as necessary to pay off debts as they became due.

The net worth sweep was the focus of the litigation. In strictly financial terms, it gave nothing to the shareholders. If Fannie and Freddie were insolvent, then Treasury exchanged nothing for nothing. Ten percent of nothing is nothing, and the net worth of an insolvent firm is nothing. If Fannie and Freddie were solvent and so could pay off creditors, but were not able to earn enough to pay back Treasury's investment through recurrent 10 percent dividends, then the net worth sweep just formalized this state of affairs. Treasury would receive the entire residual value of the GSEs in either case. If the GSEs earned more than this, however, the net worth sweep benefited Treasury at the shareholders' expense. It simply transferred the residual value of the GSEs from the shareholders to Treasury.

In one of its briefs, the government provides the following explanation for the net worth sweep:

> From the earliest months of the PSPAs [preferred stock purchase agreements], the Enterprises had insufficient capital to pay the 10% dividend to Treasury, and thus consistently drew funds *from* Treasury in order to make the dividend payments back *to* Treasury. As Plaintiffs allege, this created a "harmful feedback loop" that "requir[ed] the Companies to draw down Treasury's funding commitment, which, in turn, required the Companies to pay increased dividends to Treasury." At the time the Third Amendment was executed in August 2012, both Enterprises projected that this circular practice likely would continue over the long term because the Enterprises still could not afford the 10% dividend, which had grown to $11.7 billion for Fannie Mae and $7.2 billion for Freddie Mac. . . .[5]

Because the cap on the Treasury commitment became fixed on January 1, 2013, each dollar drawn from Treasury merely to pay the Treasury dividend was one less dollar available to the Enterprises to draw on in the event the Enterprises suffered losses due, for example, to a decline in the housing market or broader economic turbulence. Accordingly, the prospect of the Enterprises continuing this circular practice raised concerns in the marketplace over the adequacy of the remaining Treasury funds. In particular, market forecasts predicted that the Enterprises' ongoing payment of the 10 percent dividend would completely exhaust Treasury's funding commitment within ten years, leading to potential downgrades in the Enterprises' credit ratings.[6]

According to the government, the problem in 2012 was that the GSEs were not profitable enough to afford the 10 percent dividends. They could obtain additional funds from Treasury to pay the dividends back to Treasury. But this increased the size of Treasury's cash infusion, which in turn increased the dividends that would be due next time round, in a vicious circle—a "death spiral," as the government put it. This could happen only a limited number of times before Treasury's commitment would be exhausted. As the GSEs approached their funding limit, their counterparties—private creditors, banks that relied on their guarantees—would become increasingly reluctant to do business with them.

The plaintiffs argue that the government simply misread the contract—disregarding text that allows the GSEs to defer payments if they were willing to pay a higher interest rate—and that there were alternative arrangements that would have solved the circularity problem. But the nub of the issue lies elsewhere. Even if it was necessary for Treasury to effectively waive the dividend payments in the short term (which is what it did by providing the funds for its own payment), and so be compensated for the risk and time value of money to be received in the future, Treasury should have received the amount of money (in the form of additional dividends) that would fairly give it such compensation. If the GSEs were insolvent or close to insolvency, then, yes, all future profits could well be fair compensation. But if they were viable firms that were likely to make large profits in the future, then the net worth sweep overcompensated Treasury.

As it turned out, the GSEs recovered in 2013. In that year, the firms paid Treasury almost $130 billion. As of January 2017, Treasury has received payments worth $247 billion from Fannie and Freddie, an amount that exceeds its investment by almost $70 billion (Kiel and Nguyen 2016). If we extrapolate their 2015 profits of $17.3 billion forward,[7] Fannie and Freddie will earn at least tens and probably hundreds of billions of dollars more, all of which will go to Treasury (Frame et al. 2015, 42–49). It may well be that the government was not surprised by any of this. Documents released at the time of this writing suggest that government officials did not believe that the GSEs were in a death spiral. They believed (correctly, as it turned out) that the GSEs stood on the verge of "the golden years of GSE earnings," and they sought through the net worth sweep to ensure that the companies never returned to profitability (Morgenson 2016a; 2016b).

Was the Rescue Justified?

The best discussion I have found on this issue was written by a quartet of economists—W. Scott Frame, Andreas Fuster, Joseph Tracy, and James Vickery (Frame et al. 2015). Their careful look at the data indicates that the rescue accomplished both its immediate objectives and contributed to the resolution of the liquidity crisis. After the takeover in early September 2008, the price of the GSEs' debt fell, as did the yields of agency-guaranteed MBSs, indicating that the market lowered its estimate of their risk of insolvency. The Lehman debacle then intervened, and the GSEs' yields increased again, in line with the effects of Lehman's collapse on other financial institutions. The government rescued the GSEs; among other actions, the Fed implemented a program of buying agency-guaranteed MBSs and GSE debt. As the market unfroze, the GSEs became active in guaranteeing mortgages again. They have guaranteed more than half of the new mortgages since 2008.

Frame et al. argue that the rescue was a success because it enabled the GSEs to continue securitizing and guaranteeing mortgages and to honor their debts. If the GSEs had stopped operations in the mortgage market, originations would have collapsed, exacerbating the downward spiral of housing prices and housing-related derivatives, which would have thrown additional firms into insolvency. If the GSEs defaulted on their debts, countless more financial institutions that owned GSE debt would have failed. Frame et al. approve the decision to wipe out common and preferred equity owned by private investors.

Frame et al. also fault the government. The "focus on the financial performance of the two firms conflicted to some degree, however, with other public policy objectives during this period" (Frame et al. 2015, 47). First, the GSEs (under FHFA's direction) frequently exercised their contractual right to return mortgages to sellers who had misrepresented the quality of the loans. As a result, mortgage originators tightened underwriting standards, which raised the cost of mortgages, delaying the recovery of the housing market. Second, the GSEs refused to participate in Treasury's program of encouraging banks to partially forgive the mortgages of underwater borrowers, which could also have helped the housing market recover. Third, the GSEs have become stronger, rather than weaker, which may mean that their elimination—long desired by policymakers—will be delayed indefinitely. The second and third criticisms echo a Treasury department press release from August 17, 2012, which justified the net worth sweep as a way of ensuring that the GSEs "will be wound down" and that their earnings "will be used to benefit taxpayers."[8] Ironically, the government has found itself unable to kill the zombies because of their essential role in maintaining the mortgage market. It is just not clear that private institutions will step in and guarantee or package mortgages if the GSEs are eliminated. The government won't take this risk. So while HERA authorized only a short-term involvement by the government in the GSEs—on the understanding that if they should need a rescue, then their days would be numbered—the financial transactions that rescued them have also given the government the power to maintain (and operate) them indefinitely (Wallach 2015, 60–62).

Frame et al.'s arguments are in serious tension with the legal constraints that governed the rescue. HERA gave the government the power to place the GSEs into a conservatorship, not the power to take them over and operate them in any way that might advance public policy or benefit taxpayers. With the benefit of hindsight, we can see what was at stake. If Congress had simply taken over the GSEs in June 2008, it could have used them however it wanted to, but it would have owed compensation to shareholders. (In July 2008, when HERA was passed, the price would have been almost $32 billion.[9]) If Congress had left the GSEs to their fate, then their collapse would have contributed to overall financial ruin. Congress chose a path that was neither fish nor fowl—one that mirrored the GSEs' traditional hybrid public-private role. The government would have the power to take them over, but would have to operate them to the benefit of stakeholders. At the same time, it imposed restrictions on the ability of those stakeholders to challenge the government's decisions in court, perhaps with the hope that the government would have enough flexibility to help the market as a whole. This fateful decision would be the source of litigation.

The Litigation: The Plaintiffs' Claims

Numerous institutions and people who owned common or preferred stock in the GSEs brought lawsuits.[10] Their complaint was, at bottom, simple.

Before the net worth sweep, Fannie and Freddie had recovered to the extent that they could have paid all their debts, fulfilled their obligations to pay 10 percent dividends to Treasury, and still been worth something. That residual was owned by the plaintiffs.[11] The net worth sweep transferred that residual from the plaintiffs to Treasury. This exaction was not authorized by law.

The actual arguments were more complex. HERA gave FHFA considerable discretion to manage the GSEs after they were put in conservatorship. Once FHFA determined that Fannie and Freddie were undercapitalized—and Fannie and Freddie *were* undercapitalized in September 2008, as were all major financial institutions, if one uses the crisis-driven prices at the time—then FHFA could place them in conservatorship. Conservators normally are given wide discretion to manage the firms under their control, and FHFA was no exception. The law stripped courts of the power to block FHFA's action unless they were egregious.

The plaintiffs argued that FHFA's actions *were* egregious. So were Treasury's. FHFA and Treasury both violated the law—FHFA by driving the GSEs into what will eventually be liquidation rather than "conserving" them, Treasury (as well as FHFA) by engineering the net worth sweep. And if HERA authorized these actions, then Congress violated the Constitution by passing a law that enabled FHFA and Treasury to expropriate profits from the shareholders.

The Merits: Procedural Irregularities

The plaintiffs argue that FHFA and Treasury engaged in numerous procedural irregularities. Several plaintiffs argue that Fannie and Freddie were not undercapitalized or in violation of the law in any way in September 2008. FHFA failed to make a showing that they were and failed to give the GSEs an opportunity to raise capital if necessary, as was required by HERA. Instead, FHFA and Treasury "bullied" the directors of both GSEs into accepting the conservatorship.

Once FHFA took control of Fannie and Freddie, it was required by law to manage the GSEs in the interests of all stakeholders—shareholders as well as creditors. When FHFA negotiated deals with Treasury, it should have treated these deals as arms-length relationships and strived for the best terms that it could get, just as a private company would if it were negotiating for loans or investments from Treasury. Yet FHFA and Treasury are arms of the government; they serve the same master. The heads of the two agencies—Treasury secretary Henry Paulson (later replaced by Timothy Geithner) and FHFA director James Lockhart (succeeded by Edward DeMarco)—worked together. The plaintiffs argue that FHFA and Treasury entered an arrangement under which Treasury supplied capital for the companies on onerous terms. These terms would ultimately reap a windfall for Treasury, while in the meantime the two agencies manipulated the GSEs so as to help other financial institutions survive the liquidity crisis—just as Treasury and the Fed used AIG to bail out AIG's counterparties using Maiden Lane III (see chapter 4). They directed the GSEs to continue to buy, guarantee, and securitize mortgages to support the mortgage market, which was not necessarily the same thing as nursing them back to profitability.

The plaintiffs argued that FHFA violated HERA and the Administrative Procedure Act (APA)[12] (a statute that prohibits agencies from acting "arbitrarily and capriciously") because HERA authorized it to "conserve" the GSEs, not use them as ATMs to benefit Treasury and private firms. Treasury also violated HERA as well as the APA by collaborating with FHFA in the extraction of wealth from the GSEs.

The government responds that HERA gives FHFA immense discretion. Congress passed the statute after the financial crisis began and did not want lawsuits to interfere with the government's rescue efforts. HERA strips away the protections that regulated parties receive under the APA. In the one case to address the shareholders' complaints so far—*Perry Capital LLC v. Lew*—the court held that, as a consequence, its ability to review the net worth sweep on the merits was extremely limited.[13]

And even if FHFA's actions were subject to judicial review, the government could argue that it discharged its obligations properly. Two law professors—Adam Badawi and Anthony Casey—make just this argument (Badawi and Casey 2014). They argue that if the GSEs had been ordinary private institutions subject to corporate and bankruptcy law, they would have been treated in roughly the same way. Once it became clear in September 2008 that the GSEs could not pay their debts as they became due, the fiduciary duties of the directors of the GSEs would have extended to the creditors of the firms as well as the shareholders. The directors would then have faced limited choices. They could have sought a loan from a private actor, but no private actor at the time had the funds that the GSEs needed—tens or even hundreds of billions of dollars—and even if a consortium of private lenders could have been put together, they would have demanded extremely onerous terms, very likely similar to those FHFA arranged with Treasury.

More likely, the directors would have caused the GSEs to declare bankruptcy. Here again, it seems likely that in this counterfactual world a loan like Treasury's would have been arranged. The standards for reviewing such loans in bankruptcy law are deferential. A judge would approve it if otherwise the firm would fail and no better terms were available. Because the GSEs sought and failed to receive private financing prior to bankruptcy, we can be confident that Treasury's terms were the best available, and without them, they would have failed. The norms of bankruptcy law confirm the broad discretion of the conservator, and for that reason the net worth sweep of 2012 would have been approved as well.

The problem with Badawi and Casey's argument is that it discounts the reason that the government was involved in the first place—that a major liquidity crisis was in process and that the GSEs did not have the power to enter bankruptcy on their own, even if that would have helped them. In ordinary bankruptcy, the laws of the competitive market operate as normal. A deferential standard of review is acceptable because multiple private creditors compete for the debtor's business. The competition will impose some discipline on the terms of financing. By contrast, in a liquidity crisis only one creditor can save the debtor: the government. There is no competitive market that offers emergency loans during a liquidity crisis. This means that the government can dictate terms. It can also neglect the interests of other stakeholders or discriminate among them for political reasons. The risk of abuse is far higher than it is in a normal bankruptcy. We will see this problem again when we turn to the rescues of General Motors and Chrysler (see chapter 6).

If the court was right that HERA stripped away the normal protections of the APA, the plaintiffs could not make these arguments based on a statute. Instead, the plaintiffs need to attack HERA, not the agency actions made under its authority. This would mean a takings claim under the US Constitution. If the court was wrong, then the question remains whether the agencies acted consistently with HERA. Either way, one cannot avoid the merits.[14]

The Merits: The September 2008 Transaction

Although the litigation focuses on the net worth sweep of 2012, we should address the original credit transaction of September 2008. Treasury made available $100 billion, later increased to $200 billion, and still later increased even more, in return for preferred stock that gave it a liquidation preference for the amount contributed, dividends worth 10 percent of Treasury's contributions, warrants to purchase 79.9 percent of the GSE's equity for a nominal amount, and various fees.

Fannie and Freddie' stock prices collapsed when the conservatorship was imposed, and on that basis some of the plaintiffs argue that the conservatorship was a taking without fair compensation.[15] Fannie's stock fell from $7.04 per share to $0.73 between September 5 and September 8. Freddie's fell from $5.10 to $0.88. Together, this amounted to a loss of $41 billion for shareholders. This loss does not even include alleged losses resulting from the government's use of these firms to help others in the market once the conservatorship was in place and from the net worth sweep in 2012.

But the decline in stock price doesn't tell us very much. Fannie's shares had traded at $30, and Freddie's at $25, earlier in 2008. Most of the decline in their price should be attributed to their exposure to housing prices, not to the government's actions. Investors might have believed that the government placed the GSEs in the conservatorship because it realized that the firms were in trouble.

The crucial question—one that parallels the question in the AIG litigation—is not what the market thought at the time, but whether the fundamental value of the GSEs' assets exceeded their liabilities. According to the GSEs' June 2008 balance sheets, they were solvent at that time. Fannie's equity was $41.2 billion on assets of $885.9 billion, and Freddie's equity was $12.9 billion on assets of $879 billion. Their capital/asset ratios exceeded regulatory requirements. The GSEs argued in September 2008 that they remained solvent.

But there are several reasons for skepticism.[16] First, these numbers reflected book values. With the decline in housing values and the rise of default rates, there was good reason to believe that the historical values did not reflect the actual values of the GSEs' assets. Second, their balance sheets included substantial deferred tax assets. These assets derived from standard tax rules, which would have allowed the GSEs to save taxes on future profits by allowing them to offset from those profits losses of the past for the purpose of calculating tax liability. But these assets would have value only if the GSEs ever returned to profitability, which was far from certain. For these reasons, Frame et al. (2015, 34) argue that the GSEs were effectively insolvent, which is why they believe that the shareholders were rightly wiped out. However, the authors do not try to estimate the fundamental value of the GSEs' assets at the time of the crisis. The question of whether Fannie and Freddie were insolvent or merely illiquid remains open. Of course, FHFA's decision to put Fannie and Freddie in a conservatorship rather than liquidate them was presumably based on the assumption that they were solvent, at least as a legal matter.

If the value of Fannie's and Freddie's assets was temporarily depressed by the liquidity crisis, then the government made a killing. Imagine that the real value of these assets was at, or close to, par. This means that the Fed could have made a fully secured emergency loan to them, as it did to all the other major financial institution in 2008. For those loans, the Fed charged low interest rates of a few percentage points at most (aside from AIG). Using the Fed loans as a baseline, the warrants and even a portion of the 10 percent dividend vastly exceeded the amount of consideration that the Fed believed was appropriate for its other loans.

The plaintiffs can win their case only if Fannie and Freddie were solvent, but again this means solvent in terms of fundamental values, not crisis values. On this view, the government seized control over two valuable firms and extinguished the shareholders' property interests in them—both to enrich the Treasury and to help other financial institutions that owned GSE debt. However, even if the plaintiffs can show that Fannie and Freddie were solvent, they face obstacles.

First, the government can argue that the transactions that created the conservatorships were voluntary and therefore not "takings" in the traditional sense. The boards of the two GSEs agreed to put the firms in conservatorships so the FHFA was not required to use force. However, this argument is not very strong. HERA gave FHFA the authority to place the GSEs in conservatorship under very broad conditions.[17] These conditions included a determination that they were unlikely to be able to pay creditors as debts became due. This means that Fannie and Freddie could be seized if they faced a liquidity crisis regardless of whether they were insolvent in fundamental-value terms. In September 2008, Fannie and Freddie faced just such conditions, as did all financial firms, and therefore FHFA's legal authority to act was clear. It would have been pointless for the boards to resist.

Second, the government can argue that the terms of the transactions were fair—the shareholders received just compensation even though they received almost nothing. Now, if the firms were solvent, it is hard to argue that almost nothing could be just compensation, but a better argument is that fair terms would have reduced shareholders to very close to zero. This argument is based on credit risk. In the uncertain conditions of September 2008, the probability that the GSEs would collapse was very high. This means that as Treasury contributed tens of billions of dollars to them, there was a high likelihood that Treasury would lose money on this investment.

The economist Larry Wall (2014) argues that the terms were fair, indeed generous. The 10 percent dividend was not out of line from what creditors were charging comparably weak borrowers both before and after the financial crisis. Moreover, the 10 percent dividend covered only the amount that Treasury loaned to the GSEs. Treasury also guaranteed the GSEs' debt, exposing it to as much as $200 billion in additional liability, but did not charge a separate amount for this guarantee. Finally, by deferring dividend payments in 2012–14, Treasury conferred additional benefits on the GSEs. However, all of these arguments should have been addressed in a trial.

Third, the government can argue that the shareholders never had any property rights in their shares—in the sense of a right to exclude the government from eliminating their value. On this view, the shareholders enjoyed the residual return only at the pleasure of the government, which at all times retained the right to expropriate the equity by placing the GSEs into conservatorships. However, this argument is weak. The GSEs were private organizations; they needed to raise capital from the market, and they could do so only if investors believed that their investments were secure. Fannie and Freddie were unable to raise much-needed capital in 2008, and it turns out that investors were wise to shun them. Anyone who bought shares during that period faced expropriation from the government in September 2008 and thereafter. The government cannot simultaneously seek to attract private investment in a corporation and reserve the right to expropriate that investment for reasons unrelated to the financial health of the corporation—that is, the enrichment of the Treasury and of other firms in the credit market. Yet according to the plaintiffs, that is just what the government did.

In sum, the argument that the government expropriated the shareholders' property at the time of the rescue in September 2008 can't be rejected out of hand, but it is nevertheless weak.

The Net Worth Sweep

Once the conservatorship was in place, the government enjoyed a free hand to operate Fannie and Freddie. It used this free hand to implement the net worth sweep of 2012, under which Fannie and Freddie gave up all their future profits to the government in return for forgiveness of the 10-percent dividends. The government argued that the net worth sweep was needed to avoid depleting Treasury's loan commitment to the GSEs, which was being exhausted by the senseless contributions of cash to fund the dividends paid back to Treasury. But that argument can be right only if the future discounted value of the dividends exceeded the equity value owned by the shareholders.

Here again, we have a question of fact, which has not been addressed in the litigation. If Fannie and Freddie were insolvent or close to insolvent, then the net worth sweep did not impair the rights of the shareholders. If they were solvent, then the net worth sweep did impair the rights of shareholders. If there was any probability, however small, that Fannie and Freddie would recover, the net worth sweep therefore took property from the shareholders without giving them anything in return. If the probability was small enough, perhaps this taking was de minimis. But by 2012, housing prices had recovered to their historical trend line despite the continued weakness of the economy. It thus seems likely that the shareholders lost a substantial amount of money.

In *Perry Capital v. Lew*, Judge Lamberth managed to avoid this question by arguing that the shareholders had no property interest in the first place once the GSEs were placed in conservatorship.[18] The opinion is not a model of clarity, but the idea seems to be that when shareholders bought GSE stock, their rights were circumscribed by the government's power to take over the firms. Effectively, a shareholder's right to dividends (if they are issued) and ultimately a portion of the liquidation value was conditional on the government's superior right to take the firms' assets for itself. Where did the government's superior right come from? The court says that even before HERA, the government had the power to put the GSEs into a conservatorship; HERA seems to have strengthen this power.

But this argument does not work. A conservator's duty is to maximize the value of a firm for the benefit of its stakeholders, including share-holders as well as creditors. That's just what a conservator is. HERA itself says that as a conservator, FHFA should "put the regulated entity in a sound and solvent condition," and "carry on the business of the regulated entity and preserve and conserve the assets and property of the regulated entity."[19] All this suggests that Congress meant to use the term "conservator" in its ordinary sense. Moreover, the GSEs were always premised on the idea that private investors would supply capital to them—and even after HERA Congress hoped that private investors would save the GSEs by recapitalizing them, so Paulson would not need to fire his bazooka. If the statute had said that the government can confiscate the shareholders' dividends, then of course no one would invest. In fact, the conservatorship language in the statute means the opposite: that the government would help preserve shareholder value by making an emergency loan if necessary.

Judge Lamberth cited earlier cases in which courts held that share-holders of regulated financial institutions lack the power to block the government from seizing control of them.[20] In those cases, the courts held that shareholders gave up the right to exclude the government in return for the benefits of deposit insurance. The cases actually say that the courts should avoid second-guessing the decisions of regulators to seize control of possibly insolvent institutions. But they do not suspend the law of takings when the government puts a financial institution in conservatorship. That shareholders cannot block a regulator from putting a financial institution in a conservatorship does not entail that the regulator can expropriate assets from the institution once the conservatorship is in operation. The fact that the regulator, as conservator, must preserve the value of the institution means just the opposite. The statute does not—and cannot—authorize regulatory agencies to operate the institutions once in conservatorship without regard to the interests of shareholders—unless the equity is worth zero, which returns us to the empirical questions that Lamberth did not reach because he never held a trial.[21] Or if it does, then the statute itself was a taking as it eliminated significant elements of the shareholders' property rights.

The validity of the takings claim depends on whether the net worth sweep actually reduced the value of the shares. If the shares were already worth nothing in economic terms, then there was no taking. But they traded at a price greater than zero; investors believed that the GSEs had turned a corner. The government's argument—that the dividend arrangement would have driven the GSEs into insolvency, and therefore the net worth sweep did not harm shareholders—is flimsy. Even if the dividend arrangement was unsustainable because of the pressures it put on the firms' liquidity, the credit transaction could have been restructured without reducing shareholder value to zero.

Lessons

There are striking parallels between the AIG and GSE bailouts. In both cases, the rescue began with a deal that plaintiffs later argued was coerced by the government. The initial deal gave the government most of the value of the companies and control over their operations but did not completely wipe out the shareholders. However, government control of the firms meant that the remaining interest of the original shareholders was thrown at the mercy of the government's discretion. In both cases, the government stands accused of using the companies to funnel resources to other financial institutions and to enrich itself, or to achieve other goals—in the GSEs' case, restructuring the government's involvement in the mortgage market—that were inconsistent with promises to honor the property rights of private investors. The merits of the arguments ultimately depend on whether the firms were insolvent based on fundamental values or instead were solvent victims of a liquidity crisis that affected everyone. If the firms were insolvent, the government's treatment of them was not harsh. If they were merely cash-constrained, the government's treatment of them raises troubling questions about policy and legality.

Taking the plaintiffs' perspective, then, we see the government undertake a two-part strategy—first of using force to seize control of the company and transfer most of its value to itself, and then of using its control over the company to achieve objectives that are inconsistent with the interests of the stakeholders or that do not treat the different stakeholders fairly. The plaintiffs agree that the government needs power to make emergency loans or investments during a financial crisis but claim that the government abused that power for political purposes.

The government's response in both cases runs on parallel tracks. First, it argues that the plaintiffs lack standing, the courts lack jurisdiction, and related procedural obstacles block relief. These are legalistic arguments, but they get at the idea that courts lack the competence to evaluate emergency action during a financial crisis. Second, it argues that the board of directors in question voluntarily submitted to the deal because the firm would have collapsed without it. Third, it argues that the firm was worth nothing, so the shareholders did not lose anything—either in the initial transaction or in the subsequent operation of the firm. Fourth, it argues that it never really controlled the firms, and even if it did, it owed no obligations to shareholders (again, because the firm was worthless).

All of these arguments turn on the question whether the firms were worth nothing or something in September 2008. If the GSEs were worth something, all four tracks of the government response fail. The shareholders and other stakeholders were harmed by the bailout and therefore have standing to challenge it. The consent of the boards of directors meant nothing because the illegitimate threat of withholding liquidity to a financial institution during a liquidity crisis deprived them of any choice. The shareholders lost whatever the GSEs were worth. And that was possibly only because the government controlled the firms.

The GSEs were worth nothing if their liabilities exceeded the fundamental values—meaning the value of their assets as streams of payoffs until maturity discounted by credit risk and time. The GSEs were worth something and deserved liquidity support on fair terms (the same terms that other financial institutions received) if their liabilities were less than the fundamental values of their assets, even though they exceeded the temporary crisis-driven values of the assets. It is tempting to argue that the answer to this question was unknowable, but the government agencies did estimate fundamental values—and turned out to make pretty good guesses. They acted on those estimates, as they were legally required to do, at every stage of the crisis. The government had no basis for treating similarly situated firms differently. Discrimination of that type would be unfair and would violate Bagehot principles and generate perverse behavior. The unavoidable conclusion is that these disputes turn on a specific and knowable empirical issue—the fundamental values of the firms' assets—and that courts should resolve that issue by holding a trial, which would likely confirm that the GSEs were solvent in the fundamental-value sense. But in the end, one can't avoid the conclusion that the government acted unlawfully. If the GSEs were solvent, then the government expropriated its property. If the GSEs were insolvent, the government should not have put them in conservatorships but should have liquidated them.

All of this might seem too legalistic. Consider a different argument the government could make. During a liquidity crisis, the primary goal of the government is to pump money into credit markets until confidence is restored. There is no clean, fair way to do this. Financial markets are too complex, and regulators are constrained in complicated and unpredictable ways by mass psychology—panic!—which itself raises the specter of political pressures that could do more harm than good. A prudent regulator cannot disregard public fear and political pressure, even if the law, strictly construed, blocks actions that would address it.

Let's consider the worst case—the plaintiffs' most lurid depiction of events—and see how the government's action could have been justified on political and psychological grounds, even if not on a strictly legal basis. Consider first the firms that were treated most gently: the banks and investment banks. The problem for the government was that these firms were independent and had strong incentives—individually rational but collectively perverse—to turn down government assistance until as late as possible. Firms feared that a government loan would stigmatize them as the weakest of the herd, causing a flight by private creditors that would undermine whatever good that government assistance might do. The government could persuade these firms to accept liquidity support only by offering it on generous terms, so that it appeared no different from an ordinary credit transaction.[22]

This outraged the public, creating political problems, but more important, this type of emergency lending could well have been insufficient for addressing the crisis. Firms accepted liquidity assistance on generous terms so they could pay their bills in the short term, but they were not willing to start lending again until the crisis was over. More aggressive action was needed, and the government responded by using AIG and the GSEs as conduits for macroeconomic support. AIG was used to take toxic collateralized debt obligations off the balance sheets of banks. This enabled private investors to evaluate their creditworthiness based on their customary and marketable assets, and extend credit to them. And the GSEs were used to ensure that mortgages would continue to be originated, so as to halt the slide in housing prices, which in turn would increase the value of housing-related assets owned throughout the market. AIG was treated differently just because of happenstance—it was the first major firm to fail after the Lehman debacle convinced the government that a crisis had been reached, while the government's refusal to save Lehman temporarily enabled it to credibly threaten not to rescue AIG unless the AIG board consented to harsh terms. The GSEs were treated differently because of their quasi-government status, which made it easier for regulators to seize control of them without alarming the market.

The government did not, and could not, make these arguments in court because they are not legal arguments. Even while Judge Engelmayer argued in the AIG case that an emergency may justify judicial deference to government action, his opinion was based on conventional legal doctrine, not a theory of extra-legal action. More to the point, while these arguments, if true, might cause us to approve the government's emergency actions in 2008, they do not provide a basis for denying compensation to shareholders of AIG and the GSEs. As I will argue in subsequent chapters, we can argue that even if the government acted properly from a policy standpoint, we can now demand that it compensate those who bore the cost of the government's actions.

6

The Bankruptcies of General Motors and Chrysler

This was the financial equivalent of putting a gun to the heads of the bankruptcy judge, GM's stakeholders, and of course Team Auto itself.

RATTNER (2010, 251)

IN THE SPRING OF 2009, THE US GOVERNMENT RESCUED GENERAL Motors and Chrysler—two of the largest manufacturers in the country, which collectively employed 268,623 workers.[1] These bailouts wiped out the shareholders of both companies and have come under criticism because they favored the claims of politically connected auto union workers at the expense of tort victims, auto dealers, and conventional financial creditors. Critics also pointed out that the bailouts departed from Bagehot's dictum. GM and Chrysler were real-economy firms; they were not financial institutions. They were also likely insolvent. They were inefficient firms that might have failed even without the financial crisis. In these two respects, the government bailouts of GM and Chrysler fundamentally differed from the bailouts of AIG and the government-sponsored enterprises (GSEs), which were illiquid but (in all likelihood) solvent financial institutions.

The GM and Chrysler bailouts are also distinctive because they took place in the course of bankruptcy proceedings. While the firms received emergency loans in the fall of 2008, the bulk of the US government investment (Canada also participated) took place after the companies declared bankruptcy the following year. Bankruptcy law provides a procedure for the liquidation or reorganization of firms and extends rights to all their stakeholders. Some of Chrysler's and GM's creditors argued to the bankruptcy courts that the bailout was illegal, but their arguments were rejected. Auto dealers whose distributorships were terminated during the rescue and reorganization have brought takings claims, which are pending.

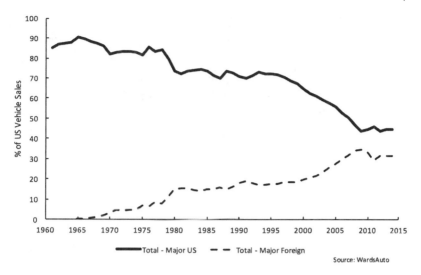

FIGURE 6.1. US vehicle market shares

For all the differences, the GM and Chrysler bailouts raise exactly the same issues as the AIG and GSE bailouts did. The government was not legally obligated to rescue any of these firms, but once it decided to launch a rescue, legal and policy constraints came to the fore. The major questions in all cases were whether the bailout was justified as a policy matter and whether the government's use of bailout money to favor some people at the expense of others could be justified on policy and legal grounds. The different economic and legal settings of the GM and Chrysler bailouts allow us to see how these tensions play out from a new and informative angle.

The Decline of the US Car Industry

The US automobile industry has experienced a steady decline since its peak in the 1950s when GM, Ford, and Chrysler manufactured 94.5 percent of the cars sold in the United States. Figure 6.1 tells the story. But it remained a significant source of jobs and economic activity on the eve of the financial crisis.[2]

In the late 1950s, foreign manufacturers made inroads in the US markets by exporting small, inexpensive cars, led by Volkswagen's Beetle. Consumers responded favorably to the lower prices as the US economy went into recession. The Detroit Three responded by manufacturing their own small cars and regained some of their lost market share in the early 1960s. But in the 1970s a series of blows permanently damaged the competitive position of the US automakers. During the oil crisis of 1973, the price of gasoline skyrocketed, which in turn led consumers to flock to small cars. The US auto industry was not prepared for the rise in demand for small cars, while foreign car manufacturers, which specialized in small cars, were. The Japanese automakers entered the market and developed a reputation for quality that American companies could not match. This was particularly important after Ralph Nader's activism for car safety brought this topic to public attention. New fuel-economy laws also favored imports. The weak economy and high gas prices of the 1970s, culminating in another shock in 1979, reduced domestic market share to less than 65 percent and forced Chrysler to obtain a bailout from the US government.

In the 1980s, the US manufacturers temporarily halted their decline, thanks to low gas prices, US economic recovery, and "voluntary" restrictions on foreign imports. The extent to which innovation and good management contributed to this recovery is less clear. Thomas Klier (2009) says that the car manufacturers wasted time with mergers and acquisitions that were eventually unwound, and that many ambitious efforts to improve productivity came to naught. But the manufacturers also spotted a shift in consumer demand in favor of larger cars as gas prices declined again and responded by producing innovative minivans, SUVs, and pickup trucks, which were immensely popular. By the early 1990s, the Detroit companies were profitable again.

However, foreign automakers fought back by improving quality, competing on price, and entering the light truck market. Gas prices edged up in the late 1990s and 2000s, throwing the competitive advantage back to the foreign companies, which had also circumvented import restrictions and reduced costs by building factories in the United States. The US companies could not respond as quickly as the foreign exporters to a shift in consumer demand back to small cars when gas prices spiked in 2007. But the biggest problem for the US companies remained low quality and high production costs. The US companies had agreed to pay the health-care costs of retired workers, which they could not afford. Compensation rules negotiated with the United Auto Workers (UAW) may also have made it difficult to motivate workers and to adjust nimbly to changing market conditions. Labor costs for the Detroit Three exceeded those of foreign exporters and foreign-owned domestic plants by as much as 45 percent (Goolsbee and Krueger 2015, 6). A 2007 agreement with the UAW attempted to address these problems, but did not go far enough to save the companies.

It is impossible to know how GM and Chrysler would have fared if the financial crisis had not dealt death blows to each. Ford had shared in the general decline of the US auto industry, but it survived the financial crisis without (much) government assistance (or at least without direct government assistance; I discuss indirect government assistance such as car buybacks below). Ford had brought in a new CEO in 2006, who launched a long-overdue restructuring of the company that allowed it to return to profitability after the crisis. The actions that Ford took—including the shedding of brands, elimination of jobs, consolidation of operations, and renegotiation of wages—all anticipated the actions of GM and Chrysler in bankruptcy. But Ford's key decision—which saved it from bankruptcy—was to borrow $23.5 billion in a secured loan in 2006. That transaction gave Ford a credit line that it could draw on during the crisis.

Ford's survival raises the question whether GM, at least, could have avoided bankruptcy by borrowing money before the crisis as Ford did. (Chrysler was in considerably worse shape.) GM's rapid return to profitability after the crisis provides further evidence for this view. If this view is correct, an argument can be made that GM's collapse was caused by liquidity problems rather than by insolvency.

The Financial Crisis Strikes GM and Chrysler

Sales of cars and light trucks in the United States fell rapidly in 2008 and 2009. Part of the decline was due to the recession. As people lost jobs and paychecks, they could not afford to buy new vehicles. The decline was also due to overcapacity. As the quality of cars improved, people replaced them less often. But a significant source of the decline was the financial crisis. Ninety percent of car buyers borrowed money to finance the purchase (Klier and Rubenstein 2012, 35). Because of the credit freeze, auto companies and third-party financers like banks could not borrow the money from wholesale markets to make the loans to consumers. They could not raise money by securitizing auto debt and selling the securities to investors (Rattner 2010, 145). Nor could consumers any longer borrow money for car purchases using the equity in their houses. When Lehman collapsed, auto sales plunged (Rattner 2010, 49 and n.2).

The Detroit automakers contributed to the downward spiral. Since they could not sell as many cars, they shut down plants and fired workers. Suppliers went bankrupt and fired *their* workers. As workers lost their jobs and paychecks, they defaulted on mortgages, car loans, and other forms of credit. This in turn forced creditors to reduce lending even more. Chrysler and GM were unable to borrow money from the private market once the crisis began.

Rescue

The government rescue unfolded over several years, but the key period extended from the fall of 2008 to the spring of 2009.[3] The CEOs of the Detroit Three realized in the fall that GM and Chrysler might not survive the financial crisis. GM and Chrysler approached the government for a loan. Ford tagged along to ensure that any assistance given to GM and Chrysler did not put it at a competitive disadvantage. Ford also worried that if GM and Chrysler collapsed, their suppliers would collapse as well, which would hurt Ford because Ford bought parts from many of the same suppliers.

The companies initially contacted Treasury, but were shunted to the Department of Commerce, and then told to plead their case to Congress. In congressional testimony, the CEOs argued that their companies were victims of the financial crisis, just as the banks were. A collapse of the auto industry would have deepened the financial crisis and the recession. The CEOs were greeted by a great deal of skepticism from politicians who believed that the companies' problems were of their own making. ("Why can't they make a Corolla?," Obama would later ask [Rattner 2010, 44].) A rescue bill was proposed, but it died in December.

Meanwhile, it became clear to executive-branch officials that Chrysler and GM would not survive without government assistance. The Bush administration believed that bankruptcy of the firms would exacerbate the financial crisis and deepen the recession. Yet there was not enough time left in the Bush administration to formulate a proper response. Officials decided to lend the companies enough money to enable them to survive into the Obama administration. On December 19, the Bush administration made bridge loans to the two companies and their financial subsidiaries—$19.4 billion to GM and GMAC and $5.5 billion to Chrysler and

Chrysler Financial. It drew on Troubled Asset Relief Program (TARP) funds appropriated under the Emergency Economic Stabilization Act (EESA)[4]—a move that sparked controversy because EESA did not mention automakers and limited assistance to "financial institutions." The government told GM and Chrysler to reduce the pay of executives and workers, modify work rules, and dilute investors. They were also told to draft plans for restructuring their businesses. The plans were due on February 17, 2009.

After he took office, President Obama appointed a team to oversee the bailouts of GM and Chrysler. Headed by Steven Rattner, the Auto Task Force, which was located in the Treasury Department, negotiated the deals and guided the firms through bankruptcy.[5] The task force concluded over the next several weeks that neither company should be allowed to fail. The collapse of the companies would not only throw thousands of autoworkers onto the streets; it would reverberate through the economy, affecting suppliers and dealerships. Government officials and private economists estimated that more than a million jobs could be lost (Goolsbee and Krueger 2015, 8). But while a good case could be made that GM was systemically important, the consensus seems to be that Chrysler was saved for "political" rather than merely economic reasons—a Chrysler failure would have damaged President Obama's political standing or perhaps people's faith in the government at a critical juncture.

The task force believed that the restructuring plans proposed by GM and Chrysler were based on unrealistically optimistic assumptions and encouraged the companies to negotiate more aggressively with their stakeholders. The government could have forced the companies into bankruptcy at any time but preferred a negotiated deal, which would have avoided the disruptions of bankruptcy. However, the ever-present threat of bankruptcy spooked auto parts suppliers, who had traditionally supplied parts on credit. If bankruptcy took place, they would never be paid, nor could GM and Chrysler pay cash on delivery. The government solved this problem by offering additional credit to the car companies, which they could use to buy parts. It also gave them additional working capital and guaranteed their warranties so car buyers would trust them.

For GM and Chrysler to avoid bankruptcy, they needed either federal financing—private financing was not available—or an agreement among all creditors of each firm to restructure them. In fact, they needed both. The government supplied credit on a continuing basis but demanded that

GM and Chrysler restructure their loans and operations. If the firms were insolvent in an economic sense, this would mean that shareholders would be wiped out and that all creditors (or most of them) would accept a haircut. Nearly unanimous consent would be required. This turned out to be impossible. Thus, bankruptcy would be necessary. The major benefit of the bankruptcy procedure is that stakeholders can be forced to accept haircuts (or nonpayment, as the case may be), albeit under the supervision of a bankruptcy judge, who ensures that the haircuts are fair and in conformity with the law.

The Chrysler Bankruptcy

An ordinary corporate bankruptcy takes years. Firms are complex, and it takes that long to evaluate their assets and business prospects, untangle the claims against them, and either liquidate or reorganize them. While in bankruptcy, firms typically continue to operate, financed by outside creditors who are given priority over the firm's prebankruptcy creditors. The bankruptcy judge tries to ensure that the capital structure of the firm that emerges from bankruptcy respects the prebankruptcy entitlements of creditors. That usually means that lower-priority creditors obtain equity, and higher-priority creditors receive debt or are paid in cash. The shareholders of the prebankruptcy firm usually receive nothing.

Everyone agreed that the auto bankruptcies could not follow this model. Because of the liquidity crisis, no private creditor would step forward to provide debtor-in-possession (DIP) financing. The government would play that role. And because the government would play that role (and was also the companies' largest- and highest-priority prepetition creditor), it would have the dominant voice in the restructuring. Moreover, the primary purpose of the auto bankruptcies was to stimulate the economy, not to restructure the companies. The macroeconomic goal of the government would shape the bankruptcy process. One indication of this was the speed of the bankruptcy. United Airlines' chapter 11 reorganization, which began in 2002, took three years. GM's and Chrysler's took one month.

The stakeholders negotiated the restructuring in advance of the bankruptcy filing and then asked the judge to approve the plan. This strategy is thought to be permitted by section 363 of the Bankruptcy Code, which permits the debtor's "assets" to be sold during bankruptcy—with "assets" defined broadly to include the debtor itself.[6] The plan is negotiated against the background of the normal procedures of the Bankruptcy Code. If the parties can't agree to a plan before bankruptcy, then bankruptcy sets forth procedures that enable stakeholders to propose and vote on various plans, which must comply with certain rules. The most important of those rules is the absolute priority rule, which (with certain exceptions) requires that prebankruptcy priorities be respected.

Chrysler entered into bankruptcy on April 30. Chrysler owed $8 billion to pension plans; $4.5 billion to the health plans of retired workers; $6.9 billion to banks with secured claims; $2 billion in second-lien loans to its owners, Daimler and Cerberus; and $5.3 billion to trade creditors. It also owed more than $4 billion to the US Treasury.[7] The book value of its assets was $39.3 billion. The bankruptcy court would later estimate that the liquidation value of Chrysler was no more than $1.2 billion, and could be low as $0. Like GM, Chrysler had seen an enormous drop in the demand for its cars from the preceding year, driven by the collapse of auto credit as well as a shift in consumer preference away from large, expensive gas-guzzling cars, as a result of the recession and high gas prices. Chrysler was kept alive by government loans; it did not take in enough money to fund its operations.

The Auto Task Force, creditors, and Chrysler management put together a section 363 transaction. New Chrysler would inherit the assets of old Chrysler but few of its liabilities. Old Chrysler received $2 billion that it turned over to the secured creditors, who were accordingly paid only $0.29 on the dollar. A retirement trust for Chrysler employees would own 55 percent of New Chrysler—albeit without the power to vote. The US government would own 8 percent and the Canadian government 2 percent; they were also given debt claims against the new Chrysler. Daimler's and Cerberus's equity interests and debt claims were wiped out. The plan also envisioned that Fiat would gain equity in New Chrysler in return for a commitment to give New Chrysler access to Fiat technology, which would enable Chrysler to build fuel-efficient vehicles and cut costs. Chrysler closed numerous plants and dealerships, and cut pay for its workers. The court approved the plan on May 31.

The GM Bankruptcy

GM filed for bankruptcy on June 1, 2009. GM had reported assets of $82 billion and liabilities of $172 billion—it was insolvent. A rule of thumb states that the market value of assets are 10 percent of their book value, which means that GM's assets were worth only $8 billion—it was *really* insolvent. Observers at the time were skeptical that GM could turn things around. Sales were down, revenues were down, losses were up, cash reserves were vaporizing. Shareholders would be entitled to nothing, and creditors to very little.

The section 363 deal provided that nearly all of GM's assets would be transferred to a new entity called "New GM." Secured creditors were paid in full. GM's liabilities stayed with the old company with a few exceptions. Most important, liabilities under employee benefit plans of workers covered by a UAW collective bargaining agreement were transferred to New GM. All other creditors—including victims of car crashes caused by design defects—would be required to pursue their claims against old GM, which meant they would be entitled to a fraction of their claims. The shareholders of old GM were also wiped out. New GM would inherit old GM's employees and suppliers. Thanks to agreements between GM and UAW, the employees would be paid lower wages than before and in a more flexible manner than before—comparable to the treatment of employees in the more-competitive transplant factories in the US South owned by Toyota and other foreign auto companies. GM shut plants, cut brands, fired thousands of workers, closed more than a thousand dealerships, and changed its management. New GM's owners would be Treasury (60.8 percent of the common stock), the Canadian government (11.7 percent), an employees' beneficiary association trust (17.5 percent), and old GM (10 percent). The court approved the plan on July 5, and New GM sprang into existence on July 10.[8]

Recovery of the US Auto Industry

Knowledgeable observers at the time of the bankruptcies believed that Chrysler was a basket case and deserved to die. It owned a lot of real estate and the valuable Jeep brand, but not much else. A significant faction in the White House believed that Chrysler should not be rescued, but were outvoted. Opinion on GM was less uniform. GM's brands sold better than Chrysler's, and the quality of GM's cars had been improving in recent years. The company was also a vast and storied powerhouse of American capitalism.

There were three possible justifications for the automakers' rescue. The first was macroeconomic. The failure of the automakers could aggravate the downward spiral. While the worst of the liquidity crisis was past, the economy had entered into a severe recession. Throwing additional thousands of people out of work—the thousands of people who worked for the auto companies and even more people who worked for suppliers and related firms—would further depress demand and delay economic recovery. On this view, the rescue was a kind of economic stimulus—like a jobs program, albeit one directed to autoworkers. Although GM and Chrysler were insolvent, they could—with the government's help—be reorganized and made more efficient.

The second was political. The government had bailed out the financial system, and the public saw these bailouts as gifts to fat cats on Wall Street. The Detroit bailout could be depicted as an overdue effort to help working people in the heartland. The automaker bailout therefore would boost confidence in the government and the political standing of the president.

In the various accounts of the decision making (e.g., Rattner 2010), the economic justification played a larger role for the GM rescue than the Chrysler rescue, which was seen as a political necessity. However, there is a third justification for the GM rescue, which is purely financial. On this view, GM was not insolvent in an economic sense. It couldn't borrow because of the liquidity crisis. If the government had loaned it enough money, it would have been able to pay its debts and return to profitability. The shareholders would not have lost equity.

The car industry recovered after the Great Recession. While most of the gains, as figure 6.2 shows, were made by foreign companies (including exporters and those with factories in the United States), Chrysler gained market share in each of the five years after the bankruptcy. GM did less well in regaining market share. Both companies—and Ford as well—have made large profits thanks to the economic recovery and the decline of gas prices, which returned the competitive edge to their gas guzzlers. In a careful analysis, Goolsbee and Krueger (2015) suggest the reorganization of Chrysler probably contributed to its growth, but that this growth came in part at the expense of GM.

In contrast to the rescues of financial institutions like AIG and the GSEs, the US government lost money on its investment in the auto companies—about $10 billion. But the government is not a company, and it is

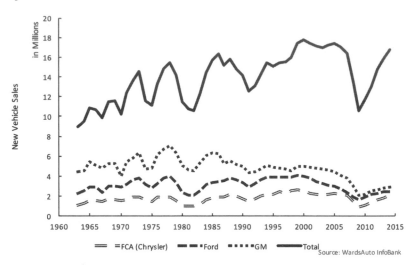

FIGURE 6.2. US new vehicle sales

much harder to determine whether it "profited" on a transaction. Part of the reason the government lost money is that it forced GM and Chrysler to make transfers to workers. The government could instead have bought GM and Chrysler for their liquidation value and then made a fortune when the companies recovered. It chose to make a deal that paid off certain constituencies. Whether the government needed to make these payoffs to return the companies to viability is unknown.

To be sure, the loss could also understate the government's true losses because it excludes car buyback legislation, the "cash-for-clunkers" scheme. The government offered thousands of dollars to automobile owners who traded in old cars that met certain criteria. This stimulated demand for new cars—to replace the traded-in old car. But since taxpayers funded the scheme, that was an additional cost to the government. On the other hand, cash-for-clunkers might have improved environmental quality and so been separately justified—or partly justified—on those grounds.[9] These considerations underline the problem with thinking of the Lender of Last Resort as a mere profit-making entity like a bank.

Were Creditors' Rights Violated?

The Chrysler and GM bankruptcies raised the same legal issue: the proper use of section 363 to implement a bankruptcy plan negotiated in advance by the firms' major stakeholders. The Auto Task Force negotiated Chrysler's 363 plan with Chrysler management, Fiat, the UAW, and JP Morgan—the major creditor, which also acted as agent for other large creditors. The task force negotiated GM's 363 plan with GM management, the UAW, and bondholders. Various small fry were either left out of the process or were represented by large fry—raising procedural questions to which I will return. The task force, representing the US government, could use US money—or the threat to withhold it—to influence the terms of the deals.

The Chrysler deal puts the problem in highest relief. Chrysler owed $6.9 billion to a group of secured creditors led by JP Morgan; $10 billion to an unsecured employee benefit plan; and smaller amounts to other unsecured creditors like suppliers. In a normal bankruptcy, the secured creditors would have been paid before the unsecured creditors. If Chrysler had been liquidated for $1 billion, all of that $1 billion would have been paid to the secured creditors and nothing to the employee benefit plan. If someone had been willing to pay $5 billion for Chrysler as a going concern, then all $5 billion would have gone to the secured creditors. Unsecured creditors would receive nothing unless Chrysler was worth more than $6.9 billion.

In the GM bankruptcy, the employee benefit plan was also treated far more generously than the other unsecured creditors. While the other unsecured creditors were collectively owed $27.1 billion—$7 billion *more* than the trust was—they received far less. The other unsecured creditors retained their claims against old GM, which was given 10 percent of new GM (plus warrants). The trust was given 17.5 percent of equity, plus a $2.5 billion note, plus $6.5 billion in preferred stocks, plus warrants.

Corporate reorganizations usually take place under section 1129 of the Bankruptcy Code, which ensures that priorities are respected.[10] If Chrysler is reorganized under section 1129—with secured creditors and unsecured creditors given interests in a New Chrysler—then the secured creditors must either be paid off in full or give their approval. Similarly, GM's unsecured creditors would receive the same payoff as the trust.

So how did Chrysler's secured creditors end up with $0.29 on the dollar while workers received more than $0.50 on the dollar? How did it happen that GM's unsecured creditors were treated worse than the employee trust? The answer is section 363. Because the creditors agreed to sell Old Chrysler's assets to New Chrysler and old GM's assets to New GM, and give each other new interests in the new corporation, the court merely had to approve the deal; it was not required to ensure that priorities were respected.

But if everyone agreed to the 363 transactions, what difference does it make that the normal procedures of section 1129 were not used? There are a few concerns. In Chrysler's case, while a majority of secured creditors voted for the transaction, not all of them did. Those that did might have believed that they would profit from lending to the reorganized entity and that this profit offset any losses. While the secured creditors had agreed among themselves by contract that the majority rules, that agreement itself might have assumed that a bankruptcy court would block attempts by the majority to expropriate value from the minority. In GM's case, most of the unsecured creditors went along, but not all.

Another criticism is that the government controlled the bankruptcies so that the creditors were not able to protect themselves. The government threatened to pull the plug on the rescues by calling its loans and refusing to extend further credit for the reorganization unless all the parties could reach an agreement. The government also made clear to the creditors—most of which had received TARP money and other support from Treasury and the Fed—that the retirement fund must be paid and that most workers must be retained. The creditors agreed to the deal because the alternative was worse.

Rattner defends the 363 transaction by pointing out that the secured creditors received more money than they would have if Chrysler had been liquidated (2010, 180-81).[11] The same point can be made about GM. His defense parallels the government's argument about AIG and the GSEs— that if the government had not made emergency loans to these companies, their stakeholders would have received nothing. But this argument is beside the point in all three cases. None of the companies was liquidated, and so the question is how the value generated by government intervention should be distributed. The government's insistence that stakeholders are entitled to no more than their share of the liquidation value is wrong legally—most clearly in the bankruptcy setting, but also in the other two settings. Chrysler wasn't liquidated, it was reorganized. Under bankruptcy law, high-priority creditors should be paid in full out of the reorganized firm.

The bankruptcy courts approved the 363 transactions on the ground that the payoffs to subordinate creditors were the result of the government infusion of capital.[12] They believed that the government put more capital into the firms than the secured creditors were entitled to. The government might have done this because it believed that the extra capital could be used to enhance the value of the firms as going concerns or because it believed that the transfers to workers and other creditors would have valuable macroeconomic benefits. In either case, the secured creditors had no grounds for criticizing the government's behavior.

The problem with this argument is that the government could dictate terms. In a normal bankruptcy, outside creditors compete to be the DIP. This ensures that the DIP is paid the market price of the credit it supplies. Because of the lingering effects of the liquidity crisis and the vast size of the corporations, the government alone could serve as the DIP. This means that the government was a monopolist and could charge an above-market price. Unlike an ordinary monopolist, the government's interest was not to maximize its profits, and so the interest rate it charged was not particularly high. The government instead used its monopoly power—or could have used its monopoly power—to favor the stakeholders it cared about. The secured creditors could not protect themselves because no other firm could serve as DIP—which in normal circumstances would have cut out the unsecured creditors and given more value to the secured creditors in return for the right to finance the reorganization.

The bankruptcy courts were thrown off because they did not understand how the liquidity crisis interfered with normal bankruptcy procedure. For this reason, they interpreted the absence of DIP candidates or bidders for the firm as evidence that the firms had no going-concern value. This mistake caused them to accept the government's argument that the secured creditors had no grounds for complaint.

Should an Auction Have Been Held?

Academic critics of the 363 transactions also fault the bankruptcy courts for not forcing the government to prove that the firms' going-concern value was less than their liquidation value (Roe and Skeel 2010; Baird 2012). In a typical bankruptcy, anyone can propose a reorganization plan, and the court is supposed to accept the plan that generates the most value—as long as it respects prebankruptcy entitlements and is viable. If someone proposes a 363 transaction, then the court should give other people a chance to propose a better 363 transaction. This the courts failed to do. While they provided a little more than a week for others to propose a 363 transaction—

hardly enough time, in any event—they put significant constraints on the types of bids they would consider (Roe and Skeel 2010, 749, 765). The courts said that other plans would need to preserve retiree and supplier liabilities. But the issue was precisely whether a plan that preserved these liabilities would maximize value. No one had the chance to propose a plan that generated more value but gave less to the employees and suppliers. Such a plan would have given a larger payoff to the higher-priority creditors, as is required.

The major response to this argument—which can be found in the judicial opinions—is that there was not enough time for a normal auction process. In a deepening recession, the government was justified in pushing through a plan that would keep the firms alive even if the distribution was not legally impeccable. It's hard to know whether this argument is right or not. The Auto Task Force feared that people would stop buying cars from a firm in bankruptcy, but no one stopped buying airline tickets when United was in bankruptcy. In light of people's complacency about the risks of driving and their fear of flying, one would think that an airline bankruptcy would spook them more than an auto bankruptcy. And, indeed, there was no evidence that people inclined to buy a GM and Chrysler car were deterred while the companies were in bankruptcy. Moreover, firms operate normally in bankruptcy—the automakers would have continued manufacturing cars while in bankruptcy, whether the bankruptcy proceeding took one month or three years. All this suggests that a longer, and fairer, bankruptcy process would have been possible. On the other hand, no one knew that the Chrysler bankruptcy would run so smoothly, and by the time this became clear, the momentum behind the GM deal was irresistible. The accounts of the complexity of negotiations—the number of stakeholders, the number of issues, the intricacy of the companies with their worldwide operations and thousands of employees, the limited administrative resources of the government, the meddling of politicians in Congress and state governments—all explain why the bankruptcy courts may have believed that they had no choice but to defer to the deals they were presented with.

Another defense is that everyone knew that the automakers were for sale (Rattner 2010, 107–08)—and had known at least since late 2008. The normal marketing period before a section 363 sale—designed to ensure that the best price is obtained for the debtor—would have been a meaningless formality. While this is true, the absence of bidders is a problem rather than a justification. Because only the government could buy the automakers or finance their reorganization, a market test was impossible. I will return to this issue below.

Bankruptcy during a Liquidity Crisis

Academic bankruptcy experts worry that the Chrysler and GM cases will set harmful precedents that bring back the bad old days when insiders used prepackaged deals to squeeze out creditors with higher priority (Adler 2010; Baird 2012; Roe and Skeel 2010). A legal rule known as the *sub rosa* doctrine is supposed to prevent insiders from using section 363 to circumvent the protections in section 1169, which both ensure that procedures are fair and preserve, as much as practical, the credit priorities that parties had agreed to. The criticism is off-base. The special circumstances of these cases—the large role of the government and the existence of a liquidity crisis—remove Chrysler and GM from the mainstream of bankruptcy. The Chrysler and GM bankruptcy courts themselves acknowledged these special circumstances, opening the way for future courts to treat the cases as sui generis rather than precedential.

The real importance of the Chrysler and GM bailouts lies in what they tell us about emergency government action during a liquidity crisis. And the liquidity crisis did play a significant role. The liquidity crisis—and the recession it spawned—provided the major justification for the bailouts.

Because of the liquidity crisis, which by the time of the bankruptcies was tailing off, it was possible that Chrysler and GM's assets were temporarily undervalued. While the companies did not deal in CDOs and MBSs, their business depended heavily on credit transactions, and the credit spigot was turned off during the crisis. This means that the liquidation values offered to the courts reflected crisis-driven prices rather than fundamental values. The undervaluation gave the government a golden opportunity to restructure the firms without ensuring that creditors were paid off in full.

As a result of the liquidity crisis, only the government could play the role of DIP financer.[13] This was a problem for bankruptcy law, as we saw, because it meant that the government played an outsized role in distributing the value of the firms. But the larger point is the same as the one we saw in the AIG and GSE bailouts. Because the government is a credit monopolist during the financial crisis, it can transfer wealth among the public in a way that is normally barred by law—unless the courts prevent it.

One of the strange effects of the government's omnipresence in financial markets is that many of the bankruptcy creditors were beholden to the government. Even as they were negotiating with the Auto Task Force for a larger slice of the pie, Chrysler's secured creditors were benefiting from TARP investments and Fed loans. As Mark Roe and David Skeel (2010, 760) note, "One wonders why the Treasury was tough on Chrysler's lenders in this dimension, while propping them up elsewhere." The government could have achieved the same effect by being more generous in bankruptcy and less generous outside bankruptcy. Indeed, the same funds from TARP were being used to lend to Chrysler and to lend to JP Morgan, Chrysler's largest secured creditor. Recall how the government made loans both directly to AIG's counterparties and benefited them by causing AIG to pay them off at par. If the Chrysler model had been followed, the government would have loaned them more money directly while causing AIG to demand a haircut.

The critics argue that because the major secured creditors were beholden to the government for TARP money, they were in no position to press for a fair distribution in bankruptcy—especially for the smaller secured creditors that had received no TARP money (Rattner 2010, 174). It is in that sense that their consent to the 363 transaction was coerced—at least in the Chrysler case. But we could turn this criticism on its head. Maybe the government was generous to the banks so that the banks could be generous to Chrysler. The banks were not coerced but bribed. This may explain why government's actions did not raise the borrowing costs of unionized firms (Anginer and Warburton 2014), as many critics predicted. If the government funneled resources to workers without actually harming the creditors, then access to credit at similar firms would not be harmed.

But whether the banks were coerced or bribed, the bottom line is this. During a liquidity crisis, the automakers' assets were undervalued, so the creditors lost the backstop bankruptcy protection that they would normally receive—the liquidation value of their claims. And during a liquidity crisis, only the government can lend, and so the government was given an opportunity to redistribute wealth in a way that violates normal bankruptcy entitlements, which protect priorities. The problem was not so much that the bankruptcy courts failed to enforce bankruptcy law. It would have taken an unusually sophisticated and self-confident bankruptcy judge to call off the normal rules because a liquidity crisis gave the government inordinate power. And if a bankruptcy court had demanded that priorities be respected, it would have risked causing the government to withdraw credit. The bankruptcy court is in no position to force the government to respect priorities when the government's participation in the bankruptcy is voluntary.

Bankruptcy law is the wrong place for protecting creditors. The problem was just that the liquidity crisis gave the government extraordinary power to intervene in the market, power that it could abuse—and this power could be used outside of bankruptcy as well as inside of it.

The Auto Dealers' Takings Claim

In late 2010 and early 2011, auto dealers whose contracts had been terminated by GM and Chrysler brought suit against the US government, arguing that the government had coerced GM and Chrysler to terminate the contracts, which violated the dealers' constitutionally protected property rights.[14] The Court of Federal Claims and, on appeal, the Federal Circuit have allowed the suit to go forward. The dealers' rights under their franchise agreements constitute property for purposes of the takings clause. And in response to the government's arguments that it was GM and Chrysler, not the government, that terminated the agreements, the courts sensibly replied that if GM and Chrysler acted at the behest of the government, then they were merely agents.

The question then arises whether GM and Chrysler were coerced. The dealers argue that they were—that the Auto Task Force would not have released money to the companies unless they terminated the dealers. Rattner (2010, 251) describes the government-imposed deadline for the GM deal as a gun to the head. The government argues that the automakers would have terminated the contracts even if the government had not offered financing or had not conditioned the financing on the terminations. The two courts agreed that the plaintiffs should be given a chance to show that GM and Chrysler had been coerced.

What would it mean for the government to coerce an automaker? The plaintiffs will obviously not be able to produce evidence of physical coercion, and the meaning of economic coercion is not clear. A threat is often said to mark an act of coercion. If the government says, "we will not make a loan unless you terminate dealers," is that a threat? Or is it simply a reasonable condition? The only way to answer this question is to ask what a private DIP lender would have done under these circumstances. One possibility is that a private DIP lender would condition the loan on dealership closures because it believes the dealerships waste money that would otherwise be used to pay it back. If that is the case, then we cannot object if the government adopted the same posture. However, another possibility is that a private DIP lender would be indifferent to the continued existence of the dealership relationships, or would even favor them—as it would if those relationships are profitable and hence improve the probability of repayment. If that is the case, then the government's insistence that the dealerships be closed would have to be motivated by a nonpecuniary goal—for example, generating short-term money that can be used to pay off constituents like the autoworkers. If plaintiffs can prove that the automakers would have in this way benefited by maintaining the franchises in question, then they ought to win on the coercion issue. However, most commentators believe that too many franchises existed—state laws blocked needed closures—and if they are right, the plaintiffs should lose on this issue.

If the plaintiffs can jump this obstacle, however, they face another, higher one. The appeals court held:

> The complaints contain no allegations regarding the but-for economic loss of value of the plaintiffs' franchises from which to establish an economic loss. Absent an allegation that GM and Chrysler would have avoided bankruptcy but for the government's intervention and that the franchises would have had value in that scenario, or that such bankruptcies would have preserved some value for the plaintiffs' franchises, the terminations actually had no net negative economic impact on the plaintiffs because their franchises would have lost all value regardless of the government action.[15]

The dealers probably cannot show that their franchises would have had value in bankruptcy without government intervention because the automakers were in terrible financial shape when they entered bankruptcy. If government money had been withheld and the companies had been liquidated, then the franchises would have been worth nothing at all. Dealers can make money only if they can sell cars. While it is possible to argue that the auto companies would not have been liquidated but instead could have been nursed back to life during a lengthy bankruptcy proceeding that over-lapped with the beginning of an economic recovery, and that they would have continued to sell cars to the dealers that the dealers would have re-sold at a profit, the plaintiffs have the burden of proof, and it would be difficult to carry it.

The court's holding echoes those of the courts in the AIG and GSE cases, and reflects the same error. If the government can avoid liability, then it can take property during liquidity crises and redistribute wealth without regard to people's property rights. The liquidity crises artificially suppress the value of property, but the government should be liable for the real value of the property it takes rather than the crisis-driven value. The but-for world must be defined as one in which the automakers re-ceived pure liquidity loans and independently decided whether to main-tain or terminate the franchises based on their economic interest. If they would have maintained the franchises, then the government's intervention caused economic loss.

The bankruptcies make clear what is at stake. Workers, suppliers, and dealers all had contracts with the automakers prior to the bankruptcy. The Auto Task Force determined that the value should be transferred to the workers and suppliers because without their support, the reorganized firms would not succeed. The task force also determined that many (but not all) dealers should be terminated. Did the companies consent to these deci-sions because they needed government money or because they indepen-dently agreed with the task force? That is the question that needs to be answered at trial.

Was the Use of TARP Funds to Rescue the Automakers Lawful?

The government used TARP funds at several stages to rescue GM and Chrysler. EESA, however, does not authorize the government to rescue the auto industry. The statute authorizes the government to "purchase troubled assets from any financial institution."[16] At the time, people used the term "troubled assets" to refer to mortgage-related securities, and this definition is included in the statute, but the statutory definition also en-compasses "any other financial instrument . . . the purchase of which is necessary to promote financial market stability."[17] A "financial institution" is defined as any "institution, including, but not limited to, any bank, savings association, credit union, security broker or dealer, or insurance company."[18]

The government argued that EESA authorized it to lend to, and make equity investments in, the auto companies because the notes and equity the government purchased were "financial instruments" and the automakers were "institutions." Moreover, both GM and Chrysler owned finance companies that loaned money to consumers so that they could buy cars—GM's (which was known as Ally Financial) was one of the largest financial institutions in the country. The government argued that if GM failed, then Ally would fail as well, and so the government could save GM to save Ally. But the government possessed separate authority to save Ally and Chrysler Financial. The government's argument implied that it could invest in any firm it wanted to—all firms are institutions and all firms issue notes and equity. But Congress did not give the government unlimited authority. Congress had rejected an earlier, broader draft that Treasury had submitted to it, rejected legislation for an auto bailout, and assumed in its deliberations that EESA was focused on the financial industry alone.[19]

Conclusion

The automaker bailouts have come into a lot of criticism from commentators who believe that the government violated the "rule of law" (Zywicki 2011). The use of TARP funds for an emergency loan to a nonfinancial institution may have violated EESA; the failure to respect priorities violated bankruptcy law, or at least its spirit; the government meddled in the operations of the companies, using its control to force them to pursue policies like green energy, which were not necessarily in the interest of the company's stakeholders; and the government was able to do all this because of the deferential posture of the courts.

The omnipresence of the government on all sides of the negotiating table deserves additional comment. Many of the creditors who lost "in" bankruptcy were at the same time receiving payoffs from the government outside bankruptcy. I already mention that many bank creditors received TARP financing or Fed loans. The dealers successfully lobbied Congress for a law that allowed the franchise terminations to be reevaluated in arbitration. All parties that received interests in New Chrysler or New GM benefited from the cash-for-clunkers plan, which enhanced demand, as well as from the usual array of government subsidies for automakers. In his memoir, Rattner (2010, 134–41) insists that Obama authorized a "commercial" negotiation. However, by his own admission, the Chrysler bailout was a political decision. So was, very likely, the decision to replace executives and block GM from moving its headquarters out of Detroit.

We see again an illustration of my argument that a liquidity crisis gave the government the opportunity to shuffle around property interests in violation of people's entitlements. The GM/Chrysler case is less clear than AIG and the GSEs, however. It was probably harder to value GM and Chrysler, whose long-term value depended on imponderables like the price of gasoline and the actions of their competitors. The government may well have been justified in believing that the going-concern value of the companies fell below their liabilities. But this just means that the government took advantage of their high-priority creditors rather than their shareholders.

The law provided little protection to these creditors for the same reason that the shareholders of AIG and GSEs have had trouble asserting their claims. In all the cases, the government acted nominally as a volunteer, one that intervened and rescued firms when it could have done nothing at all. The law provides the strongest protections against government coercion. But in the setting of a liquidity crisis, the distinction between coercion and noncoercion collapsed. The government became a credit monopolist, and all firms needed to deal with it. The government could, and did, use its monopoly power to redistribute wealth. The question now to be asked is what we can do about it.

7

Takings and Government Action in Emergencies

[T]wenty percent of something [is] better than
100 percent of nothing.[1]

THE BAILOUTS OF AIG, FANNIE MAE AND FREDDIE MAC (THE GSES),
and the automakers differ in detail, but the cases raise the same issues
about government power. Underlying every claim is the charge that the
government abused its powers when it rescued the firms. While the government may choose not to lend, if it decides to lend, it must do so on fair
terms. "Fair" terms here mean terms that reflect legitimate policy considerations—like credit risk or moral hazard—rather than political connections,
public approval, or policy considerations that are irrelevant to the problem
at hand. The harsh terms used in the AIG and GSE deals did not reflect
legitimate factors. The government used harsh terms in the AIG rescue to
appease public outrage and to persuade Congress to approve the Emergency Economic Stabilization Act (EESA).[2] The government used harsh
terms in the GSE rescues apparently as a way of driving them out of business so as to make room for new policy initiatives for housing. In both
cases, the government may have seen an opportunity to make money for
the Treasury that was absent in other bailouts or sought to use the institutions as vehicles to channel funds to favored constituencies—influential
Wall Street banks or vulnerable homeowners, as the case may be.

The automaker bailouts raise more complicated legal questions, but the
underlying objections are the same. The government used its lending power
to redistribute wealth from disfavored to favored constituencies. Ironically,
the major victims of the wealth redistribution were the big banks, many of

which were beneficiaries of the wealth redistribution in the AIG and GSE bailouts. That is probably why these banks did not raise a legal challenge to the bankruptcies. However, other victims—including some small creditors plus the auto dealers—did seek help from courts. The creditors argued that the bankruptcy process was abused; the auto dealers argued, like the AIG and GSE shareholders, that value was taken from them by the government, value that was redistributed in part to autoworkers.

But when we speak of "legitimate considerations," what do we mean? The question can be put as follows. We want the government to engage in an "optimal" rescue during a financial crisis, but we are not sure that the incentives of government officials will lead them to engage in an optimal rescue. The question is what institutional design should be used to align their incentives with the interests of the public. And what role might courts play in that institutional design?

A major argument of this book is that the government did not fully follow Bagehot's dictum—both for a good reason and for a bad reason. The good reason is that Bagehot's dictum demands too much passivity from the government—it underestimates the difficulty of reviving the credit market, which requires the government to force financial institutions to lend. The Fed and Treasury did well by departing from Bagehot's dictum in this respect.

The bad reason is that Bagehot's dictum requires evenhandedness, and evenhandedness was not always in the interest of the government. Government officials gained political and practical advantages by making scapegoats of certain financial institutions. The question now arises how the government can be prevented from doing this again.

When lawyers wonder how government abuse can be stopped, they first look to the federal courts. To obtain a remedy from the federal courts, people need to point either to statutes or to constitutional law. I will focus in this chapter on constitutional law and, specifically, the takings clause, which we discussed in previous chapters.[3] The plaintiffs have argued that the government took their property without compensating them and are so entitled to "just compensation."

The government responds with four major arguments. First, it argues that its discretion to lend included the discretion to bargain for terms that were favorable to it. Second, it argues that most plaintiffs consented to these transactions; they were deals, not takings. Third, it argues that the plaintiffs benefited from the rescue loans relative to the baseline of bankruptcy, and so had no cause to complain. Finally, it argues that emergency conditions justified its actions.

The arguments on both sides take place in typical formulaic legalese. In this chapter, I will discuss them in light of the underlying constitutional values that the takings clause reflects. My argument is that the government's position reflects confusion about the meaning of consent and price during a liquidity crisis; properly understood, the government's actions are no different from taking someone's house or land without compensation.

Preliminaries: A Tale of Two Crises

The savings and loan (S&L) crisis in the 1980s also produced litigation, now mostly forgotten. When regulators realized that they could not rescue the ailing thrifts because of limited resources and objections from Congress, they cobbled together a clever but deeply flawed strategy. The regulators told healthy thrifts and banks that if they purchased weak thrifts, the acquiring firm would be allocated an asset called "supervisory goodwill," which was just a positive amount equal to, and offsetting, the negative value of the acquired thrift so that the hole it created in the acquirer's balance sheet was filled up by regulatory fiat. The purpose of this accounting gimmick was to enable the acquiring firms to remain in compliance, as a formal matter, with legal rules that required them to maintain an adequate ratio of capital to assets, signaling financial health. In reality, of course, by acquiring a thrift that was insolvent or close to insolvency, the acquiring firm was reducing its own economic solvency to dangerously low levels. But the acquiring firms were willing to take this risk, which gave them a chance to profit if economic conditions improved.

In 1989, Congress passed the Financial Institutions Reform, Recovery, and Enforcement Act,[4] a law that resolved the S&L mess by creating a government entity to sell off the assets of bankrupt thrifts, and that overhauled thrift regulation. The law also eliminated supervisory good will, which plunged many of the acquiring firms into bankruptcy. The shareholders of the firms sued the government, arguing that the law breached a contract that they made with the regulators. After many years of what came to be known as the Winstar litigation (after one of the plaintiffs), the courts held in favor of the shareholders.[5]

From a legal standpoint, the Winstar litigation raises different issues from the cases we have discussed. The government made a contract and then breached it rather than taking property without just compensation. But the underlying concern is the same. In the S&L crisis, the government was forced to engage in politically unpopular and financially expensive actions to address a problem that was blamed on excessive and irresponsible risk taking by executives at financial institutions. To try to minimize the political and financial cost of the emergency response, the government violated the rights of stakeholders—with the effect of transferring value from them to the treasury. The courts played their normal role in such cases: they held the government to account. If the courts acted properly in the Winstar litigation, why should they behave differently now?

The Case for Government Liability Revisited

PRINCIPLES

The takings clause of the Constitution requires the government to pay "just compensation" when it expropriates property from citizens. This clause was of great importance; the founders worried that the government might come under the control of unscrupulous persons who would use the powers of government to enrich themselves and their supporters rather than to serve the public interest. Experience during the Articles of Confederation period gave them reason to worry. In some states, citizens used their new political power to push legislatures to release them from debts.

However, the takings clause raises puzzles. When the government taxes people, it also "takes" their property. Yet the states at the time of the founding imposed taxes to finance military defense, government operations, and development—and no one thought the takings clause prohibited taxation. States also issued regulations that imposed costs on people. A strictly enforced takings clause would interfere with many government functions that we take for granted.

Over centuries of evolution, a takings jurisprudence took shape. Today, it has three basic elements. First, ordinary taxation, as well as user fees and the like, are not takings. These exactions are imposed on classes of people to raise revenue or to fund government services. Second, regulations are not takings unless they "go too far"—eliminating all or most of the value of property without good reason. Such takings are known as "regulatory takings." Third, expropriation of land (above all) and other assets (including money and goods) are generally considered takings that require just compensation. These are called "per se takings." Takings law does not apply, of course, to punishments such as fines that are levied after a trial determines that a person has committed a crime or a civil wrong.

Courts have attempted to achieve a balance. The government must be able to expropriate property to finance public goods; it also must be able to regulate people's behavior so that they do not harm each other. But a market economy can function only if people expect that their property rights will be respected. The law tries to encourage the government to raise revenue by imposing nondiscriminatory taxes on broad classes of people based on their economic activity, while discouraging it from discriminating against, or *singling out*, specific individuals or groups who are politically unpopular. As Justice Hugo Black put it, the takings clause bars the "Government from forcing some people alone to bear public burdens which, in all fairness and justice, should be borne by the public as a whole."[6] The market economy can function only if government clearly and consistently protects property rights—which means setting out in advance which types of investments will be protected and to what extent. This in turn means that the government may not expropriate the property of people on the basis of political expedience—if, for example, certain people are vulnerable because they are temporarily unpopular and lacking in political power.

It is clear how the per se takings rule follows from these principles. If the government must build a road from point A to point B, it will face choices about the precise route. Route 1 would cut through one neighborhood, requiring the demolition of numerous houses in that neighborhood; route 2 would cut through another neighborhood. In the absence of a takings law, the government can choose the route that destroys the houses of its enemies and not its friends; it could refuse to compensate the victims. Takings law (in principle) ensures that no one is hurt, everyone is compensated, and so political considerations of this sort should not influence the government's choice of routes.

Regulation raises more difficult questions. A law requiring factories to install scrubbers in their smokestacks deprives shareholders of some of their returns. One could imagine a takings regime that required the government to compensate the shareholders, but this does not seem practical. But if regulation always lay outside the ambit of takings law, then the government could expropriate property by styling ordinary takings as regulations—for example, by requiring permits that are prohibitively expensive before building on land or by zoning out residential uses in a traditional residential neighborhood, rendering the houses valueless. So takings limitations encompass some types of regulations.

A last category of activity has turned out to be the most perplexing. When the government buys property from people, the transaction is not deemed a taking because of the seller's consent. But these transactions are not always as voluntary as they seem. Suppose a municipality refuses to grant a permit to build on land unless the owner agrees to set aside a portion of the land for public use. An owner makes the deal and then sues, charging that the government took part of his land. The government will argue in response that because the owner consented to the deal, the owner was not coerced, and no taking could have taken place. The problem with this argument is that while the initial permitting scheme may be constitutionally permissible because the criteria for approval ensure that the construction does not harm neighbors, or make too much noise, or place too great a burden on the city's resources, this rationale does not extend to the case where the city withholds the permit to obtain land for free. The Supreme Court calls the requirement for approval an "unconstitutional condition" unless there is a "nexus" between it and the legitimate state interest. The nexus requirement means that the condition serves the policy embodied in the statutory scheme. A government may condition a construction permit on the taking of safety precautions or payments to offset safety inspection costs to the city, but it may not condition the permit on a transfer of property that gives the government or the public something that it wants but is not entitled to under the law.

TAKINGS THROUGH MARKET MANIPULATION

The theory of takings implicitly rests on the idea that a market exists. When the government takes your house, a court recognizes your property interest in your house and awards compensation based on the market price of that interest. By contrast, if the government were to demand saliva samples—perhaps because of a disease outbreak—there would be no taking because people do not have a property interest in their own saliva. If people objected, they would need to find another clause in the Constitution to invoke—most likely, the due process clause.

This creates a paradox. Property rights exist in the first place only because the government recognizes them. Suppose that you go to the park every day, and this activity gives you a great deal of pleasure. One day a fence blocks your path; it turns out the government has sold the park to a private developer. There is no taking. While you have derived a great deal of pleasure from sitting at your customary spot under the tree, you do not have a property interest in that spot. And you don't have a property interest in the spot just because the government has never recognized such an interest. It could if it wanted to—but it hasn't.

Couldn't the government therefore expropriate people's property without paying compensation under the takings clause simply by withdrawing legal recognition of the property right? The answer is no. Courts allow governments to create property rights but not to eliminate them—at least, not unless the government can give good reasons, for example, rooted in public health and safety, as when the government removes a drug from the market because it harms people's health.

And yet the paradox is not resolved. Property rights do not enforce themselves. For property rights to be valuable, the government must be ready to enforce them. If someone trespasses on your lawn, you can call the police, as you can if someone steals your car. If the government refused to enforce rights over property or a class of property by failing to make available police and judicial resources, then the property would be worthless.

At the same time, it is widely understood that the government has discretion over enforcement. If you call the police and they do not arrive in time to arrest the trespasser, or do not arrive at all, you will not be able to obtain a remedy in court. Even in the case of serious property thefts, the police will often do no more than fill out a report. Any lawsuit to force them to put resources into an investigation will fail. Except in egregious cases, this principle of enforcement discretion applies generally—to police protection, emergency rescue, and other government-supplied services.

Enforcement discretion exists because the lawmaker—Congress, in our federal system—cannot anticipate how resources should be best used to address threats, harms, and other problems as they arise. Congress gives the executive branch a set of laws and a budget, along with some rough guidance as to how the budget should be used. But the executive (led by the president) cannot enforce all laws in full. There are too many laws, applying to too many people, often in ambiguous ways. Many laws are quickly outdated. The executive branch sets its own priorities, loosely but not fully consistent with Congress's own priorities, and uses the budget to enforce the law accordingly. Private citizens cannot usually persuade courts to compel the president to enforce laws; courts defer to the executive's enforcement discretion. The same system operates at the state and local levels.

All of this suggests that clever, unscrupulous government officials could expropriate property by withdrawing government services, waiting for market prices to plummet, applying eminent domain to the now low-valued properties, and then restoring government services, sending prices back up. This strategy, in fact, has occurred to some public officials.[7] In *Amen v. City of Dearborn*,[8] the city government sought to redevelop a section of the city. Before buying the land from homeowners located in that area, it stopped issuing building and occupancy permits to residents, or did so only after lengthy delays, and conditioned building permits on various onerous requirements that residents elsewhere in the city were not obliged to comply with. It also purchased some houses and left them vacant, and even encouraged people to strip the houses of their fixtures, resulting in blight across the neighborhood. These efforts drove down market prices, which enabled the city to pay low prices for the houses that it eventually condemned.

A court found that the city had acted wrongfully by depriving home-owners of the monetary value of their homes. But if the city had simply refused to enforce the building code vigorously, or reduced police protection, it would not have been required to pay damages to the residents. And if it had subsequently bought land in that area, it surely would not have been required to pay the pre-blight market price. What makes *Amen* an easy case is that the city's underenforcement of the law was combined with a plan to buy the properties.

Why don't courts punish underenforcement by itself? The answer is very likely that there is no judicial standard for evaluating underenforcement. A town could always hire additional police officers to protect residents. As it adds police officers, market prices will rise. One might identify the theoretical optimal: the town should keep paying for police officers until the marginal cost (in terms of taxes) equals the marginal benefit (in terms of property values). But no one—courts least of all—is in the position to calculate the optimal tradeoff between taxation and police protection, and so courts leave it to the democratic process, as they should. The courts intervene only in extreme cases. One such case exists when deliberate underenforcement of property rights reduces market prices, enabling the government to take property without paying its full value.

The lesson is that courts have taken upon themselves an implicit obligation to ensure that the government does not underenforce property rights to save money on condemnations. Courts do not take the market as "given" even when calculating "market prices." The courts themselves maintain the market by ensuring the government enforces the rules of the market—including all the regulations of the market, like building codes— evenhandedly.

TAKINGS DURING A FINANCIAL CRISIS

While the points I have made are not unknown, they are rarely discussed. It is tempting for property scholars to think of the market as natural. When the government "intervenes" by taking someone's house, the court sets things right by compelling the government to pay for the house, as a private individual would. But the government is different from a private individual. The private individual is not responsible for enforcing property rights fairly—making sure that the police show up if trespass occurs, cleaning the streets, approving requests for building permits, and all the rest. The court's job is, within its capacities, to ensure that the government goes about this business of structuring and maintaining the market in the right way.

So far I have suggested that "structuring and maintaining the market" means more than paying for property that the government takes for its own use. It also means supplying the police and funding a judicial system that enforces property rights, even against the government, and constructing a bureaucracy that manages sewers, streets, bridges, and other infrastructure. Let me use the general term "market infrastructure" to refer to all of these functions. The value of a house and other property is a function of the quality of market infrastructure. The government's job is to maximize the value of property by investing in market infrastructure.

Liquidity support is a part of this market infrastructure. It is just as important for the government to maintain the money supply as it is for the government to supply police, street cleaners, and sewer workers. The withdrawal of any of these services reduces property values. Of course, as noted, courts will not penalize the government when the government fails to supply these benefits—except perhaps in egregious cases where people's due process rights are violated. But courts do penalize the government for withdrawing support for elements of market infrastructure when doing so enables the government to expropriate property of identified people at a suppressed price. And that is exactly what the Fed did, in the case of AIG, the GSEs, and—to a lesser extent—the automakers.

If the Fed acted wrongly toward these companies and their stake-holders, did it act wrongly toward Lehman—by failing to rescue it? Indeed, the Fed failed to rescue numerous banks and other financial institutions. Does my argument imply that all the relevant stakeholders should have a remedy against the government?

The answer is no. As illustrated by *Amen*, we need to make a distinction between underenforcement by itself (i.e., failure to supply market infrastructure as a general matter) and underenforcement that results in an expropriation at a suppressed price. In theory, the government should engage in neither type of underenforcement—it should always enforce the law optimally, as far as it can. That is why it is right to criticize the Fed for failing to rescue Lehman, even though the failure to rescue Lehman did not violate the law. In practice, the courts believe themselves—rightly, in my view—capable of correcting only the type of underenforcement that results in expropriation at a suppressed price. That did not happen to Lehman; that is why Lehman's shareholders do not, and should not, have a takings claim against the government.

If this argument is not as obvious as it should be, that is because our ideological and political biases predispose us to think that the government gave shareholders a benefit—a "bailout"—rather than took their property. Bernanke called the rescue loan a "windfall" for AIG's shareholders. The thinking is that a "bailout" cannot be a taking; a firm that receives a bailout has obtained a windfall. But that is why the word "bailout" should be avoided. Against the proper baseline—the provision of market infrastructure in the form of property rights enforcement and liquidity supply—the government took value from AIG and the GSEs. One could classify the AIG loan as a bailout only if one believed that the money offered by the government to the homeowners in *Amen* was a bailout because it was greater than zero.

It's worth dwelling on an irony here. Takings law has traditionally been championed by libertarians and other market advocates who worry that if the government can take property too easily, it will interfere with people's freedom and undermine the market, which depends on secure property rights. Thus, the core of takings law has focused on expropriation of property and indirect forms of expropriation accomplished through regulation and conditional discretionary benefits. It is tempting to argue that takings law should not be concerned with "bailouts" because "bailouts" are in-imical to the free market. The problem with this argument is that if we use the accurate rather than pejorative term here—namely, "liquidity sup-port"—we realize that only takings law can prevent the state from oppor-tunistically withdrawing support from the market to expropriate property. The financial infrastructure without which "real" markets would not work, or not work very well, depends on the government backstop, and liquidity support is one of the essential components of that backstop. The economic principles underlying takings law apply just as much to overpriced bailouts as to conventional expropriations of property.

It is, of course, possible to respond that the government should not provide liquidity support—that liquidity support is not like enforcement of contract and property rights but instead a subsidy that interferes with free markets by "socializing losses." An extreme version of this view is that we do not need central banks at all; the money supply should be entirely private. A more respectable view is that central banks should abandon the Lender of Last Resort (LLR) function because, eventually, financial mar-kets will correct themselves and, in the long term, generate more wealth than they would if the government intervenes. But these views are not in-corporated in the law or in central bank tradition.

The Government's Defense: A Reprise

With this argument in mind, we can revisit the government's legal de-fense. Recall that the government argues that the Fed has discretion how to structure loans; that the loans were consented to; and that it had the right to demand unfavorable terms to deter moral hazard. Looking at these arguments through the lens of *Amen*, we can see their difficulties with great clarity.

The Fed has discretion over the terms of the loans that it makes, just as a city has discretion over the prices it may offer to homeowners for their houses. We give these institutions discretion because there is no obvi-ous right answer in either case. Optimal liquidity support, like optimal enforcement of property rights, is a highly complex question, calling on both expertise and (wholly absent in the case of the Fed) values informed by democracy. Discretion just means that if a legal challenge is brought, courts are unwilling to substitute their judgments for that of the experts— the Fed or the city, as the case may be.

However, discretion can never be unlimited. Courts have limited the discretion of cities when underenforcement is used to target unpopular individuals—and, more pertinently, when underenforcement is used to suppress prices to accomplish a taking on the cheap. They have in the same way and for the same reasons limited the discretion of administrative agencies, which is all that the Fed is.

The government also argues that AIG and the GSEs consented to its loans. This is the same argument that the City of Dearborn made in *Amen*. Because the homeowners sold their houses to the city, they cannot claim that the city used coercion to expropriate them. But the actual coercive measure was the withdrawal of property-rights enforcement—something over which the homeowners had no control. Similarly, in the case of AIG, the coercive measure was not the loan but the threat to withdraw liquidity support, on which AIG and every other firm relied on, just as they relied on enforcement of property rights to their office buildings.

Next is the government's policy argument that it demanded harsh terms to deter moral hazard. Dearborn made no such argument because that argument would have been palpably absurd. The innocent citizens in the targeted area had done nothing wrong, nothing that would justify the partial expropriation of their homes. If they had done something wrong, the city should have held civil or criminal proceedings to identify their misdeeds and fashion suitable remedies. The argument makes no sense for the emergency rescues, either. The government never proved legal wrongdoing by AIG, the GSEs, or the automakers.

Finally, the government can argue that it needs discretion when facing a financial crisis, and a court—applying rigid legal rules with the benefit of hindsight—can only interfere with that discretion. This argument has a long pedigree. Government officials have often claimed that they should have greater discretion during emergencies than they do during normal times because laws can only be passed to address predictable, recurrent threats, and Congress cannot act speedily enough to provide new laws during emergencies.

The last great debate about emergency power took place in the wake of the 9/11 terrorist attack. Government officials felt that existing legal and constitutional rules did not give them the powers they needed to address the threat. The executive branch was able to secure new powers from Congress in short order, but it also engaged in counterterrorism activities—coercive interrogation, mass surveillance, detention, and "targeted killing"—of dubious legality. These activities continued for years but were eventually either stopped or given formal statutory authorization. Calls to prosecute government officials who overstepped the bounds of the law were rejected. And because of secrecy laws and rules of official and sovereign immunity, victims of government misbehavior could not win their cases in court, and so received no compensation or other remedy for the abuse they suffered.

Discretion is claimed for government officials in ordinary times as well. When police officers quell riots with billy clubs or chase criminal suspects with guns blazing, people who bring suit based on injuries they receive run headlong into legal barriers that protect police from lawsuits except when their behavior is egregious. The laws reflect worries about hindsight bias, which if applied to punish police officers may result in excessive caution by those needed to main public order.

Fed and Treasury officials did not need to worry about their personal safety, but they faced a financial emergency every bit as acute as the post 9/11 terrorist crisis. Like terrorism fighters, they were required to make very difficult decisions, on which the well-being of a great many people depended, under extreme uncertainty, and under conditions that demanded quick reactions to constantly changing events that left no time for the information gathering and analysis that was really necessary. It is predictable that many errors would be made and wrong to punish people for those errors, except, again, in egregious cases.

But this argument conflates different issues. No one thinks that Geithner or Bernanke should pay out of their own pockets if they are found to have made errors that cost people a great deal of money. Police officers are almost never held personally liable for harming people. The question is whether the government should pay damages to people who are harmed by wrongful behavior by the agents.

Nor should courts be given the power—again, except in egregious cases—to block the actions of emergency responders. Such a power would just substitute the judgment of an unqualified judge for the judgment of an expert.

The question is whether the government should pay damages to victims when, after the emergency is over, a court determines that the agents violated the law and caused harm. The standard view in American law is—yes.[9] And, indeed, the US government has, by statute, agreed to pay damages to people when government agents commit torts against them, break contracts, and commit other legal wrongs. This system produces several benefits. It compensates victims. It clarifies the meaning of often vague statutes and legal norms so that, if necessary, the public can debate them and Congress can revise them. And it deters the government from acting wrongfully in the first place.[10]

The principles that govern ordinary policing should carry over to Fed actions as well. While the law cannot realistically put many controls on the LLR—and for that reason, the LLR must be given a great deal of discretion—it can put some controls on it. The LLR may need to go beyond the law, but if it does so, the government should be prepared to pay damages to victims.

The Measure of Damages

One of the trickiest problems faced by the plaintiffs in the bailout cases is the calculation of damages. In a traditional takings case, the measure of damages is the fair market value of the thing taken. This measure of damages compensates the victim for the taking—she can, in principle, use the money to purchase a replacement of the thing that was taken. It also ensures that government officials will take into account the costs they impose on citizens when they embark on projects that require the expropriation of property—at least, to the extent that government officials worry about budgets. However, this measure breaks down when the expropriation takes place during a financial crisis.

A fair market value can be calculated only if there is a market. A market exists if there are willing buyers and willing sellers of the property that is taken. If the government takes someone's house, a court can calculate damages by comparing the house to other houses in the neighborhood that have been sold around the time of the taking. The price of comparable houses reflects the price that willing buyers and willing sellers agree on, and so the price, with adjustments for differences in the size and amenities of the houses, can be imputed to the house that is taken.

During a financial crisis, the credit market collapses. This means that the relevant forms of property—credit-related assets like collateralized debt obligations—stop trading. There are willing sellers but no (or few) willing buyers because the buyers hoard cash rather than spend it. In extreme cases, trading stops completely. In normal cases, trading might still take place, but so rarely that it is impossible to derive a market value for comparable goods. A gap opens up between the market price and the present discounted value of the future payoffs (interest and principal). An instrument with a present value of $100 might find no buyers or buyers who are willing to pay only a low price (say $10) because they need to hold onto as much money as possible.

As we saw in *Amen*, courts have recognized that fair market value is not always the right measure of damages for takings (Serkin 2005). Let's consider a second example. During World War II, the government shut down the aluminum market, forbidding people to buy and sell aluminum in most cases. The price of aluminum plunged. Then the government confiscated the aluminum supplies and goods of a business, which sued the government. An appellate court held that because the (lawful) control of the market drove down the market price, damages for the (unlawful) taking could not be based on the market price. Instead, the lower court was to use its "sense of fairness" to calculate damages.[11] In another case, the US government persuaded the Philippine government to ban export of certain communications equipment, which the US military than seized from some Americans in the Philippines. A court held that since the export ban suppressed the market price of the equipment, the market price cannot be used to calculate damages.[12] Thus, market value is not invariably used to determine damages in a takings case.

In the bailout cases, however, the courts used fair market value, at least implicitly. In the AIG litigation, the Court of Federal Claims denied damages because it believed that if the government had not made the loan to AIG, AIG would have entered bankruptcy and its shares would have become worthless. AIG's shares had traded at prices that suggest that the 79.9 percent share transferred to the government was worth more than $20 billion, and that is the amount that the plaintiffs sought as damages. The court argued that people were willing to pay so much for the shares only because the government loan would save AIG. Take away the loan, and AIG was worth nothing, so when the government took the equity, it didn't harm anyone.

To understand the problem with this reasoning, recall that the government could issue the loan to AIG in the first place only because it believed that AIG's "real" value—the present discounted future value of its profits—was very high. The law required the government to make this determination; and the evidence indicates that government officials believed that AIG's real value was substantial. This of course means that the real value was not zero. If the market value of AIG was zero, that is only be-cause potential buyers were hoarding their cash rather than buying finan-cial assets, which is the rational thing to do when credit markets are frozen.

The case is not quite on all fours with the two cases discussed earlier, where the government's actions drove down the market price of goods in a way that predictably would save it money when it expropriated those goods. But it is close. The government did drive down the market price of financial assets by failing to rescue Lehman—though it certainly did not intend to. But the larger problem with the traditional reliance on fair mar-ket value in this context is just that there was no fair market value. Fair market value requires working markets, and the government intervened in the first place because markets were not working. If the whole premise of the AIG bailout was that markets had failed, the government could not fairly cite market prices as the reason that it could pay AIG's shareholders nothing for their shares.

If market value cannot be used to calculate damages, then how should damages be calculated? A court's "sense of fairness" does not get us very far. The measure of damages should be keyed to the constitutional policy that the takings clause serves. One theory is that the takings clause pro-vides people with insurance against government abuse. So one might ask, if a financial institution bought insurance against a government expropria-tion of financial assets during a credit crisis, what would that policy look like? A possible answer is that the insurance would cover the par value of the assets—just as credit default swaps do. A more sophisticated answer is that the insurance would cover the real value of the assets. What is the real value? As we have seen, a financial crisis is a *temporary* disruption in markets. It lasts only as long as creditors are afraid to lend money. It is pre-dictable, then, that within a year or so, credit will be flowing again. At that point, market prices will return to fundamentals. In the case of the 2007–8 financial crisis, it became clear that assets had become overvalued as a re-sult of the real estate bubble. Their real value was accordingly a function of the actual value of real estate. It was reasonable to expect property values at a national level to return to the historical trend line. The government and firms it contracted with apparently used that trend line to calculate the fundamental values of the assets, on the basis of which the govern-ment made its emergency loans. Those values are appropriate for calculat-ing damages for the taking.

One might respond to this argument that in the fall of 2008, anything could have happened. It was possible, for example, that as the financial crisis continued, people would cancel their insurance policies because they needed cash on hand. If they did, AIG's valuable insurance subsidiaries would have gone bankrupt, and the US government would never have been paid back. But while it's true that this was possible, it's always true that extreme events can upset the assumptions used to determine assets values. Wars could break out, technological innovation could disrupt supply and demand, Martians could invade. There is no alternative to extrapolating from history, and nothing in history suggested that a major financial crisis would eliminate the demand for insurance.

Similar, albeit somewhat weaker, arguments can be made about the auto dealers' claims. The auto dealers argued that the government expropriated the value of their franchises by compelling GM and Chrysler to terminate the franchises. The Federal Circuit agreed that this takings theory is viable, but held that the dealers must prove that their franchises would have been worth something if the government had not financed GM's and Chrysler's recovery. *If* the automakers' collapse resulted from the financial crisis (rather than their own poor business judgments), and *if* the dealers would have flourished if the automakers had not collapsed, then the "real" value of the franchises was positive rather than zero, and the government should be required to pay damages. But these ifs are pretty big ones. The causal chain from the credit freeze to the dealers' franchise terminations is longer than the one from the credit freeze to AIG's collapse, and so the argument for damages is correspondingly weaker.

* * *

Takings law is a backstop against government abuse. Shareholders, creditors, and other stakeholders have rightly invoked it in the post-crisis litigation. But the undeveloped nature of takings law makes it less than ideal for cleaning up the mess left by a financial meltdown. The courts lack the guidance they need for addressing complicated issues of financial valuation that lie outside their experience. We can do better by reforming the law. That is the topic of the next chapter.

8 Politics and Reform

I'm being called Mr. Bailout, I can't do it again
HANK PAULSON (QUOTED IN WESSEL 2009, 14)

THE ARGUMENT SO FAR HAS BEEN A SIMPLE ONE. CONGRESS DID NOT give the Lender of Last Resort (LLR) adequate powers for responding to the crisis. Government agencies, motivated largely by the Bagehot-inspired central bank prescriptions for resolving a financial crisis, circumvented the law where they could and broke it where they couldn't. But law wasn't the only constraint on the agencies. Politics was as well. While I have touched on politics from time to time, I must now focus on them before recommending measures for reform.

Politics

The financial system that prevailed on the eve of the crisis seemed to benefit everyone. Consumers, including low-income consumers traditionally shut out of loan markets, received cheap credit, including inexpensive and accommodating mortgages. The housing industry—builders, real estate agents, construction workers—benefited from the credit-fueled demand for housing. Car dealers and automakers benefited from the strong demand fueled by cheap credit, as did the auto buyers who received that credit. Small banks and mortgage brokers churned out mortgages and sold them to Fannie or Freddie (GSEs) or an investment bank for a generous fee, transferring risk off their balance sheets in the process. Large financial institutions made money packaging mortgages, selling mortgage-derived and other asset-backed securities, and setting up complex trades between investors who bet for and against the housing market. Sovereign wealth funds, pension funds, and other institutions benefited from the ample supply of safe securities with relatively high yields.

The fact that everyone was making money and that low- and moderate-income people were getting cheap loans must have quieted any doubts. It was in no one's interest for this merry-go-round to spin off its rails—not until a few skeptics bet against housing, and even they did not want or expect the financial system to collapse. Experts detected flaws in particular aspects of the systems—the operations of Fannie and Freddie, the confusing complexity of the loans, and the opacity of the derivatives market. But the apparent success of the system made reform impossible.

When savings and loans (S&Ls) began failing in the early 1980s, the relevant agency—the Federal Saving and Loan Insurance Corporation (FSLIC), the S&L counterpart to the Federal Deposit Insurance Corporation (FDIC)—understood that many more thrifts were on the verge of insolvency or were already insolvent. It, too, faced stiff ideological and political winds. The collapse of the thrifts embarrassed the Reagan administration, which was committed to the free market and therefore opposed to government rescues, and the administration responded passively throughout the crisis. Indeed, the Reagan administration and Congress initially made the crisis worse by enacting the Garn-St. Germain Depository Institutions Act,[1] which allowed thrifts to enter into businesses with which they had no experience, like commercial real estate lending. As the crisis worsened, the FSLIC sought funds from Congress to wind up the insolvent firms and absorb the losses, but Congress balked. As Romer and Weingast (1991) observe, thrifts, which sought to remain alive as long as possible in the hope that they would be rescued by an economic upswing, were able to exploit veto gates in the House and Senate. Cooperative members of Congress from districts and states in which thrifts held significant political power used parliamentary maneuvers to block reform. Deprived of resources to shut down the thrifts, regulators kept them open by encouraging mergers between healthy and sick institutions. But this just put off the day of reckoning and vastly increased the price tag of the rescue, which eventually came in the 1990s.

The subprime crisis took a different form, but some parallels existed. The regulators enjoyed more autonomy because the Fed, which played a very limited role in the thrift crisis, took the lead in 2007 and 2008, and is self-funding. Congress did not interfere as much with the rescue in

2007–8. Because the critical phase arrived quickly and threatened the financial system and the economy, Congress acted when finally called upon.

But political divisions opened up rapidly. The public and politicians in both parties opposed bailouts as a matter of principle. For the right, bailouts interfere with the free market; for the left, bailouts reward the rich. The regulators possessed the legal authority and the resources to make emergency loans but felt the political heat. In an effort to mollify their political masters and the public, the regulators tried to punish firms when they could and to hide their loans when they couldn't.

In the Bear bailout in March 2008, Paulson tried to thread the needle by ensuring that Bear's shareholders received a low payoff. The stock had been trading around $80 just one month earlier. JP Morgan offered $4 but, apparently at the government's insistence, reduced the purchase price to $2 (FCIC 2011, 290). Paulson's gambit failed, partly for operational reasons, and the price was later raised to $10. But the political problem was not just that Bear's shareholders received money; it was that Bear's creditors were not forced to take a haircut. Paulson could not demand haircuts without undermining the purpose of the rescue, which was to restore confidence to the financial system by ensuring creditors that they would be paid in full.

Despite the negative political reaction to the prospect of bailouts, the Bush administration was able to secure the passage of the Housing and Economic Recovery Act of 2008[2] in July. The key was that the statute did not actually bail out the GSEs; it merely authorized government agencies to rescue the GSEs if that became necessary. Moreover, Paulson argued that the authorization would make a bailout less rather than more likely, and the statute contained punitive terms that would enable the government to take over the firms.

Fears about the political reaction also contributed to the regulators' biggest blunder—the failure to rescue Lehman. In the wake of the Bear rescue, both parties in Congress and both presidential candidates—John McCain and Barack Obama—announced their opposition to further bailouts (Geithner 2014, 175). Paulson got the message. In a conference call with other government officials, he declared, "I'm being called Mr. Bailout, I can't do it again" (Wessel 2009, 14). Paulson and Bernanke also apparently believed that Lehman's collapse would not harm the financial system, while usefully countering moral hazard that had built up in the system as a result of the Bear rescue. Politics, then, probably did not play a determinative role; it reinforced a failure of judgment. The pattern repeated itself with AIG. Having learned their lesson from Lehman, Paulson and Bernanke turned around and rescued AIG. But the punitive terms, again justified by moral hazard, were also seen as a way of mollifying the public—even though the punitive terms in Maiden Lane III for AIG were generous terms for the investment bank counterparties.

As the crisis unfolded, the cleavages deepened. "Wall Street" was identified as the culprit of the crisis and the beneficiary of the rescue. This greatly damaged the credibility of the big banks among the public and Congress, but the banks continued to influence events behind the scenes. Top government officials (including Paulson) and countless deputies and other subordinates had been recruited from Wall Street, and they were connected with Wall Street executives through networks of mentorship and mutual interest. And because the big banks—as long as they were solvent—retained their freedom of action, the government needed to treat them gently in return for their cooperation in solving the crisis.

The crisis also fueled populist opposition to Wall Street. The left demanded government aid—effectively, bailouts—to homeowners, who were portrayed as victims of unscrupulous mortgage lenders. On the right, the initial impetus of the Tea Party movement was President Obama's plan to help homeowners who could not pay their mortgages.

These political pressures filtered into the different parts of government in different ways. While all of the agencies were designed to play a role in rescuing the financial system, their roles—and hence their missions—differed. Sheila Bair, for example, saw her primary job as ensuring that the FDIC fund was not depleted so that insured depositors would be protected. Bernanke, Geithner, and Paulson believed that she put the fund's solvency over the health of the financial system. Indeed, by insisting that the fund pay out only those with insurance, Bair was (according to her critics) putting the fund at *greater* risk because if the shadow banking system collapsed, depositors would run on banks, destroying the FDIC fund. Bernanke, Geithner, and Paulson tried to persuade her to make the FDIC guarantee more broadly available. Although Bair eventually agreed, authorizing FDIC's participation in the Temporary Liquidity Guarantee Program (TLGP) and the Public-Private Investment Funds (PPIF), she did so only after delay and friction.

Bernanke saw the Fed as the ultimate LLR, but he also defined its role in narrower terms than he might have. The Fed traditionally earns financial returns through its operations and every year turns over its "profits" (revenues minus operating expenses) to Treasury. As the financial crisis unfolded, Bernanke began to worry that the Fed's payments to Treasury would be reduced by its losses. He believed that if the Fed turned over no money to Treasury—or lost money—the political repercussions would be severe. This might explain why Bernanke frequently interpreted section 13(3) of the Federal Reserve Act[3] to mean that the Fed could lend only to solvent institutions, while 13(3) is not so limited; and why Bernanke on several occasions obtained letters from Paulson that verified that a particular lending program might lose money (Bernanke 2015, 220). Bernanke initially sought a "guarantee" from Treasury, which would mean (for example) that if one of the Fed's borrowers failed to repay a $1 billion loan, then Treasury would give $1 billion to the Fed, which in turn would give it back to Treasury at the end of the year. As Paulson (2010, 114–15) saw it, the Fed needed political, not legal, cover for these loans, and Paulson was willing to oblige. But if the letters were not legally required, then Bernanke could not have believed that the Fed was legally prohibited from making loans that could lose money—either that, or he believed that he was breaking the law.[4] Bernanke's concerns help explain why he refused to rescue Lehman, and why he told Paulson that it would be necessary to go to Congress for additional money.

Treasury is, by custom, the fiscal authority. With congressional authorization, it spends the government's money. That is why Paulson took the lead negotiating with Congress for the Emergency Economic Stabilization Act (EESA),[5] and why EESA authorized spending through Treasury. And this is why Bernanke asked Paulson to write letters supporting Fed programs that could have produced losses. Treasury was allowed, through EESA, to make risky investments and buy risky assets, and thus was permitted to take losses.

As a non-independent agency under the direct supervision of the president, Treasury is also a more "political" agency than the Fed and FDIC— that is, more sensitive to popular opinion as channeled through the presidency than the Fed and FDIC, whose major concern is to retain their legitimacy with Congress. This, too, was reflected in its actions. Paulson (and later Geithner) regularly consulted with the president and Congress. Paulson, stung by the negative reaction to the Bear rescue, and philosophically opposed to intervening in markets, was initially more cautious about bailouts than the Fed. Geithner, once installed in Treasury, found himself under pressure from Congress to use Troubled Asset Relief Program

(TARP) funds on foreclosure relief, despite his doubts about its effectiveness (Geithner 2014, 209–10). By contrast, the Fed and FDIC showed little interest in this issue.[6]

While the Fed, Treasury, and FDIC were the main players, they needed to contend with numerous other agencies with authority over other pieces of the financial system. The Office of the Comptroller of the Currency (OCC) and the Office of Thrift Supervision (OTS) were the primary regulators of the national banks and the federal S&Ls. These agencies lacked LLR authority but tried to protect the institutions they regulated from shutdowns. The Securities and Exchange Commission (SEC) used its emergency powers to implement a temporary short-sale ban—apparently, at the behest of the Fed and Treasury—and otherwise did little of value.[7] The Federal Housing Finance Agency (FHFA) operated the conservatorships of Fannie and Freddie; Geithner later complained that it obstructed efforts to revive the mortgage market (Geithner 2014, 171–74).[8]

The division of authority led to frictions even among the primary LLR agencies. Wachovia, a giant national bank, was on the verge of collapse in September 2008. The government helped broker a deal in which Citigroup would acquire Wachovia with government support. Before the merger was completed, Wells Fargo made a more attractive bid for Wachovia. Geithner believed that FDIC should block or discourage Wells Fargo's bid, but Bair allowed it to go through, in part because Wells Fargo was financially healthier than Citigroup. She feared that Citigroup would choke on Wachovia, exposing FDIC's insurance fund to massive liabilities. Geithner was infuriated by Bair's decision. He believed that the government's credibility was at stake, but the real source of disagreement appears to be that Geithner wanted to help Citigroup, which would have benefited from Wachovia's deposit base.[9]

This episode can be read in two ways—as a good-faith disagreement about the proper crisis response and as a clash between bureaucratic missions. Under the former interpretation, the agencies disagreed about timing and tactics: whether to provide assistance to Citigroup by favoring it over Wells Fargo, even though Wells Fargo offered the better deal, or to provide assistance to Citigroup later through a direct infusion of funds (as happened). Bair believed that the latter approach was more transparent and fairer; Geithner believed that the press of events did not allow for it. As a bureaucratic clash, the dispute can be seen as one in which each agency protected its turf. The FDIC sought to preserve the bank insurance fund. Geithner sought to protect a major bank with which the Federal Reserve Bank of New York enjoyed a close relationship.

All that said, the initial reactions to the bailouts showed more consensus than disagreement among the three LLR agencies. This probably reflected their relative political insulation. Even Paulson was protected by Bush's lame-duck status. By contrast, Congress could not avoid politics. Members of Congress, unlike President Bush, faced reelection battles in November 2008. By the time of EESA, much of the public had come round to bailouts, but intense dissent remained, and EESA was initially voted down in the House. It was eventually passed only after $150 billion of pork had been added to the Senate version of the bill.[10] The many payoffs — such as the repeal of an excise tax on toy arrows (Washington Post 2008) — were interest-group transfers that were unrelated to the policy questions raised by the law. The substantive provisions of EESA reflected the influence of the finance industry. Mian, Sufi, and Trebbi (2010) find a statistically significant correlation between Wall Street campaign contributions to an elected official and that official's vote in favor of EESA.[11]

Much of the debate about the government's response to the financial crisis concerns whether the regulators went easy on banks because of the banks' political influence. In their well-regarded book, *13 Bankers*, Simon Johnson and James Kwak argue that top government officials were psychologically captured by the banks. Many of them hailed from Wall Street, and many others expected to make their fortune on Wall Street after their tenure in government ended. But the evidence is complicated. Consider the authors' complaint about the terms of a government equity injection in nine major banks on October 13, 2008:

> But as Pandit recognized, the government was giving the banks capital cheaply. . . . In short, Paulson, a former CEO of Goldman Sachs, was pushing free money at his former colleagues. . . . According to Swagel [a Treasury assistant secretary at the time], the government had to offer attractive terms because it could not force the banks to agree to any investment, and it is true that some bankers claimed that they did not need government capital. However, the government did have considerable negotiating leverage, thanks to its regulatory authority, its ability to threaten *not* to bail out banks later should they need it, and the fact that banks would be taking a risk by walking away without money that

their competitors had. And the government officials involved fully appreciated the strength for their position. During the meeting, Paulson responded to an objection by saying, "Your regulator is sitting right there," referring to the director of the Office of the Comptroller of the Currency and the chair of the Federal Deposit Insurance Corporation. "And you're going to get a call tomorrow telling you you're undercapitalized and that you won't be able to raise money in the private markets." (Johnson and Kwak 2010, 154–55)

The problem was that the healthier firms would have gained a competitive advantage over the weaker firms by walking away—receipt of money from the government is stigmatizing, and experience during the crisis showed that depositors and other creditors would very likely have shifted their funds to the banks that declined the government capital, lowering their costs. Moreover, the government's threats were hollow. Johnson and Kwak would have us believe that the government would have shut down the healthiest of the banks—and this in the midst of a financial crisis—while keeping weaker banks open; and that the government could have refused to bail out a too-big-to-fail bank after Lehman. While there is evidence that the banks did enjoy influence over regulators,[12] this was a second-order problem. The real problem was that the regulators lacked the power to coerce the banks during a financial crisis. With their limited powers, the regulators needed the cooperation of the banks, and to obtain that cooperation, they needed to offer something in return.

In a similar vein, Mian and Sufi (2014) argue that regulators focused their relief efforts on banks when they should have offered relief to homeowners—additional evidence of the excessive influence of the banks. For these authors, this approach was perverse because, in their view, homeowner relief would have been a more effective way of generating economic recovery. Homeowners had cut back on spending because of debt overhang, while banks had stopped lending, even after the liquidity crisis passed, because homeowners could not spend. The solution was to jumpstart homeowner spending, not bank lending, and that required debt relief for homeowners. And while the government did launch homeowner relief programs, relatively meager resources were allocated to them.

But Mian and Sufi, like Johnson and Kwak, are too hard on the regulators. The failure to rescue homeowners was due to the operational complexity of offering relief to millions of people rather than to a handful of banks. The evidence suggests that the homeowner relief programs failed because of the complexity of the markets that they attempted to help (Agarwal et al. 2012; 2015). If this evidence holds up, it vindicates the judgments of the regulators against Mian and Sufi's criticisms.

While many of the retail-level choices of the regulators are open to question, the ultimate judgment must be that, overall, they acted properly. Political pressures affected their behavior at the margin, but did not cause them to deviate from their mission, which was to protect and rescue the financial system. Moreover, the regulators—especially at the Fed and in Treasury—showed, and acted on, an impressive level of expertise and experience. There is no evidence that anyone in Congress—not even someone as intelligent and otherwise informed about financial matters as Barney Frank, who headed the House Financial Services Committee— had the slightest idea what was going on.

The political lesson of the crisis was that regulators, not Congress, should have the primary authority to respond to financial crises, and that regulators need more, not less power, so that they can avoid, as much as possible, worrying about the political reaction to their decisions and calling on Congress for additional authority and funds. The regulators engaged in abuses but in the main acted properly, while Congress could do little more than serve as a rubber stamp. This conclusion is bolstered by the findings by Mian, Sufi, and Trebbi (2014), who show, using cross-country as well as US evidence, that financial crises predictably lead to polarization among the public between debtors and creditors and hence gridlock at the political level. EESA was a near thing, and passed only because of significant interest-group payoffs. Congress did too little because of political gridlock. Recall as well that during the thrift crisis, the regulators initially sought to do the right thing—to wind down the thrifts—but they were thwarted by Congress and driven to take unwise measures.

But if the regulators also abused their powers, as I have argued, then how is it possible to give them more power without also giving them more power to abuse?

Reform

The overwhelming negative reaction to the bailouts played an important role in the design of the Dodd-Frank Act, a law intended "to protect the American taxpayer by ending bailouts,"[13] as Congress announced in the preamble of the law. President Barack Obama agreed that "because of this law, the American people will never again be asked to foot the bill for Wall Street's mistakes" (Obama 2013). But years later Timothy Geithner admitted that Dodd-Frank would not end bailouts. In response, Republicans in the House of Representatives issued a scathing report entitled "Failing to End 'Too Big to Fail': An Assessment of the Dodd-Frank Act Four Years Later" (Republican Staff of the Committee on Financial Services 2014). Republicans argued that the Dodd-Frank Act increased the likelihood of future bailouts by encouraging financial institutions to grow so large that the government would have to rescue them if they could not pay their bills.

Dodd-Frank tried to end bailouts in two ways. First, it addressed the causes of financial crises—excessive risk taking by banks and other financial institutions. Pre-Dodd-Frank law encouraged financial regulators to impose ex ante regulations on financial institutions of all types. Ex ante regulations—for example, capital requirements—raise the cost of making risky loans or purchasing risky assets; this reduces the amount of risk in the system. Dodd-Frank ordered regulators to take aim at too-big-to-fail nonbank financial institutions, which had been underregulated prior to the crisis. It also introduced the Volcker rule, which limits the freedom of banks to trade financial instruments except when trading reduces rather than increases risk or serves an important commercial function. Dodd-Frank strengthened the hand of agencies, giving them more power to resist the perennial complaints of banks that they are being overregulated.

Second, the Dodd-Frank Act tried to end bailouts by curtailing the power of agencies to rescue floundering financial institutions. It created a new bureaucratic layer—called the Financial Stability Oversight Council—to ensure a broad level of consensus across agencies before a financial rescue could be launched. It blocked Treasury from using the Exchange Stabilization Fund to support money market mutual funds, and limited FDIC's power to issue system-wide guarantees to financial institutions—slapping the wrists of both institutions for overstepping their authority during the crisis. More important, it amended section 13(3) of the Federal Reserve Act to require that emergency loans take place through a "program or facility with broad-based eligibility."[14] This provision was intended to ban bailouts similar to those of Bear Stearns and AIG, which were directed to a single company rather than a group of companies. By contrast, the credit facilities were open to any company that satisfied certain criteria. Facilities like those would remain lawful under the amendment.

The first response was sensible. While no one can agree about how strictly the financial system should be regulated, no one denies that regulation is justified. Underregulation of the financial system contributed to the financial crisis, and now we need to hope that regulators can figure out how to strengthen regulation without choking off lending. This mostly boils down to determining what capital requirements should be—how strict they should be, and how they should vary in response to the riskiness of the portfolios of regulated firms. Too much regulation squeezes off economic growth, but too little regulation raises the probability of another financial crisis to unacceptable levels.

But the tradeoff between economic growth and the risk of financial crisis reveals another fact, which was recognized by Geithner: no amount of regulation will reduce the probability of crisis to zero. Optimal regulation is consistent with another financial crisis sometime in the future. The Dodd-Frank Act will not end bailouts because it cannot prevent financial crises from occurring, and if a financial crisis occurs, bailout is the correct response. This means that Congress's second response to the crisis—restrictions on the LLR—was perverse rather than wise.

Congress may well have understood the dilemma. While it took away from the LLR with one hand, it gave the LLR more powers with another. Congress created a much-needed resolution authority for nonbank financial firms. It named it the Orderly Liquidation Authority (OLA) and placed it under the control of FDIC.[15] OLA can lend money to insolvent nonbank financial firms—Lehman may have been the prototype—so that they can be kept alive long enough to ensure that counterparties will be protected. This OLA was given powers beyond the classic Bagehot prescription—which limited loans to solvent firms—and the traditional powers of the Fed under 13(3). It reflects one of the major lessons of the recent financial crisis: that it may be necessary to make emergency loans to insolvent firms to protect the system.

But doesn't the availability of government bailouts create perverse incentives for financial institutions? This, again, is the moral hazard argument, which we have seen again and again. However, as I have argued, the existence of moral hazard does not by itself mean anything. Any insurance scheme creates moral hazard. If moral hazard is partly controllable through ex ante regulation, and the insurance is needed, then the residual moral hazard not prevented by the regulation is simply part of the price of the insurance. People would take greater precautions against fire if fire departments did not stand ready to rescue them. People would be less likely to move into flood zones if the government refused to supply emergency workers to pluck them from floods. The problem is that even without a government response, fires would occur and floods would destroy houses. Government insurance that helps the genuinely unfortunate will help the reckless as well.

A financial crisis is a more complex problem than a fire or a flood because a financial crisis is, to a large extent, a purely psychological phenomenon—a crisis of confidence, as it is so often put. A popular way to address moral hazard is to insist that creditors take a haircut if they benefit from a government rescue. This gives them an ex post incentive to take care when lending money. The problem with this approach, however, is that the risk of haircuts will exacerbate the panic once it begins. In the United Kingdom, bank depositors were not fully insured by the government but were permitted to retain 90 percent above £2,000, up to £35,000. UK regulators were forced to abandon the deductible and raise the ceiling after the Northern Rock bank run in September 2007.

One can understand this problem by considering the fire analogy. The government does not charge people for calling the fire department, though it certainly could. Imagine that you must pay a $5,000 fee if the fire department comes to your house to put out a fire. The prospect of being required to pay such a fee, like any insurance deductible, will encourage people to take precautions against fire. But the problem is that people, hoping to avoid paying the fee, might be tempted to put out a small fire themselves using a hand fire extinguisher fetched from the closet, instead of calling the fire department. If the hand fire extinguisher proves inadequate, the fire could spread to other houses. By fully rather than partially insuring people against fire, the government reduces the risk of perverse behavior once the "crisis" begins.

The only practical way to address moral hazard in the financial setting is through strict ex ante regulation. This regulation includes capital regulations, underwriting requirements, and all the rest. Of course, it will remain possible for the government to punish financial institutions after the crisis if they violate those regulations, especially if their regulatory violations contributed to the crisis—as occurred in 2007–8. But it is important that the fines and other punishments take place after the crisis, not in an ad hoc way during the crisis through the imposition of harsh rescue terms, and that they are directed only at the firms that violated the rules, not at the firms that followed the rules.[16] If firms that follow the rules are punished, there is no incentive to follow the rules in the first place.

WHAT AUTHORITY DOES THE LLR NEED?

The old powers of the LLR must not only be restored but augmented. The traditional LLR was based on a bank-centered view of the world that was destroyed by the financial crisis. That view drew a line between traditional banking—where banks loaned out deposits—and other types of financial activity. The LLR was the *lender* of last resort—the institution that took over the banks' lending function when banks stop making loans. Other financial institutions, which traded and speculated, did not receive protection from the LLR.

The new LLR must also be the "market-maker of last resort" or the "dealer of last resort." Because so much of maturity transformation takes place through a range of nonbank institutions—broker-dealers, hedge funds, money market mutual funds, special purpose vehicles owned by financial holding companies that also own bank subsidiaries—that convert short-term loans into tradeable securities, the LLR must be authorized to provide liquidity support to these institutions.

What powers does this new LLR need to perform this broader LLR function? At a minimum, it needs the powers that the Fed, Treasury, and FDIC used, mostly illegally, during the last financial crisis. These include the powers to

- buy financial assets, including notes, loans, bonds, and stock;
- make unsecured and undersecured, as well as secured, loans to financial institutions (and accept low-quality collateral);
- transact with financial institutions of all types, on equal terms, not just banks;
- seize financial institutions under the power of eminent domain with just compensation determined by a judicial valuation at a later date, and to control their activities;
- guarantee the outstanding and new debt of financial institutions;
- order supervisory agencies, like the OCC and the SEC, to take steps that are necessary to address the crisis (e.g., to order short-sale bans).[17]

While these powers are impressive, financial economists and others who have given thought to the LLR in the wake of the crisis seem to agree that they are necessary.[18] History suggests as much. The LLR, lacking political support and legal authority, underreacted to the liquidity crises of the 1930s (Carlson and Wheelock 2013). And the LLR reacted too slowly to the financial crisis that began in 2007.

The recent financial crisis shows why all these powers are necessary and the conventional Bagehot approach is inadequate. Because of the fear of stigma, even liquidity-constrained financial institutions will be inclined to delay before borrowing from emergency credit facilities. The LLR needs the authority to force firms to borrow, and also to force healthy firms to borrow at the same time to prevent the market from picking off the weakest firm. Moreover, the crisis showed that when financial institutions accept emergency loans, they face strong incentives to hoard cash when the system as a whole benefits only if they lend into the market a portion of the money they borrow. For this reason, the LLR needs the authority to order firms to enter financial transactions. Finally, the crisis showed that financial institutions that should be given emergency money may not be able to offer collateral for a loan, and it may be very difficult to value the collateral in any event. The LLR needs the authority to make capital injections, unsecured loans, and partially secured loans; and to buy assets.

A significant act of legislation would be needed to put these reforms into place. In most cases, the Fed and related LLR agencies lack the power to engage in the actions listed above, and need congressional authorization in the form of a legislative act. In a few cases, the law explicitly prohibits the Fed to take actions. For example, with limited exceptions, the Fed is prohibited by law from making loans to undercapitalized banks. Congress should eliminate this prohibition.

Protections

The LLR, because of its vast powers, should be permitted to act only after a financial crisis has begun. The law should, as now, provide that the LLR's authorities are triggered upon agreement by a supermajority of top economic officials, including the president. These officials should also release a statement that describes objective indicators of crisis, such as a collapse of lending or other signs of loss of confidence.

Vast powers create opportunities for abuse; the LLR cannot be given un-limited power. Judicial review during a crisis is impractical, as the 2007–8 crisis showed. People negatively affected by the government's actions could not persuade courts to intervene.[19] Judges are unwilling to interfere with emergency actions by expert agencies. Courts move too slowly and lack expertise. However, this view, if taken to its logical extreme, would elimi-nate any constraint on the government. A robust legal regime to correct abuses *after* the crisis can be put into place. As noted, where the LLR uses force to acquire firms and other assets, the owners will be able to sue the government for damages based on a proper valuation that uses fundamen-tal rather than crisis-driven asset values. In addition, where the LLR uses its regulatory and supervisory authorities to order firms to shed assets and make loans, the firms will be entitled to sue after the crisis and receive a remedy if they can show that the LLR's actions were unreasonable. The usual post-crisis analyses by independent government agencies with the power to compel testimony and discover documents from the LLR will facilitate the litigation by collecting facts and making them publicly avail-able.

Because of the paucity of statutory law on these issues, most of the liti-gation has involved constitutional claims, for which precedents are limited. This puts courts in a difficult position. To remedy this problem, Congress should pass a statute that provides a procedure for making claims against the government after a financial crisis. The most important feature of this statute would be a provision that makes clear that the "fundamental" or "real" values calculated at the time of the rescue loans provide the basis for calculating damages in post-crisis litigation. If the government makes loans, buys assets, issues guarantees, or supplies other financial services at a price that does not reflect the fundamental value, the government must subsequently compensate counterparties for the difference between the price charged and the fundamental value. The law would prevent the government from using its credit monopoly to extract wealth from firms during a liquidity crisis.

This simple rule would make an important difference in the govern-ment's behavior. Recall that during the crisis, the government used high asset valuations in order to justify loans to firms that it wanted to save. After the crisis, it claimed low asset valuations in order to justify its failure to lend to some firms (like Lehman) and to overcharge others (like AIG).

A simple consistency requirement—one that forced the government to use consistent valuations—would block the government from showing favoritism while allowing it the flexibility it needs to respond to the crisis.

Administrative Organization

The complex division of responsibility between financial regulatory agencies hampered the crisis response. How should the LLR be designed to do better? It is tempting to argue that all powers should be handed to a single agency, eliminating at a stroke the problem of interagency rivalries. However, it is doubtful that such a powerful agency would be politically acceptable, while existing agencies are too deeply entrenched in the government's institutional structure to be swept aside. The Dodd-Frank Act eliminated the OTS, but addressed the entrenched status of the other agencies by layering a coordinating body, the Financial Stability Oversight Council (FSOC) above them.[20] The FSOC searches for risks in the financial system, identifies systemically risky institutions, and orders the breakup of too-big-to-fail entities, but it does not enjoy any rescue authority aside from a coordinating function.

This seems inadequate, but it is not clear what the alternative is. The problem with the existing regulatory structure, revealed by the financial crisis, is that the different agencies develop constituencies that they try to protect: for the OCC, big New York banks; for the OTS, thrifts; for FDIC, Main Street banks; for the Fed, big Wall Street financial institutions. The Federal Emergency Management Agency (FEMA) or the National Guard does not favor constituencies, but sees its mission as protecting people and restoring order.[21] It is possible to think that a financial agency could be given a similar purely ex post mission, detached from ex ante regulatory responsibilities that might cause it to favor some entities over others. But the connection between ex ante regulation and ex post response seems necessary to ensure that agencies possess enough information and expertise about the financial system to be able to act wisely during a crisis.

If we use history as our guide, the Fed seems to be the agency that shows the least favoritism and the most consideration for the general public rather than for specific groups. Because of their power over the money supply, central banks are in a better position than other agencies to address a financial crisis. This role has been understood for a long time and is central to the mission and self-conception of central banks. The Fed already has the broadest powers and the greatest level of sophistication among all the financial agencies. While practical and institutional constraints cannot be wished away, Congress should gradually transfer additional powers to the Fed, such as the power to buy assets, make unsecured loans, and acquire equity, while removing LLR powers from other agencies, to the extent politically feasible.

At the same time, it may be necessary to add voices to the LLR that are not as closely tied to the financial community. If Mian and Sufi (2014) are correct that the LLR undervalued homeowner relief because it was excessively influenced by banks, then it may be necessary to ensure that the LLR includes a role for housing agencies that treat homeowners as their constituents.

Centralization and Independence of the LLR

The financial crisis exposed significant gaps in the LLR's authority. While Congress filled one gap with the OLA, it perversely widened the others. It should have enhanced the powers of the LLR and gathered as many of those powers as possible into the hands of the Fed, subject to a strong procedural trigger that requires consensus among top economic officials and the president that a financial crisis has begun. The reason is simple. The LLR powers currently available to the Fed and other agencies reflected a simpler world in which the banking system was the primary source of short-term liabilities, so that the FDIC fund plus the Fed's residual lending powers sufficed to stop a crisis, even to prevent a crisis from starting. A new system that extends the LLR to the shadow banking system is needed. And the LLR power must be lodged in an institution that enjoys substantial independence from politics, so that it can resist the ideological and political pressures that hampered the congressional response during the last crisis.

Congress did not create such an LLR for numerous reasons—mostly political reasons, including distrust of the Fed and popular resentment at the bailouts of Wall Street firms. The most important policy reason for restricting the LLR is the theory that a generous LLR encourages financial institutions to behave recklessly—a theory that was adopted in Dodd-Frank itself. But moral hazard is not a justification for depriving the LLR of the powers that it needs to rescue the financial system. The necessity of an LLR is (within mainstream economic and political circles) uncontested. And if an LLR is necessary, then it should be supplied with the powers that it needs. Moral hazard justifies ex ante regulation such as capital requirements, which are independent of the LLR's power, and (conceivably) requirements that the LLR penalize the firms that it rescues—for example, with high interest rates, as in the original Bagehot formulation. Both ex ante regulation and ex post penalizing are consistent with a powerful and robust LLR.

As an analogy, imagine that a town is plagued by residential fires, caused by the carelessness of homeowners who do not install smoke detectors and who store flammable materials in their basements. The town could sensibly address this problem by enacting a fire code that it enforces with inspections. It could also address this problem by directing the fire department to replace hoses with squirt guns and tanker trucks with horse-drawn carriages. The second approach would certainly address moral hazard; residents, fearful that the fire department will not save their houses, would be more careful. But not all fires are caused by carelessness, and not all careless fires should be allowed to burn since, by a process similar to financial contagion, fires may spread from house to house. The town does better with an adequately equipped fire department along with a fire code. And so with the LLR.

Another possible criticism of my proposal is that it would violate the "rule of law." Numerous scholars have argued that the Fed and Treasury violated the rule of law during the financial crisis, and many of them also argue that the Fed needs to be stripped of powers so that it cannot violate the rule of law again (Samples 2010; White 2013; Zywicki 2011).[22] On inspection, it becomes clear that while the authors believe (in most cases, correctly) that the Fed violated the law during the crisis, their main complaint is that Congress has given the Fed too much discretionary power, which enables it to act arbitrarily. However, the constitutional limitations on delegation of power to agencies—embodied in the nondelegation doctrine—are minimal. The requirement that the LLR use its powers to unfreeze the financial system[23] would supply the intelligible principle required by the nondelegation doctrine under recent precedents.[24]

A more serious version of this criticism, emphasized by the former deputy governor of the Bank of England, Paul Tucker, is that, as a matter of political economy (as opposed to legal principles) an unconstrained central bank is both undesirable and unsustainable (Tucker 2014): undesirable because we live in a democracy, and an independent agency with vast powers may act against the will of the people; and unsustainable because for just that reason the agency will be regarded with suspicion and ultimately subject to constraints.[25] Tucker advocates two types of constraints—procedural and substantive. The procedural constraints include reporting requirements, triggering rules that require the agreement of top officials, and the like. Few people would disagree with such requirements, which are mostly in place. As a substantive constraint, he argues that the LLR should never be allowed to lend to insolvent firms because such loans put at risk funds that go to the Treasury, and hence raise "fiscal" issues that are the province of Congress and the people.

Tucker's worries are well grounded. The restrictions on the LLR in the Dodd-Frank Act, along with routine threats by Congress to impose further restrictions on the Fed, reflect just those worries. The problem with his argument is that, as we saw during the financial crisis, lending to insolvent firms—or firms that are likely to be insolvent—may well be a sensible approach to a crisis. Many such firms often have counterparties that are solvent, and lending to insolvent firms, enabling them to pay their counterparties, may be a more efficient way of helping the counterparties than lending to them directly. And because of the difficulty of asset valuation during a crisis, a determined LLR can often avoid the restriction proposed by Tucker by making inflated estimates.

While the idea that the LLR should not invade the fiscal province of the legislature draws on a long history, going back to Bagehot and beyond, it is time to retire it. The fiscal versus monetary distinction is illusory during a financial crisis. The LLR can value most collateral only with difficulty, with the valuation depending on whether the crisis conditions will ameliorate in the near future. As a result, the LLR's collateral valuations are based on the LLR's prediction about the effectiveness of its current and future actions, giving it a huge amount of effective discretion even under the strict Bagehot approach. Moreover, if the LLR acts weakly rather than aggressively and fails to resolve the crisis, the negative fiscal consequences—lower tax receipts, higher transfer payments—could exceed losses on loans made to insolvent firms.

The LLR will be able to survive in a democracy, regardless of how powerful and independent it is, as long as the public believes that it serves the public interest. Depriving it of the powers it needs will not advance that goal.

Acknowledgments

I BENEFITED FROM DISCUSSIONS WITH NUMEROUS COLLEAGUES AND friends, and from comments on previous drafts. Thanks in particular to Bill Bratton, Tony Casey, Darrell Duffie, Richard Epstein, Itay Goldstein, Anil Kashyap, Arvind Krishnamurthy, Randy Kroszner, David Musto, Steve Schwarcz, David Skeel, Lior Strahilevitz, Philip Wallach, and David Zaring, and to participants at seminars and conferences at Wharton, the University of Chicago Booth School of Business, Columbia Law School, and Stanford Business School. Kathrine Gutierrez, Adam Holzman, Paul Mathis, and Hannah Waldman provided valuable research assistance.

The book contains some passages excerpted from two articles: "What Legal Authority Does the Fed Need During a Financial Crisis?," published in the *Minnesota Law Review*; and "Principles of Bailout Regulation" (with Anthony Casey), published in the *Notre Dame Law Review*.

My thinking about the AIG bailout was heavily influenced by my friend Bob Silver, a partner at Boies, Schiller & Flexner, where I was of counsel at the time of the AIG litigation. He helped the firm develop the legal strategy that was pursued in that case by the plaintiffs, and I helped him, mainly as a sounding board. Bob died after the case went to trial. I dedicate this book to his memory.

Although I no longer work at the firm and have no financial interest in the outcome of the AIG case, my involvement in that case, on behalf of the plaintiffs, has no doubt colored my view of it.

Notes

INTRODUCTION

1. Starr Int'l Co. v. United States, 121 Fed. Cl. 428, 444 (2015).

2. Pub. L. No. 111-203, 124 Stat. 1376 (2010).

3. Many S&Ls did receive a subtle form of government assistance—regulatory forbearance—which could be seen as a de facto partial bailout, but the S&Ls were eventually allowed to fail.

4. Firms that lend to too-big-to-fail firms and are rescued when the latter are bailed out in otherwise normal economic conditions are given bad incentives, but, as I will argue, the proper response is regulation, not restrictions on bailouts.

5. As is discussed in chapter 5, the government was unable to compel Fannie and Freddie to help the mortgage market as much as it wanted to. The problem was that the "government," in this context, was two different agencies that disagreed about how to manage the two institutions.

CHAPTER ONE

1. In the following, I rely mainly on these sources: Pozsar (2011; 2014); Mehrling (2011); Gorton (2012); Krishnamurthy (2010); Brunnermeier (2009); Krishnamurthy, Nagel, and Orlov (2014); Duffie (2010). Other citations are below.

2. The major exception was Raghuram Rajan (2005), whose argument was famously pooh-poohed by Larry Summers and other major economists at a meeting sponsored by the Fed.

3. Apparently, the term was coined by McCulley (2007).

4. See Pozsar et al. (2012, 10–11), for a more complete description. The authors provide a still stylized but more complex account with seven stages: (1) loan origination by finance companies; (2) loan warehousing by conduits set up by various types of financial institutions and funded by commercial paper; (3) the packaging of loans into ABSs by investment banks; (4) the warehousing of ABSs by investment banks and other financial institutions; (5) the structuring of ABSs into CDOs by investment banks; (6) ABS intermediation by finance companies, hedge funds, and other institutions; (7) funding of all these steps by money

market mutual funds, other mutual funds, pension funds, insurance companies, and others (2012, 10–11). All these steps can take place within a financial holding company as well. See also Pozsar (2014).

5. On the various theories of shadow banking, see Gennaioli, Shleifer, and Vishny (2013) and the discussion within.

6. See Gerardi et al. (2008, 140): "Most analysts simply thought that a 20 percent nationwide fall in prices was impossible."

7. This kind of bubble-thinking, while hard to reconcile with typical economic models, is well documented historically. See, e.g., Kindleberger (2000). For a recent discussion, see Brunnermeier and Oehmke (2013).

8. See, e.g., Beltran, Cordell, and Thomas (2013).

9. See Gorton and Metrick (2012). While not all segments of the repo market were affected (see Copeland, Martin, and Walker [2014]), and the magnitude of the run was not all that great, it affected systemically important institutions like Goldman, Morgan Stanley, and Citigroup. See Krishnamurthy, Nagel, and Orlov (2014).

10. LIBOR is one of many interest-rate benchmarks that are used by creditors as an input in interest rates they charge. It is calculated from the submissions of a group of banks, which are asked to estimate their cost of funds for short-term unsecured loans.

11. For a discussion, see Goldstein and Razin (2013); Goldstein (2013).

12. See, e.g., Acharya and Mora (2015).

13. For discussions of these and other views, see Gorton and Winton (2003); Schularick and Taylor (2012).

14. Pub. L. No. 95-128, 91 Stat. 1147 (1977).

15. See, e.g., Bolotnyy (2014); Kaufman (2014).

16. See, e.g., Corbae and Quintin (2015); Campbell and Cocco (2015).

17. Fannie Mae and Freddie Mac, the GSEs, were the major but not only instruments of housing policy. I will discuss them in chapter 5.

18. Many people apparently thought that the CDS market was highly liquid; it turned out not to be, especially once the crisis began. See, e.g., Junge and Trolle (2013).

19. There are many other theories about why crises occur, some of them having nothing to do with network structure. For example, Gorton and Ordoñez (2014) focus on the role of information about collateral values. In earlier models, crises were essentially random events. While the recent literature is imaginative and instructive, for all practical purposes—and certainly from the standpoint of regulators—a crisis remains impossible to predict.

20. See also Fahlenbrach, Prilmeier, and Stulz (2012).

21. This popular view is not supported by the evidence. See Fahlenbrach and Stulz (2011).

22. This problem was early on identified as a major factor in the crisis, based on the theory that mortgage originators violated underwriting standards because they did not bear the risk of default. See Keys et al. (2009). However, the evidence for this theory is weak. See, e.g., Bubb and Kaufman (2014).

23. For a sample of the large literature, see, e.g., Baghai, Servaes, and Tamayo (2014); C. Opp, M. Opp, and Harris (2013); Bolton, Freixas, and Shapiro (2012); Pagano and Volpin (2010); Griffin and Tang (2012).

24. Pub. L. No. 106-102, 113 Stat. 1338 (1999).

25. Pub. L. No. 73-66, 48 Stat. 162 (1933).

26. On Bear Stearns, for example, see SEC (2008).

27. By contrast, public-sector borrowing from foreign creditors could and did cause crises in socialist countries.

28. See Brunnermeier (2009, 81). Regulators recognized these forms of arbitrage and moved to address them, but only partially.

29. For a valuable history of financial innovation, see Olegario (2016).

30. For an accounting of predictions, see Bezemer (2010). On the failure of commentators and government officials in the United Kingdom, see Hindmoor and McConnell (2015). By contrast, FCIC (2011, xvii) argues that the crisis was predictable: "The captains of finance and the public stewards of our financial system ignored warnings and failed to question, understand, and manage evolving risks within a system essential to the well-being of the American public. Theirs was a big miss, not a stumble. While the business cycle cannot be repealed, a crisis of this magnitude need not have occurred."

31. For more about the collapse of repo, see Kacperczyk and Schnabl (2013).

32. As far as I know, only one person publicly argued that the bursting of the housing bubble would cause a financial crisis—the investor Peter Schiff (see Schiff 2007). While Schiff did predict a financial crisis, in his view the crisis would accompany a general collapse of the US economy. This has not happened (at least, not yet).

CHAPTER TWO

1. Recent scholarship suggests that the contribution of the subprime market to the credit crisis is exaggerated; defaults on prime mortgages were just important if not more. See Adelino et al. 2016.

2. Pub. L. No. 110–289, 122 Stat. 2654 (2008).

3. Pub. L. No. 110–343, 122 Stat. 3765 (2008).

4. Credit for originating the principles is usually given to Henry Thornton, a British banker and politician, who died in 1815. See Goodhart (2011).

5. For a discussion and survey, see Domanski, Moessner, and Nelson (2014).

6. However, Bignon, Flandreau, and Ugolini (2012) argue that Bagehot and others at the time supported the penalty rate as a way of encouraging banks to start borrowing from (and hence lending to) each other rather than depending on the central bank when the crisis is over but interest rates remain too low for banks to make much of a profit from lending.

7. Under the Fed's current regulations, the penalty rate is 50–100 basis points above the market interest rate. See Federal Reserve (2016d).

8. Compare Gorton (2012, 134–39) (arguing that moral hazard is important) and Selgin (2013) (critiquing Gorton). For evidence from the crisis, see Strahan and Tanyeri (2015) (finding evidence that bailouts did not increase moral hazard in money market mutual fund markets); Brandao-Marques, Correa, and Sapriza (2013) (finding evidence of moral hazard); Black and Hazelwood (2012) (same).

9. See, e.g., Ritholtz (2009).

10. The estimate comes from ProPublica; see Kiel and Nguyen (2016). There are many reasons for taking this estimate with a grain of salt, but it is good enough.

11. The Fed was not literally a monopolist. Money did exist elsewhere, in the pockets of wealthy people and in the vaults of sovereign wealth funds and other institutions. The Fed's unique position arose from its power to make money, ultimately backed by Congress's power to tax. Private money holders mostly hoarded their cash, bought Treasuries and the like, riding out the crisis while the Fed acted.

12. See, e.g., Aït-Sahalia et al. (2012); Brunetti, di Filippo, and Harris (2011); Carpenter, Demiralp, and Eisenschmidt (2014); Duygan-Bump et al. (2013).

13. Pub. L. No. 111–203, 124 Stat. 1376 (2010).

14. The most prominent example is MetLife's battle with the government.

CHAPTER THREE

1. Cf. Wallach (2015).

2. Pub. L. No. 111-203, 124 Stat. 1376 (2010).

3. Pub. L. No. 110-343, 122 Stat. 3765 (2008).

4. 12 U.S.C. § 347(b).

5. Id. § 343(3)(A).

6. Id. § 1821(f).

7. Id. § 1823(c)(4)(G)(I).

8. 12 U.S.C. § 347b(a).

9. Id. § 353.

10. The Fed's discount-window lending appears to have satisfied other legal requirements, including collateral requirements. See Gilbert et al. (2012).

11. One important legal requirement for these loans was the prohibition on lending to undercapitalized banks for more than a few days under the Federal Deposit Insurance Corporation Improvement Act of 1991, Pub. L. No. 102-242, 105 Stat. 2236 (codified at 12 U.S.C. § 1831t). The Fed appeared to comply with this requirement for the most part. See Gilbert et al. (2012).

12. 12 U.S.C. § 343.

13. The collateral used in the TSFL decreased in quality over time, raising the question whether the "good collateral" requirement was consistently satisfied. But, unlike the PDCF collateral, the TSLF collateral never fell below investment-grade. See Federal Reserve (2016f).

14. The data are available at Federal Reserve (2016f), under "Data."

15. My account follows GAO (2011, 22–26, 178–84).

16. The loan was routed through JP Morgan, but the Fed recognized that the loan was functionally a loan to Bear.

17. The data set posted at the Federal Reserve discloses the type of collateral but uncharacteristically does not break it down by rating. See Federal Reserve (2016b). Oddly, the data set shows the collateral as of 2010 rather than when the loan was originated in March 2008.

18. 12 U.S.C. § 353.

19. For similar arguments, see Porter (2009); Mehra (2010, 236). For a summary of the (negative) response from legal commentators, see Wallach (2015, 53–54).

20. See Federal Reserve (2016e).

21. Starr Int'l Co. v. United States, 121 Fed. Cl. 428, 466 (2015), rev'd, 856 F.3d (Fed. Cir. 2017). The plaintiffs have announced that they will seek review by the Supreme Court.

22. Through TALF, the Fed effectively made loans to businesses, which were secured by various securities, consistent with section 13(3). For a description of the program, see GAO (2011, app. XII).

23. Mostly during the Great Depression, though the Fed offered to extend (secured) credit on several occasions since then.

24. See the careful analysis in Stanton and Wallace (2011). While their views have been criticized, their basic results seem to stand up to further analysis. See Flavin and Sheenan (2015); Longstaff and Myers (2014); Wojtowicz (2014); Vyas (2011); Fender and Scheicher (2009). For an overview of the debate, see Augustin et al. (2014).

25. Data available at Federal Reserve (2016e), under "Data."

26. See Federal Reserve (2016e, under "Data").

27. The collateral descriptions are available at the Fed's website, Federal Reserve (2016e).

Geithner (2014, 186) says that the Fed could not lend to Lehman because it didn't believe that Lehman could repay it, yet a page later notes that the PDCF was trading Treasury securities for BBB-minus rate securities.

28. A more recent study, which was released as this book went to press, also argues that Lehman was not insolvent and owned enough assets to secure a loan from the Fed. Ball (2016).

29. 31 U.S.C. § 5302.

30. Id.

31. It is possible to argue that by rescuing money market funds, Treasury indirectly rescued European banks—which relied on funding from the money market mutual funds—and in this way prevented the euro from collapsing and hence the dollar from appreciating against the euro. But Treasury did not make this argument, no doubt because no one would have believed it.

32. Emergency Economic Stabilization Act of 2008, Pub. L. No. 110-343, § 101(a)(1).

33. Id. § 101(a)(9).

34. Id. § 101(a)(5).

35. U.C.C. § 9–102(a)(47). Similar definitions can be found in federal law. See, e.g., 26 U.S.C. § 731(c)(2)(C); 18 U.S.C. § 514(a)(2); see also United States v. Sargent, 504 F.3d 767 (9th Cir. 2007) (postage statements are not financial instruments); United States v. Howick, 263 F.3d 1056 (9th Cir. 2001) (phony Federal Reserve notes are fictitious instruments).

36. See, e.g., Omega Envtl., Inc. v. Valley Bank NA, 219 F.3d 984, 986 (9th Cir. 2000) (holding that a certificate of deposit is an instrument); see also In re Newman, 993 F.2d 90 (5th Cir. 1993) (holding that an annuity contract is not an instrument because it is not transferred in the regular course of business); FDIC v. Kipperman, 392 B.R. 814, 833–34 (B.A.P. 9th Cir. 2008) (holding that surety bonds are not instruments because they are not transferrable by delivery in the ordinary course of business and do not provide for the payment of any sum certain).

37. Ind. State Police Pension Tr. v. Chrysler LLC, 576 F.3d 108, 122 n.13 (2d Cir. 2009). (*Chrysler II*).

38. Parker v. Motors Liquidation Co., 430 B.R. 65, 94 (S.D.N.Y. 2010) (*In re Motors II*).

39. Challenges to Treasury's authority were dismissed on grounds of standing in *In re Motors II* and *Chrysler II*.

40. A&D Auto Sales, Inc. v. United States, 748 F.3d 1142 (Fed. Cir. 2014).

41. For a description of the programs, see GAO 2010.

42. 12 U.S.C. § 1823(c)(1)(A)–(C) (emphasis added).

43. Id. § 1823(c)(4).

44. Id. § 1823(c)(4)(G) (emphasis added).

45. For a discussion, see GAO 2010.

46. For a discussion of the legal debate, see Wallach (2015, 152–53).

47. For an overview of the debate, see Baker (2012).

CHAPTER FOUR

1. Starr Int'l Co., Inc. v. United States, 121 Fed. Cl. 428, 451 (2015).

2. Id. at 436.

3. For a discussion, see Zaring (2014).

4. Regulators would worry during the crisis that if AIG entered into bankruptcy, the subsidiaries would have been adversely affected. It remains unclear whether this worry was

justified. In theory, the subsidiaries would not have been affected because their financial health was supposed to be independent of the financial health of the holding company. In practice, they might have been.

5. See Schwarcz (2015) for a helpful account.

6. For this reason, Laux and Leuz (2009) dispute the argument that fair value accounting contributed to the financial crisis. Banks were able to avoid marking down their assets. For another view, see Bhat, Frankel, and Martin (2011).

7. AIG's securities-lending business invested in later-vintage MBSs that were backed by a larger portion of badly performing subprime mortgages. While losses were higher, they were not high enough to threaten the solvency of the insurance subsidiaries.

8. The details of the bailout—which encompasses the initial loan, the Maiden Lane II and III facilities, and various restructurings, which took place over several years—are complex, and I abstract away from them. They can be found in various government documents. For a lucid academic account, see Sjostrom (2009; 2015).

9. See, e.g., Fiderer (2010). See also SIGTARP (2009), which takes no position on the intentions of government officials but concludes that the design and effect of Maiden Lane III was to benefit AIG's counterparties, and that available alternative arrangements would have limited or eliminated the extent of this benefit.

10. Under NYSE rules, a stock will be delisted if its price is too low. Firms can avoid delisting by engaging in a reverse stock split. However, if AIG's goal was to avoid delisting, it did not need to limit the reverse stock split to issued shares.

11. Starr Int'l Co. v. Fed. Reserve Bank of N.Y., 906 F. Supp. 2d 202 (S.D.N.Y. 2012).

12. 12 U.S.C. § 343.

13. *Starr Int'l Co.*, 906 F. Supp. 2d 202 at 244.

14. Id. at 251 n.39.

15. Id. at 250, quoting P. Dougherty Co. v. United States, 207 F.2d 626, 634 (3d Cir. 1953) (emphasis added by the *Starr* court).

16. The Second Circuit affirmed the district court's opinion on the ground that federal law preempted Delaware law. The court did not discuss whether federal common law created any duties. Starr Int'l Co. v. Fed. Reserve Bank of N.Y., 742 F.3d 37 (2d Cir. 2014).

17. Starr was able to allege that the Credit Agreement was wrongful because the statute of limitations under the Tucker Act, the relevant statute, extended back six years.

18. Koontz v. St. Johns River Water Mgmt. Dist., 133 S. Ct. 2586 (2013); Dolan v. City of Tigard, 512 U.S. 374 (1994); Nollan v. Cal. Coastal Comm'n, 483 U.S. 825 (1987).

19. 12 U.S.C. § 357.

20. Id. § 24 (Seventh).

21. See, e.g., Land v. Dollar, 330 U.S. 731 (1947); Suwannee S.S. Co. v. United States, 279 F.2d 874 (Ct. Cl. 1960). The doctrine has been applied in other contexts as well. See Aerolineas Argentinas v. United States, 77 F.3d 1564 (Fed. Cir. 1996); Alyeska Pipeline Serv. Co. v. United States, 624 F.2d 1005 (Ct. Cl. 1980). Technically, illegal exaction cases are based on the due process clause, not the takings clause of the Constitution.

22. Starr Int'l Co. v. United States, 106 Fed. Cl. 50, 83 (2012).

23. Id. at 436.

24. Both the government and Starr agreed that AIG was solvent; and the government believed that AIG was solvent at the time of the Credit Agreement, so AIG's solvency was not an issue in the case. Some commentators have expressed skepticism on this question. In a recent paper, McDonald and Paulson (2015, 103) conclude that "AIG's problems were not purely about liquidity." However, while they show that AIG's CDS and MBS assets declined

in value, they do not show that they declined in value enough to wipe out AIG's equity. The contemporary view of government officials and the repayment of the loan remain the best evidence that AIG was solvent.

25. 31 U.S.C. § 9102.

26. Transcript of Proceedings held on October 6, 2014 at 1246, Starr Int'l Co. v. United States, 121 Fed. Cl. 428 (2015). Also, discussing the use of TARP funds to invest in AIG, Paulson testified that he "was worried that $40 billion more into AIG would so enrage the American public and Congress that it would make it hard for me to get the last 350 if we needed it, and so I was—that was—that was my biggest concern." Id.; see Kessler (2014).

27. Pub. L. No. 110-343, 122 Stat. 3765 (2008).

28. See also Paulson (2010, 111–12).

29. Subsequently, the price was raised.

30. According to the FRBNY, the CDOs had a market value of $29.3 billion and a par value of $62.1 billion. FRBNY (2016).

31. For a sympathetic account, see Boyd (2011, 293–94).

32. See Acemoglu, Ozdaglar, and Tahbaz-Salehi (2015).

CHAPTER FIVE

1. The litigation has been discussed in a few academic articles; see Badawi and Casey (2014); Davidoff Solomon and Zaring (2015); Epstein (2014); Silva (2015).

2. For this brief history, I draw on Acharya et al. (2011, 14–20) and Frame et al. (2015), and I ignore GSEs other than Fannie and Freddie. Another valuable source is McLean (2015), who describes the politics surrounding Fannie and Freddie and their rescue.

3. E.g., Frame and White (2005).

4. Pub. L. No. 110-289, 122 Stat. 2654 (2008).

5. Motion to Dismiss All Claims by Defendants Federal Housing Finance Agency at 23–24, Perry Capital v. Lew, 70 F. Supp. 3d 208 (D.D.C. 2014) (1:13-cv-01025-RLW). For readability, I have deleted some citations; I have also retained the italics in the original.

6. Id.

7. YCharts (2016a); YCharts (2016b).

8. Perry Capital LLC v. Lew, 70 F. Supp. 3d 208, 218 (D.D.C. 2014), aff'd 848 F.3d 1072 (D.C. Cir. 2017).

9. On July 1, 2008, Fannie's market capitalization was $21.09 billion; Freddie's was $10.48 billion.

10. Useful discussions of the litigation can be found in Badawi and Casey (2014); Epstein (2014); Silva (2015).

11. Or at least partly owned. Treasury also received warrants that would have enabled it to seize almost 80 percent of Fannie's and Freddie's stock. Some of the plaintiffs contested the validity of these warrants, but we will put this issue aside.

12. Pub. L. No. 79-404, 60 Stat. 237 (1946).

13. 70 F. Supp. 3d 208.

14. When the government acts arbitrarily, plaintiffs can also make arguments based on the due process clause of the Constitution, but the clause provides little help in this case because it does not normally authorize courts to award damages, unlike the takings clause.

15. See Complaint Against the USA at 50–59, Wash. Fed. v. United States, No. 1:13-cv-00385-MMS (Ct. Fed. Cl. 2013).

16. As discussed by Frame et al. (2015, 34).

17. 12 U.S.C. § 4617(a).

18. 70 F. Supp. 3d 208.

19. 12 U.S.C. § 4617(b)(2)(D).

20. Golden Pac. Bancorp v. United States, 15 F.3d 1066 (Fed. Cir. 1994); Cal. Hous. Sec., Inc. v. United States, 959 F.2d 955 (Fed. Cir. 1992).

21. The court also evaluated the plaintiffs' argument as a regulatory takings claim under Pennsylvania Coal Co. v. Mahon, 260 U.S. 393 (1922), and rejected it because the decision to pay dividends is "discretionary" and "liquidation rights only ripen *during liquidation.*" Perry Capital LLC v. Lew, 70 F. Supp. 3d 208, 243–44 (D.D.C. 2014). However, this is always true of dividends, and dividends are certainly property. The discretion of the corporation is not unlimited; if it were, no one would invest. The court tries to bolster its analysis by pointing out the government's supervisory relationship to the GSEs, but as discussed above, the government's powers were limited by statute.

22. After the Troubled Asset Relief Program was put into effect, the government pressured the major banks to accept equity injections. The banks gave into the pressure, but in part because the terms were generous.

CHAPTER SIX

1. General Motors (2010), Chrysler Group (2010).

2. In this section, I rely mainly on Klier (2009).

3. I rely on the short, lucid accounts in Bickley et al. (2009) and Klier and Rubenstein (2012); and on Rattner (2010).

4. Pub. L. No. 110-343, 122 Stat. 3765 (2008).

5. The actual heads of the task force were Larry Summers and Timothy Geithner. While they delegated day-to-day operations to Rattner, they were involved in the major decisions.

6. 11 U.S.C. § 363.

7. The figures are taken from the bankruptcy court. In re Chrysler, LLC, 405 B.R. 84 (Bankr. S.D.N.Y. 2009). Other sources—e.g., the Congressional Oversight Panel—calculate them somewhat differently. See Congressional Oversight Panel (2009, 23–28).

8. In re Gen. Motors Corp., 407 B.R. 463 (Bankr. S.D.N.Y. 2009); Congressional Oversight Panel (2009, 28–31).

9. Mian and Sufi (2012) provide evidence that the program caused a few hundred thousand cars to be bought a few months earlier than they would otherwise have been bought, and so had minimal economic effect.

10. 11 U.S.C. § 1129.

11. See also Goolsbee and Krueger (2015, 21).

12. See In re Gen. Motors Corp., 407 B.R. at 499; In re Chrysler, 405 B.R. at 99.

13. Thus, the argument that the absence of other bidders indicates that the bankruptcies were fair (Lubben 2009; Morrison 2009) is wrong. This would be true only for a bankruptcy during normal economic times. But by the same token, those who complain that there was no market test (e.g., Roe and Skeel 2010) cannot explain how a market test would have been possible.

14. See A&D Auto Sales, Inc. v. United States, 748 F.3d 1142.

15. Id. at 1158.

16. Pub. L. No. 110-343, § 101(a)(1).

17. Id. § 3(9)(A)-(B).

18. Id. § 3(5).

19. For a concise account, see Congressional Oversight Panel (2009, 70–79). The Second Circuit held that the relevant provision of EESA (which limited financial support to "finan-

cial institutions") was vague enough to encompass automakers, but did not address the argument that the funds were not used to restore liquidity, as EESA required. Ind. State Police Pension Tr. v. Chrysler LLC, 576 F.3d 108 (2d Cir. 2009). There is a further argument made by the bankruptcy courts that the money was used to maintain employee morale (and avoid a possible strike) and to ensure that suppliers would not boycott the firms. If so, then the excess payments would not violate the Bankruptcy Code. But these claims are dubious. Both employees and suppliers would have had very strong incentives to continue to do business rather than become unemployed or shut down operations.

CHAPTER SEVEN

1. Starr Int'l Co. v. United States, 121 Fed. Cl. 428, 436 (2015) (quoting AIG financial adviser John Studzinski).

2. Pub. L. No. 110-343, 122 Stat. 3765 (2008).

3. In the AIG case, the plaintiffs prevailed under the due process clause (the illegal exaction theory), not the takings clause, but I regard the two arguments as in substance the same. For expository simplicity, I will refer to takings in this chapter.

4. Pub. L. No. 101-73, 103 Stat. 183 (1989).

5. See United States v. Winstar Corp., 518 U.S. 839 (1996).

6. Armstrong v. United States, 364 U.S. 40, 49 (1960).

7. For a discussion of the cases, see Romero (2006).

8. 718 F.2d 789 (6th Cir. 1983).

9. An important qualification is that, generally speaking, the government is not required to compensate people if it destroys rather than takes property for its own use during an emergency. See Lee (2015). This exception is rather puzzling but, in any event, does not apply to the financial crisis, where the government actions in question were expropriations.

10. In theory. Government officials do not pay damages out of their own pockets; the question is whether they internalize the budgetary consequences of their actions.

11. Wilson Athletic Goods Mfg. Co. v. United States, 161 F.2d 915, 918 (7th Cir. 1947).

12. Turney v. United States, 115 F. Supp. 457 (Ct. Cl. 1953).

CHAPTER EIGHT

1. Pub. L. No. 97-320, 96 Stat. 1469 (1982).

2. Pub. L. No. 110-289, 122 Stat. 2654 (2008).

3. 12 U.S.C. § 343.

4. In Paulson's (2010, 115) words, the letter "was an indirect way of getting the Fed the cover it needed for taking an action that should—and would—have been taken by Treasury if we had had the fiscal authority to do so."

5. Pub. L. No. 110-343, 122 Stat. 3765 (2008).

6. Bair (2012, 49–53, 128) expressed concern about homeowners, but there was little that FDIC could do for them.

7. It was also asked to relax mark-to-market accounting standards but refrained from doing so, instead issuing an ambiguously worded statement recognizing that those standards allow firms to abandon marks during liquidity crises. For a discussion, see Laux and Leuz (2009).

8. See also Frame et al. (2015, 47–49).

9. See Bair (2012, 88); and Geithner (2014, 135–37).

10. The figure comes from Mian, Sufi, and Trebbi (2010).

11. See also Dorsch (2013).

12. See, e.g., Duchin and Sosyura (2012); Acemoglu et al. (2013).

13. Dodd-Frank Wall Street Reform and Consumer Protection Act, Pub. L. No. 111-203, 124 Stat. 1376 (2010) (codified as amended in 12 U.S.C. §§ 5301–5641).

14. See 12 U.S.C. § 343. In 2015, the Fed adopted regulations implementing the law.

15. 12 U.S.C. §§ 5381–5394.

16. How precise the rules should be raises additional questions. The recent crisis was caused in part by regulatory arbitrage—financial institutions circumvented the rules without violating them. This is a common problem in the law, and in some settings—tax evasion through tax shelters—Congress has passed laws that permit punishment even of evasive behavior that is technically consistent with the rules. A similar approach may be warranted for evasion of financial regulations.

17. During the financial crisis, the SEC, apparently under pressure from the Fed, briefly banned short sales on financial stocks. At the time, some analysts believed that short-selling artificially suppressed the equity value of banks, creating concerns about their insolvency that could create a downward spiral. The academic consensus, however, is that bans on short sales, here and abroad, caused harm. See, e.g., Boehmer, Jones, and Zhang (2013).

18. See, e.g., Gorton (2015); Madigan (2009); Acharya (2015); Acharya and Mora (2015); Levitin (2011); Goodhart (1999); Carlson and Wheelock (2013). For an older view, see Goodfriend and King (1988).

19. See, e.g., Kahan and Rock (2009).

20. Pub. L. No. 111-203.

21. This is not to say that these institutions perform blamelessly. FEMA, in particular, has been subject to criticism for decades and has been reorganized numerous times. See Hogue and Bea (2006).

22. Cf. Merrill and Merrill (2014) (arguing that the OLA is unconstitutional); Selgin (2013).

23. And the similar principles that can be found in EESA.

24. See Whitman v. Am. Trucking Ass'ns, Inc., 531 U.S. 457 (2001).

25. On congressional efforts to rein in the Fed by requiring it to submit to audits and other requirements, see Tschinkel (2015). On the history of political pressure on the Fed, see Conti-Brown (2016).

References

Acemoglu, Daron, Simon Johnson, Amir Kermani, James Kwak, and Todd Mitton. 2013. "The Value of Connections in Turbulent Times: Evidence from the United States." NBER Working Paper Series No. 19701.

Acemoglu, Daron, Asuman Ozdaglar, and Alireza Tahbaz-Salehi. 2015. "Systemic Risk and Stability in Financial Networks." *American Economic Review* 105 (2): 564–608.

Acharya, Viral. 2015. "Financial Stability in the Broader Mandate for Central Banks: A Political Economy Perspective." Hutchins Center on Fiscal and Monetary Policy at Brookings Working Papers Series No. 11.

Acharya, Viral V., and Nada Mora. 2015. "A Crisis of Banks as Liquidity Providers." *Journal of Finance* 70 (1): 1–43.

Acharya, Viral V., Stijn Van Nieuwerburgh, Matthew Richardson, and Lawrence J. White. 2011. *Guaranteed to Fail: Fannie Mae, Freddie Mac, and the Debacle of Mortgage Finance.* Princeton, NJ: Princeton University Press.

Adelino, Manuel, Antoinette Schoar, and Felipe Severino. 2016. "Loan Originations and Defaults in the Mortgage Crisis: The Role of the Middle Class." *Review of Financial Studies* 29 (7): 1635–70.

Adler, Barry E. 2010. "A Reassessment of Bankruptcy Reorganization After Chrysler and General Motors." *American Bankruptcy Institute Law Review* 18 (1): 305–18.

Agarwal, Sumit, Gene Amromin, Itzhak Ben-David, Souphala Chomsisengphet, and Douglas D. Evanoff. 2014. "Predatory Lending and the Subprime Crisis." *Journal of Financial Economics* 113 (1): 29–52.

Agarwal, Sumit, Gene Amromin, Itzhak Ben-David, Souphala Chomsisengphet, Tomasz Piskorski, and Amit Seru. 2012. "Policy Intervention in Debt Renegotiation: Evidence from the Home Affordable Modification Program." NBER Working Paper Series No. 18311.

Agarwal, Sumit, Gene Amromin, Souphala Chomsisengphet, Tomasz Pikorski, Amit Seru, and Vincent Yao. 2015. "Mortgage Refinancing, Consumer Spending, and Competition: Evidence from the Home Affordable Refinancing Program." NBER Working Paper Series No. 21512.

Aït-Sahalia, Yacine, Jochen Andritzky, Andreas Jobst, Sylwia Nowak, and Natalia Tamirisa. 2012. "Market Response to Policy Initiatives During the Global Financial Crisis." *Journal of International Economics* 87 (1): 162–77.

Anderson, Keith T., and Rick Rieder. 2008. "Report to the Secretary of the Treasury from the Treasury Borrowing Advisory Committee of the Securities Industry and Financial Markets Association." US Department of the Treasury, July 30. https://www.treasury.gov/press-center/press-releases/Pages/hp1094.aspx.

Anginer, Deniz, and A. Joseph Warburton. 2014. "The Chrysler Effect: The Impact of Government Intervention on Borrowing Costs." *Journal of Banking & Finance* 40 (March): 62–79.

Arentsen, Eric, David C. Mauer, Brian Rosenlund, Harold H. Zhang, and Feng Zhao. 2015. "Subprime Mortgage Defaults and Credit Default Swaps." *Journal of Finance* 70 (2): 689–731.

Armantier, Olivier, Eric Ghysels, Asani Sarkar, and Jeffrey Shrader. 2011, revised 2015. "Discount Window Stigma during the 2007–2008 Financial Crisis." *Federal Reserve Bank of New York Staff Report* No. 483.

Ashcraft, Adam, Morten L. Bech, and W. Scott Frame. 2010. "The Federal Home Loan Bank System: The Lender of Next-to-Last Resort?" *Journal of Money, Credit & Banking* 42 (4): 551–83.

Augustin, Patrick, Marti G. Subrahmanyam, Dragon Yongjun Tang, and Sarah Qian Wang. 2014. "Credit Default Swaps: A Survey." *Foundations and Trends in Finance* 9 (1–2): 1–196.

Badawi, Adam B., and Anthony J. Casey. 2014. "The Fannie and Freddie Bailouts through the Corporate Lens." *New York University Journal of Law and Business* 10 (2): 443–78.

Bagehot, Walter. 1873. *Lombard Street: A Description of the Money Market*. London: Henry S. King.

Baghai, Ramin P., Henri Servaes, and Ane Tamayo. 2014. "Have Rating Agencies Become More Conservative? Implications for Capital Structure and Debt Pricing." *Journal of Finance* 69 (5): 1961–2005.

Bair, Sheila. 2012. *Bull by the Horns: Fighting to Save Main Street from Wall Street and Wall Street from Itself*. New York: Free Press.

Baird, Douglas G. 2012. "Lessons From the Automobile Reorganizations." *Journal of Legal Analysis* 4 (1): 271–300.

Baker, Colleen. 2012. "The Federal Reserve as Last Resort." *University of Michigan Journal of Law Reform* 46 (1): 69–134.

Ball, Laurence. 2016. "The Fed and Lehman Brothers." Unpublished manuscript.

Beltran, Daniel O., Valentin Bolotnyy, and Elizabeth C. Klee. 2015. "Un-Networking: The Evolution of Networks in the Federal Funds Market." Board of Governors of the Federal Reserve System Finance and Economics Discussion Series No. 2015-055.

Beltran, Daniel O., Larry Cordell, and Charles P. Thomas. 2013. "Asymmetric Information and the Death of ABS CDOs." Board of Governors of the Federal Reserve System International Finance Discussion Papers No. 1075.

Berger, Allen N., Lamont K. Black, Christa H. S. Bouwman, and Jennifer Dlugosz. 2015. "The Federal Reserve's Discount Window and TAF Programs: 'Pushing on a String?'" Unpublished manuscript.

Bernanke, Ben S. 1983. "Nonmonetary Effects of the Financial Crisis in the Propagation of the Great Depression." *American Economic Review* 73 (3): 257–76.

———. 2002. "Remarks by Governor Ben S. Bernanke On Milton Friedman's Ninetieth Birthday." Presented at the Conference to Honor Milton Friedman, University of Chicago, IL, November 8. http://www.federalreserve.gov/boarddocs/Speeches/2002/2002 1108/default.htm.

———. 2007. "Testimony: The Economic Outlook." Presented before the Joint Economic Committee, US Congress, March 28. https://www.federalreserve.gov/newsevents/testi mony/bernanke20070328a.htm.

———. 2015. *The Courage to Act: A Memoir of a Crisis and Its Aftermath*. New York: W. W. Norton.

Bezemer, Dirk J. 2010. "Understanding Financial Crisis Through Accounting Models." *Accounting, Organizations and Society* 35 (7): 676–88.

Bhat, Gauri, Richard Frankel, and Xiumin Martin. 2011. "Panacea, Pandora's Box, or Placebo: Feedback in Bank Mortgage-Backed Security Holdings and Fair Value Accounting." *Journal of Accounting and Economics* 52 (2–3): 153–73.

Bickley, James M., Bill Canis, Hinda Chaikind, Carol A. Pettit, Patrick Purcell, Carol Rapaport, and Gary Shorter. 2009. "U.S. Motor Vehicle Industry: Federal Financial Assistance and Restructuring." Congressional Research Service.

Bignon, Vincent, Marc Flandreau, and Stefano Ugolini. 2012. "Bagehot for Beginners: The Making of Lender of Last Resort Operations in the Mid-Nineteenth Century." *Economic History Review* 65 (2): 580–608.

Black, Lamont, and Lieu Hazelwood. 2012. "The Effect of TARP on Bank Risk-Taking." Board of Governors of the Federal Reserve System International Finance Discussion Papers No. 1043.

Boehmer, Ekkehart, Charles M. Jones, and Xiaoyan Zhang. 2013. "Shackling Short Sellers: The 2008 Shorting Ban." *Review of Financial Studies* 26 (6): 1363–1400.

Bolotnyy, Valentin. 2014. "The Government-Sponsored Enterprises and the Mortgage Crisis: The Role of the Affordable Housing Goals." *Real Estate Economics* 42 (3): 724–55.

Bolton, Patrick, Xavier Freixas, and Joel Shapiro. 2012. "The Credit Ratings Game." *Journal of Finance* 67 (1): 85–112.

Boyd, Roddy. 2011. *Fatal Risk: A Cautionary Tale of AIG's Corporate Suicide*. Hoboken, NJ: Wiley.

Brandao-Marques, Luis, Ricard Correa, and Horacio Sapriza. 2013. "International Evidence on Government Support and Risk Taking in the Banking Sector." IMF Working Paper No. 13/94.

Brunetti, Celso, Mario di Filippo, and Jeffrey H. Harris. 2011. "Effects of Central Bank Intervention on the Interbank Market During the Subprime Crisis." *Review of Financial Studies* 24 (6): 2053–83.

Brunnermeier, Markus K. 2009. "Deciphering the Liquidity and Credit Crunch 2007–2008." *Journal of Economic Perspectives* 23 (1): 77–100.

Brunnermeier, Markus K., and Martin Oehmke. 2013. "Bubbles, Financial Crises, and Systemic Risk." In Vol. 2B of *Handbook of the Economics of Finance*, edited by George M. Constantinides, Milton Harris, and Rene M. Stulz, 1221–88. Amsterdam: Elsevier.

Bubb, Ryan, and Alex Kaufman. 2014. "Securitization and Moral Hazard: Evidence from Credit Score Cutoff Rules." *Journal of Monetary Economics* 63 (April): 1–18.

Calomiris, Charles W., and Stephen H. Haber. 2014. *Fragile by Design: The Political Origins of Banking Crises and Scare Credit*. Princeton, NJ: Princeton University Press.

Calomiris, Charles W., and Urooj Khan. 2015. "An Assessment of TARP Assistance to Financial Institutions." *Journal of Economic Perspectives* 29:53–80.

Campbell, John Y., and João F. Cocco. 2015. "A Model of Mortgage Default." *Journal of Finance* 70 (4): 1495–1554.

Canis, Bill, and Baird Webel. 2013. "The Role of TARP Assistance in the Restructuring of General Motors." Congressional Research Service.

Canis, Bill, and Brent D. Yacobucci. 2010. "The U.S. Motor Vehicle Industry: Confronting a New Dynamic in the Global Economy." Congressional Research Service.

Carlson, Mark A., and David C. Wheelock. 2013. "The Lender of Last Resort: Lessons from the Fed's First 100 Years." Federal Reserve Bank of St. Louis Working Paper No. 2012–056B.

Carpenter, Seth, Selva Demiralp, and Jens Eisenschmidt. 2014. "The Effectiveness of the Non-Standard Policy in Addressing Liquidity Risk During the Financial Crisis: The Experiences of the Federal Reserve and the European Central Bank." *Journal of Economic Dynamics and Control* 43 (June): 107–29.

Cheng, Ing-Haw, Sahil Raina, and Wei Xiong. 2014. "Wall Street and the Housing Bubble." *American Economic Review* 104 (9): 2797–2829.

Chodorow-Reich, Gabriel. 2014. "The Employment Effects of Credit Market Disruptions: Firm-Level Evidence from the 2008–9 Financial Crisis." *Quarterly Journal of Economics* 129 (1): 1–59.

Chrysler Group LLC. 2010. "Form 10-K: Annual Report Pursuant to Section 13 or 15(d) of the Securities Exchange Act of 1934 for the Year Ended December 31, 2009."

Congressional Oversight Panel. 2009. "September Oversight Report: The Use of TARP Funds in the Support and Reorganization of the Domestic Automotive Industry."

———. 2011. "January Oversight Report: An Update on TARP Support for the Domestic Automotive Industry."

Conti-Brown, Peter. 2016. *The Power and Independence of the Federal Reserve.* Princeton, NJ: Princeton University Press.

Copeland, Adam, Antoine Martin, and Michael Walker. 2014. "Repo Runs: Evidence from the Tri-Party Repo Market." *Journal of Finance* 69 (6): 2343–80.

Corbae, Dean, and Erwan Quintin. 2015. "Leverage and the Foreclosure Crisis." *Journal of Political Economy* 123 (1): 1–65.

Cornett, Marcia M., Jamie J. McNutt, Philip E. Strahan, and Hassan Tehranian. 2011. "Liquidity Risk Management and Credit Supply in the Financial Crisis." *Journal of Financial Economics* 101 (2): 297–312.

Coval, Joshua, Jakub Jurek, and Erik Stafford. 2009. "The Economics of Structured Finance." *Journal of Economic Perspectives* 23 (1): 3–25.

Covitz, Daniel, Nellie Liang, and Gustavo A. Suarez. 2013. "The Evolution of a Financial Crisis: Collapse of the Asset-Backed Commercial Paper Market." *Journal of Finance* 68 (3): 815–48.

Davidoff, Steven M., and David Zaring. 2009. "Regulation by Deal: The Government's Response to the Financial Crisis." *Administrative Law Review* 61 (3): 463–542.

Davidoff Solomon, Steven, and David Zaring. 2015. "After the Deal: Fannie, Freddie and the Financial Crisis Aftermath." *Boston University Law Review* 95 (2): 371–426.

Domanski, Dietrich, Richhild Moessner, and William Nelson. 2014. "Central Banks as Lender of Last Resort: Experiences during the 2007–2010 Crisis and Lessons for the Future." Board of Governors of the Federal Reserve System Finance and Economics Discussion Series No. 2014-110.

Dorsch, Michael. 2013. "Bailout for Sale? The Vote to Save Wall Street." *Public Choice* 155 (3/4): 211–28.

Duchin, Ran, and Denis Sosyura. 2012. "The Politics of Government Investment." *Journal of Financial Economics* 106 (1): 24–48.

Duffie, Darrell. 2010. "The Failure Mechanics of Dealer Banks." *Journal of Economic Perspectives* 24 (1): 51–72.

Duygan-Bump, Burcu, Patrick Parkinson, Eric Rosengren, Gustavo A. Suarez, and Paul Willen. 2013. "How Effective Were the Federal Reserve Emergency Liquidity Facilities? Evidence from the Asset-Backed Commercial Paper Money Market Mutual Fund Liquidity Facility." *Journal of Finance* 68 (2): 715–37.

Dwyer, Gerald P., and Paula Tkac. 2009. "The Financial Crisis of 2008 in Fixed Income Markets." Federal Reserve Bank of Atlanta Working Paper Series No. 2009-20.

Elliott, Matthew, Benjamin Golub, and Matthew O. Jackson. 2014. "Financial Networks and Contagion." *American Economic Review* 104 (10): 3115–53.

Ellul, Andrew, and Vijay Yerramilli. 2013. "Stronger Risk Controls, Lower Risk: Evidence from U.S. Bank Holding Companies." *Journal of Finance* 68 (5): 1757–1803.

Epstein, Richard A. 2014. "The Government Takeover of Fannie Mae and Freddie Mac: Upending Capital Markets with Lax Business and Constitutional Standards." *New York University Journal of Law and Business* 10 (2): 379–442.

Fahlenbrach, Rüdiger, Robert Prilmeier, and René M. Stulz. 2012. "This Time Is the Same: Using Bank Performance in 1998 to Explain Bank Performance during the Recent Financial Crisis." *Journal of Finance* 67 (6): 2139–85.

Fahlenbrach, Rüdiger, and René M. Stulz. 2011. "Bank CEO Incentives and the Credit Crisis." *Journal of Financial Economics* 99 (1): 11–26.

FCIC (Financial Crisis Inquiry Commission). 2011. *The Financial Crisis Inquiry Report: Final Report of the National Commission on the Causes of the Financial and Economic Crisis in the United States.* Washington, DC: US Government Printing Office.

FDIC (Federal Deposit Insurance Corporation). 2008. "Emergency Economic Stabilization Act of 2008 Temporarily Increases Basic FDIC Insurance Coverage from $100,000 to $250,000 Per Depositor." Press Release, October 7. https://www.fdic.gov/news/news/press/2008/pr08093.html.

———. 2011. "The Orderly Liquidation of Lehman Brothers Holdings Inc. under the Dodd-Frank Act." *FDIC Quarterly* 5 (2): 31–49.

Federal Reserve (Board of Governors of the Federal Reserve System). 2009. "Authority of the Federal Reserve to Provide Extensions of Credit in Connection with a Commercial Paper Funding Facility (CPFF)." Federal Reserve, March 9. http://fcic-static.law.stanford.edu/cdn_media/fcic-docs/2009-03-09_Federal_Reserve_Bank_Letter_from_Legal_Division_to_Files_Re_Authority_of_the_Federal_Reserve_to_provide_extensions_of_credit_in_connection_with_a_commercial_paper_funding_facility_CPFF.pdf.

———. 2010a. "Money Market Investor Funding Facility." Federal Reserve. Last updated February 5, 2010. http://www.federalreserve.gov/monetarypolicy/mmiff.htm.

———. 2010b. "Term Securities Lending Facility." Federal Reserve. Last modified February 5, 2010. http://www.federalreserve.gov/monetarypolicy/tslf.htm.

———. 2016a. "Regulatory Reform: Asset-Backed Commercial Paper Money Market Mutual Fund Liquidity Facility (AMLF)." Federal Reserve. Last updated February 12, 2016. http://www.federalreserve.gov/newsevents/reform_amlf.htm.

———. 2016b. "Regulatory Reform: Bear Stearns, JPMorgan Chase, and Maiden Lane LLC." Federal Reserve. Last updated February 12, 2016. https://www.federalreserve.gov/newsevents/reform_bearstearns.htm.

———. 2016c. "Regulatory Reform: Commercial Paper Funding Facility (CPFF)." Federal Reserve. Last updated February 12, 2016. http://www.federalreserve.gov/newsevents/reform_cpff.htm.

———. 2016d. "Regulatory Reform: Discount Window Lending." The Federal Reserve. Last modified March 31, 2016. http://www.federalreserve.gov/newsevents/reform_dis count_window.htm.

———. 2016e. "Regulatory Reform: Primary Dealer Credit Facility (PDCF)." Federal Reserve. Last modified February 12, 2016. http://www.federalreserve.gov/newsevents/reform _pdcf.htm.

———. 2016 f. "Regulatory Reform: Term Securities Lending Facility (TSLF) and TSLF Options Program (TOP)." Federal Reserve. Last modified February 12, 2016. http:// www.federalreserve.gov/newsevents/reform_tslf.htm.

Fender, Ingo, and Martin Scheicher. 2009. "The Pricing of Subprime Mortgage Risk in Good Times and Bad: Evidence from the ABX.HE Indices." BIS Working Papers No. 279.

Fiderer, David. 2010. "How Paulson's People Colluded with Goldman to Destroy AIG and Get a Backdoor Bailout" *Daily Kos*, January 25. https://www.dailykos.com/story/2010 /01/28/831302/—How-Paulson-s-People-Colluded-with-Goldman-to-Destroy-AIG.

Flavin, Thomas J., and Lisa Sheenan. 2015. "The Role of U.S. Subprime Mortgage-Backed Assets in Propagating the Crisis: Contagion or Interdependence?" *North American Journal of Economics and Finance* 34 (November): 167–86.

Frame, W. Scott, Andreas Fuster, Joseph Tracy, and James Vickery. 2015. "The Rescue of Fannie Mae and Freddie Mac." *Journal of Economic Perspectives* 29 (2): 25–52.

Frame, W. Scott, and Lawrence J. White. 2005. "Fussing and Fuming over Fannie and Freddie: How Much Smoke, How Much Fire?" *Journal of Economic Perspectives* 19 (2): 159–84.

FRBNY (Federal Reserve Bank of New York). 2016. "Maiden Lane Transactions." Accessed June 20. https://www.newyorkfed.org/markets/maidenlane.html.

Friedman, Milton, and Anna J. Schwartz. 1963. *A Monetary History of the United States, 1867–1960*. Princeton, NJ: Princeton University Press.

GAO (US Government Accountability Office). 2010. "Federal Deposit Insurance Act: Regulators' Use of Systemic Risk Exception Raises Moral Hazard Concerns and Opportunities Exist to Clarify Provision." Report to Congressional Committees GAO-10-100. http://www.gao.gov/assets/310/303248.pdf.

———. 2011. "Federal Reserve System: Opportunities Exist to Strengthen Policies and Process for Managing Emergency Assistance." Report to Congressional Addressees GAO-11-696. http://www.gao.gov/new.items/d11696.pdf.

———. 2013. "Troubled Asset Relief Program: Status of Treasury's Investments in General Motors and Ally Financial." Report to Congressional Committees No. GAO-14-6. http://www.gao.gov/assets/660/658636.pdf.

Geithner, Timothy F. 2014. *Stress Test: Reflections on Financial Crises*. New York: Crown.

General Motors Company. 2010. "Form 10-K: Annual Report Pursuant to Section 13 or 15(d) of the Securities Exchange Act of 1934 for the Year Ended December 31, 2009."

Gennaioli, Nicola, Andrei Shleifer, and Robert W. Vishny. 2013. "A Model of Shadow Banking." *Journal of Finance* 68 (4): 1331–63.

Gerardi, Kristopher, Andreas Lenhert, Shane M. Sherlund, and Paul Willen. 2008. "Making Sense of the Subprime Crisis." *Brookings Papers on Economic Activity* (2): 69–145.

Gilbert, R. Alton, Kevin L. Kliesen, Andrew P. Meyer, and David C. Wheelock. 2012. "Federal Reserve Lending to Troubled Banks During the Financial Crisis, 2007–2010." *Federal Reserve Bank of St. Louis Review* 94 (3): 221–43.

Goldstein, Itay. 2013. "Empirical Literature on Financial Crises: Fundamentals vs. Panic."

In *The Evidence and Impact of Financial Globalization*, edited by Gerard Caprio, Thorsten Beck, Stijn Claessens, and Sergio L. Schmukler, 523–34. Waltham, MA: Elsevier.

Goldstein, Itay, and Assaf Razin. 2013. "Three Branches of Theories of Financial Crises." NBER Working Paper Series No. 18670.

Goodfriend, Marvin, and Robert G. King. 1988. "Financial Deregulation, Monetary Policy, and Central Banking." *Federal Reserve Bank of Richmond Economic Review* 74 (3): 3–22.

Goodhart, C. A. E. 1995. *The Central Bank and the Financial System*. Cambridge, MA: MIT Press.

———. 1999. "Myths About the Lender of Last Resort." *International Finance* 2 (3): 339–60.

———. 2011. "The Changing Role of Central Banks." *Financial History Review* 18 (2): 135–54.

Goolsbee, Austan D., and Alan B. Krueger. 2015. "A Retrospective Look at Rescuing and Restructuring General Motors and Chrysler." *Journal of Economic Perspectives* 29 (2): 3–24.

Gorton, Gary B. 2012. *Misunderstanding Financial Crises: Why We Don't See Them Coming*. New York: Oxford University Press.

Gorton, Gary. 2015. "Stress for Success: A Review of Timothy Geithner's Financial Crisis Memoir." *Journal of Economic Literature* 53 (4): 975–95

Gorton, Gary, and Andrew Metrick. 2012. "Securitized Banking and the Run on Repo." *Journal of Financial Economics* 104 (3): 425–51.

Gorton, Gary, and Guillermo Ordoñez, 2014. "Collateral Crises." *American Economic Review* 104 (2): 343–78.

Gorton, Gary, and Andrew Winton. 2003. "Financial Intermediation." In Vol. 1A of *Handbook of the Economics of Finance*, edited by George M. Constantinides, Milton Harris, and René M. Stulz, 431–552. Amsterdam: Elsevier.

Griffin, John M., and Dragon Yongjun Tang. 2012. "Did Subjectivity Play a Role in CDO Credit Ratings?" *Journal of Finance* 67 (4): 1293–1328.

He, Jie, Jun Qian, and Philip E. Strahan. 2012. "Are All Ratings Created Equal? The Impact of Issuer Size on the Pricing of Mortgage-Backed Securities." *Journal of Finance* 67 (6): 2097–2137.

Hindmoor, Andrew, and Allan McConnell. 2015. "Who Saw It Coming? The UK's Great Financial Crisis." *Journal of Public Policy* 35 (1): 63–96.

Hoggarth, Glenn, and Farouk Soussa. 2001. "Crisis Management, Lender of Last Resort and the Changing Nature of the Banking Industry." In *Financial Stability and Central Banks: A Global Perspective*, edited by Richard A. Brealey, Alastair Clark, Charles Goodhart, Juliette Healy, Glenn Hoggarth, David T. Llewellyn, Chang Shu, Peter Sinclair, and Farouk Soussa, 166–86. New York: Routledge.

Hogue, Henry B., and Keith Bea. 2006. "Federal Emergency Management and Homeland Security Organization: Historical Developments and Legislative Options." Congressional Research Service.

Ivashina, Victoria, and David Scharfstein. 2010. "Bank Lending During the Financial Crisis of 2008." *Journal of Financial Economics* 97 (3): 319–38.

Jaffee, Dwight, and John M. Quigley. 2011. "The Future of the Government Sponsored Enterprises: The Role for Government in the U.S. Mortgage Market." NBER Working Paper Series No. 17685.

Johnson, Simon, and James Kwak. 2010. *13 Bankers*. New York: Pantheon.

Judge, Kathryn. 2016. "The First Year: The Role of a Modern Lender of Last Resort." *Columbia Law Review* 116 (3): 843–925.

Junge, Benjamin, and Anders B. Trolle. 2013. "Liquidity Risk in Credit Default Swap Markets." Swiss Finance Institute Research Papers No. 13-65.

Kacperczyk, Marcin, and Philipp Schnabl. 2013. "How Safe Are Money Market Funds?" *Quarterly Journal of Economics* 128 (3): 1073-1122.

Kahan, Marcel, and Edward Rock. 2009. "How to Prevent Hard Cases from Making Bad Law: Bear Stearns, Delaware, and the Strategic Use of Comity." *Emory Law Journal* 58 (3): 713-59.

Kapur, Emily C. 2015. "The Next Lehman Bankruptcy." In *Making Failure Feasible: How Bankruptcy Reform Can End "Too Big to Fail,"* edited by Kenneth E. Scott, Thomas H. Jackson, and John B. Taylor. Stanford, CA: Hoover Institution Press.

Kaufman, Alex. 2014. "The Influence of Fannie and Freddie on Mortgage Loan Terms." *Real Estate Economics* 42 (2): 472-96.

Kessler, Aaron M. 2014. "DealBook: Paulson Testifies That 'Punitive' A.I.G. Terms Were Also Necessary." *New York Times*, October 6. http://dealbook.nytimes.com/2014/10/06 /paulson-takes-the-stand-in-a-i-g-trial/?_r=0.

Keys, Benjamin J., Tanmoy Mukherjee, Amit Seru, and Vikrant Vig. 2009. "Financial Regulation and Securitization: Evidence from Subprime Loans." *Journal of Monetary Economics* 56 (5): 700-20.

Kiel, Paul, and Dan Nguyen. 2016. "Bailout Tracker." ProPublica. Last updated March 23, 2017. https://projects.propublica.org/bailout/.

Kindleberger, Charles P. 2000. *Manias, Panics, and Crashes: A History of Financial Crises.* New York: Wiley.

Klier, Thomas H. 2009. "From Tail Fins to Hybrids: How Detroit Lost its Dominance of the U.S. Auto Market." *Economic Perspectives* 33 (2): 2-17.

Klier, Thomas H., and James Rubenstein. 2012. "Detroit Back from the Brink? Auto Industry Crisis and Restructuring, 2008-11." *Economic Perspectives* 36 (2): 35-54.

Krishnamurthy, Arvind. 2010. "How Debt Markets Have Malfunctioned in the Crisis." *Journal of Economic Perspectives* 24 (1): 3-28.

Krishnamurthy, Arvind, Stefan Nagel, and Dmitry Orlov. 2014. "Sizing Up Repo." *Journal of Finance* 69 (6): 2381-2417.

Kroszner, Randall S., and William Melick. 2009. "The Response of the Federal Reserve to the Recent Banking and Financial Crisis." Paper presented at *An Ocean Apart? Comparing Transatlantic Responses to the Financial Crisis*, a conference organized by the Banca d'Italia, Bruegel Institute, and the Peterson Institute of International Economics, Rome, September 10-11.

Laufer, Steven. 2013. "Equity Extraction and Mortgage Default." Board of Governors of the Federal Reserve System Finance and Economics Discussion Series No. 2013-30.

Laux, Christian, and Christian Leuz. 2009. "The Crisis of Fair-Value Accounting: Making Sense of the Recent Debate." *Accounting, Organizations and Society* 34 (6/7): 826-34.

Lee, Brian A. 2015. "Emergency Takings." *Michigan Law Review* 114 (3): 391-454.

Levitin, Adam J. 2011. "In Defense of Bailouts." *Georgetown Law Journal* 99 (2): 435-514.

Lewis, Michael. 2009. *The Big Short: Inside the Doomsday Machine.* New York: W. W. Norton.

Longstaff, Francis A., and Brett W. Myers. 2014. "How Does the Market Value Toxic Assets?" *Journal of Financial & Quantitative Analysis* 49 (2): 297-319.

Lubben, Stephen J. 2009. "No Big Deal: The GM and Chrysler Cases in Context." *American Bankruptcy Law Journal* 83 (4): 531-47.

Madigan, Brian F. 2009. "Bagehot's Dictum in Practice: Formulating and Implementing

Policies to Combat the Financial Crisis." Address presented at the Federal Reserve Bank of Kansas City's Annual Economic Symposium, August 21.

McCulley, Paul A. 2007. "Teton Reflections." *PIMCO Global Central Bank Focus*, September. https://www.pimco.com/insights/economic-and-market-commentary/global-central-bank-focus/teton-reflections.

McDonald, Robert, and Anna Paulson. 2015. "AIG in Hindsight." *Journal of Economic Perspectives* 29 (2): 81–106.

McLean, Bethany. 2015. *Shaky Ground: The Strange Saga of the U.S. Mortgage Giants*. New York: Columbia Global Reports.

Mehra, Alexander. 2010. "Legal Authority in Unusual and Exigent Circumstances: The Federal Reserve and the Financial Crisis." *University of Pennsylvania Journal of Business Law* 13 (1): 221–74.

Mehrling, Perry. 2011. *The New Lombard Street: How the Fed Became the Dealer of Last Resort*. Princeton, NJ: Princeton University Press.

Merrill, Thomas W., and Margaret Merrill. 2014. "Dodd-Frank Orderly Liquidation Authority: Too Big for the Constitution?" *University of Pennsylvania Law Review* 163 (1): 165–247.

Mian, Atif, and Amir Sufi. 2012. "The Effects of Fiscal Stimulus: Evidence from the 2009 Cash for Clunkers Program." *Quarterly Journal of Economics* 127 (3): 1107–42.

———. 2014. *House of Debt: How They (and You) Caused the Great Recession, and How We Can Prevent It from Happening Again*. Chicago: University of Chicago Press.

Mian, Atif, Amir Sufi, and Francesco Trebbi. 2010. "The Political Economy of the US Mortgage Default Crisis." *American Economic Review* 100 (5): 1967–98.

———. 2014. "Resolving Debt Overhang: Political Constraints in the Aftermath of Financial Crises." *American Economic Journal: Macroeconomics* 6 (2): 1–28.

Minsky, Hyman P. 1994. "Financial Instability Hypothesis." In *The Elgar Companion to Radical Political Economy*, edited by Philip Arestis and Malcolm Sawyer, 153–57. Brookfield, VT: Elgar.

Morgenson, Gretchen. 2016a. "Documents Undercut U.S. Case for Taking Mortgage Giant Fannie Mae's Profits." *New York Times*, April 12. http://www.nytimes.com/2016/04/13/business/fannie-mae-suit-bailout.html?hp&action=click&pgtype=Homepage&click Source=story-heading&module=first-column-region&region=top-news&WT.nav=top-news&_r=0.

———. 2016b. "Fannie, Freddie and the Secrets of a Bailout with No Exit." *New York Times*, May 20. http://www.nytimes.com/2016/05/22/business/how-freddie-and-fannie-are-held-captive.html.

Morrison, Edward R. 2009. "Chrysler, GM and the Future of Chapter 11." Columbia Law and Economics Working Paper No. 365.

Nelson, William R., and Roberto Perli. 2007. "Selected Indicators of Financial Stability." In *Risk Measurement and Systemic Risk: Fourth Joint Central Bank Research Conference, 8–9 November 2005*, in cooperation with the Committee on the Global Financial System, 343–72. Frankfurt, Germany: European Central Bank.

Obama, Barack. 2013. "Remarks on Signing the Dodd-Frank Wall Street Reform and Consumer Protection Act, July 21, 2010." In *Public Papers of the Presidents of the United States: Barack Obama, 2010, Book II—July 1 to December 31, 2010*, 1087–89. Washington, DC: US Government Printing Office.

Oh, Seung-Youn. 2014. "Shifting Gears: Industrial Policy and Automotive Industry After the 2008 Financial Crisis." *Business & Politics* 16 (4): 641–65.

Olegario, Rowena. 2016. *The Engine of Enterprise: Credit in America*. Cambridge, MA: Harvard University Press.

Opp, Christian C., Marcus M. Opp, and Milton Harris. 2013. "Rating Agencies in the Face of Regulation." *Journal of Financial Economics* 108 (1): 46–61.

Pagano, Marco, and Paolo Volpin. 2010. "Credit Ratings Failures and Policy Options." *Economic Policy* 25 (62): 401–31.

Paulson, Henry M. 2010. *On the Brink: Inside the Race to Stop the Collapse of the Global Financial System*. New York: Business Plus.

Porter, Thomas O. 2009. "Federal Reserve's Catch-22: A Legal Analysis of the Federal Reserve's Emergency Powers." *North Carolina Banking Institute* 13 (1): 483–514.

Posner, Eric A. 2015. "How Do Bank Regulators Determine Capital-Adequacy Requirements?" *University of Chicago Law Review* 82 (4): 1853–95.

Posner, Eric A., and Adrian Vermeule. 2010. *The Executive Unbound: After the Madisonian Republic*. New York: Oxford University Press.

Pozsar, Zoltan. 2011. "Institutional Cash Pools and the Triffin Dilemma of the U.S. Banking System." IMF Working Paper No. 11/190.

———. 2014. "Shadow Banking: The Money View." Office of Financial Research Working Paper No. 14–04.

Pozsar, Zoltan, Tobias Adrian, Adam Ashcraft, and Hayley Boesky. 2012. "Shadow Banking." Federal Bank of New York Staff Reports No. 458.

Rajan, Raghuram G. 2005. "Has Financial Development Made the World Riskier?" NBER Working Paper Series No. 11728.

———. 2010. *Fault Lines: How Hidden Fractures Still Threaten the World Economy*. Princeton, NJ: Princeton University Press.

Rattner, Steven. 2010. *Overhaul: An Insider's Account of the Obama Administration's Emergency Rescue of the Auto Industry*. Boston: Houghton Mifflin Harcourt.

Reinhart, Carmen M., and Kenneth S. Rogoff. 2010. "Growth in a Time of Debt." *American Economic Review* 100 (2): 573–78.

Republican Staff of the Committee on Financial Services, U.S. House of Representatives, 113th Congress, Second Session. 2014. *Failing to End "Too Big to Fail": An Assessment of the Dodd-Frank Act Four Years Later*. Washington, DC.

Rexrode, Christina, and Andrew Grossman. 2014. "Record Bank of America Settlement Latest in Government Crusade." *Wall Street Journal*, August 21. http://www.wsj.com/articles/bank-of-america-reaches-16-65-billion-settlement-1408626544.

Ritholtz, Barry. 2009. *Bailout Nation*. New York: John Wiley & Sons.

Roe, Mark J., and David Skeel. 2010. "Assessing the Chrysler Bankruptcy." *Michigan Law Review* 108 (5): 727–72.

Romer, Thomas, and Barry R. Weingast. 1991. "Political Foundations of the Thrift Debacle." In *Politics and Economics in the Eighties*, edited by Alberto Alesina and Geoffrey Carliner, 175–214. Chicago: University of Chicago Press.

Romero, Alan. 2006. "Reducing Just Compensation for Anticipated Condemnations." *Journal of Land Use & Environmental Law* 21 (2): 153–99.

Samples, John. 2010. "Lawless Policy: TARP as Congressional Failure." *Policy Analysis* No. 660.

Schiff, Peter D., with John Downes. 2007. *Crash Proof: How to Profit from the Coming Economic Collapse*. Hoboken, NJ: John Wiley & Sons.

Schularick, Moritz, and Alan M. Taylor. 2012. "Credit Booms Gone Bust: Monetary Policy,

Leverage Cycles, and Financial Crises, 1870–2008." *American Economic Review* 102 (2): 1029–61.

Schwarcz, Daniel. 2015. "A Critical Take on Group Regulation of Insurers in the United States." *UC Irvine Law Review* 5 (3): 537–58.

SEC (US Securities and Exchange Commission). 2008. "SEC's Oversight of Bear Stearns and Related Entities: The Consolidated Supervised Entity Program." Report No. 446-A.

———. 2016. "SEC Enforcement Actions: Addressing Misconduct that Led to or Arose from the Financial Crisis." Last modified January 14, 2016. http://www.sec.gov/spotlight /enf-actions-fc.shtml.

Selgin, George. 2013. "Misunderstanding Financial History." *Alt-M: Ideas for an Alternative Monetary Future*, July 11. http://www.alt-m.org/2013/07/11/misunderstanding-financial -history/.

Serkin, Christopher. 2005. "The Meaning of Value: Assessing Just Compensation for Regulatory Takings." *Northwestern University Law Review* 99 (2): 677–742.

SIGTARP (Special Inspector General for the Troubled Asset Relief Program). 2009. "Factors Affecting Efforts to Limit Payments to AIG Counterparties." SIGTARP Report No. 10-003

Silva, Joseph W. 2015. "Altering the Deal: The Importance of GSE Shareholder Litigation." *North Carolina Banking Institute* 19:109–34.

Sjostrom, Jr., William K. 2009. "The AIG Bailout." *Washington and Lee Law Review* 66 (3): 943–94.

———. 2015. "Afterward to the AIG Bailout." *Washington and Lee Law Review* 72 (2): 795–828.

Sorkin, Andrew R. 2014. "DealBook: A.I.G. Bailout, Revisionists' Version." *New York Times*. October 6. http://dealbook.nytimes.com/2014/10/06/a-i-g-bailout-revisionists-version /?_r=0.

Stanton, Richard, and Nancy Wallace. 2011. "The Bear's Lair: Index Credit Default Swaps and the Subprime Mortgage Crisis." *Review of Financial Studies* 24 (10): 3250–80.

Stewart, James B., and Peter Eavis. 2014. "Revisiting the Lehman Brothers Bailout that Never Was." *New York Times*, September 30, A1.

Strahan, Philip E., and Basak Tanyeri. 2015. "Once Burned, Twice Shy: Money Market Fund Responses to a Systemic Liquidity Shock." *Journal of Financial & Quantitative Analysis* 50 (1/2): 119–44.

Taylor, John B. 2009. "The Financial Crisis and the Policy Responses: An Empirical Analysis of What Went Wrong." NBER Working Paper Series No. 14631.

Tschinkel, Sheila. 2015. "Congress Auditing the Federal Reserve is a Truly Frightening Idea." *Quartz*, March 13. http://qz.com/362155/congress-auditing-the-federal-reserve-is-a -truly-frightening-idea/.

Tucker, Paul. 2014. "The Lender of Last Resort and Modern Central Banking: Principles and Reconstruction." In *Re-thinking the Lender of Last Resort*, BIS Papers No. 79, 10–42.

US Department of the Treasury. 2008. "Treasury Announces Guaranty Program for Money Market Funds." Press release, September 19. https://www.treasury.gov/press-center/press -releases/Pages/hp1147.aspx.

———. 2009a. "Commitment to Purchase Financial Instrument and Servicer Participation Agreement." https://www.treasury.gov/initiatives/financial-stability/TARP-Programs /housing/mha/Documents_Contracts_Agreements/bankunited_Redacted.pdf.

———. 2009b. "Treasury Department Releases Details on Public Private Partnership Investment Program." Press release, March 23. https://www.treasury.gov/press-center/press-releases/Pages/tg65.aspx.

———. 2009c. "Public-Private Investment Program." White paper, March 23. https://www.treasury.gov/press-center/press-releases/Documents/ppip_whitepaper_032309.pdf.

Veronesi, Pietro, and Luigi Zingales. 2010. "Paulson's Gift." *Journal of Financial Economics* 97 (3): 339–68.

Vyas, Dushyantkumar. 2011. "The Timeliness of Accounting Write-Downs by U.S. Financial Institutions During the Financial Crisis of 2007–2008." *Journal of Accounting Research* 49 (3): 823–60.

Wall Street Journal. 2008. "Paulson's Bazooka: A Weapon to Be Remembered?" *Real Time Economics* (blog), *Wall Street Journal*, September 24. http://blogs.wsj.com/economics/2008/09/24/paulsons-bazooka-a-weapon-to-be-remembered/.

Wall, Larry D. 2014. "Have the Government-Sponsored Enterprises Fully Repaid the Treasury?" *Federal Reserve Bank of Atlanta: Notes from the Vault*, March. https://www.frbatlanta.org/cenfis/publications/notesfromthevault/1403.aspx.

Wallach, Philip A. 2015. *To the Edge: Legality, Legitimacy, and the Responses to the 2008 Financial Crisis.* Washington, DC: Brookings Institution Press.

Wallison, Peter J. 2015. *Hidden in Plain Sight: What Really Caused the World's Worst Financial Crisis and Why It Could Happen Again.* New York: Encounter.

Washington Post. 2008. "The Breakdown of the Final Bailout Bill." *Washington Post*, September 28. http://www.washingtonpost.com/wp-dyn/content/article/2008/09/28/AR2008092800900.html.

Wessel, David. 2009. *In Fed We Trust: Ben Bernanke's War on the Great Panic.* New York: Crown Business.

White, Lawrence H. 2013. "The Federal Reserve and the Rule of Law." Testimony before the House Committee on Financial Services, September 11. http://www.cato.org/publications/testimony/federal-reserve-rule-law.

White, Lawrence J. 1992. *The S&L Debacle: Public Policy Lessons for Bank and Thrift Regulation.* New York: Oxford University Press.

Wojtowicz, Marcin. 2014. "CDOs and the Financial Crisis: Credit Ratings and Fair Premia." *Journal of Banking & Finance* 39 (February): 1–13.

YCharts. 2016a. "Fannie Mae (FNMA) Income Statement." Accessed July 8. http://finance.yahoo.com/q/is?s=FNMA+Income+Statement&annual.

———. 2016b. "Federal Home Loan (FMCC) Income Statement." Accessed July 8. http://finance.yahoo.com/q/is?s=FMCC+Income+Statement&annual.

Zaring, David. 2014. "Litigating the Financial Crisis." *Virginia Law Review* 100 (7): 1405–81.

Zywicki, Todd. 2011. "The Auto Bailout and the Rule of Law" *National Affairs* 7 (Spring): 66–80.

Index